Origen and
Greek Patristic Theology
By Rev. William Fairweather, M.A.

Origen and
Greek Patristic Theology

By

Rev. William Fairweather, M.A.

Wipf and Stock Publishers
199 W 8th Ave, Suite 3
Eugene, OR 97401

Origen and Greek Patristic Theology
By Fairweather, William
ISBN: 1-59752-889-7
Publication date 9/22/2006
Previously published by T. & T. Clark, 1901

"Vir magnus ab infantia."
                    JEROME.

"I love the name of Origen."
                    NEWMAN.

"Like the influence of Socrates in Greek philosophy, so the influence of Origen in Church history is the watershed of multitudes of different streams of thought."   FARRAR.

PREFATORY NOTE

THIS volume cannot claim to be written in the popular style adopted in some other volumes of the series, for the simple reason that the subject scarcely admits of being popularised. At the same time I have tried to make the book readable, and to refrain as far as possible from undue technicalities of philosophical and theological language. It has been my aim to avoid on the one hand the Scylla of catering for a public which no art or device will ever induce to concern itself about Greek Patristic Theology, and, on the other, the Charybdis of scholastic pedantry. Rightly or wrongly, I am convinced that my task will be most usefully accomplished by furnishing a brief introduction to the study of a subject on which, in English at least, there are not too many easily accessible helps. In view of the impossibility of assuming any very intimate knowledge of Origen's writings on the part of the general reader, or even of the average theological student, I have further deemed it best, while not refraining from criticism where it seemed called for, to aim at being expository rather than critical.

In no sense does the book pretend to be a treatment of the third century. Any attempt to deal with the Church life of the period is debarred by the limits of the present series. Such a method of treatment may sometimes have its advantages, but it necessarily throws into the background the personality of the individual. In the following pages it has been my endeavour to concentrate attention upon the life and writings, the doctrine and influence, of the great teacher of the Greek Church. Chapter I. is introductory, and intended to lead up to the main subject by showing to what extent the way had already been prepared for Origen. I regret that considerations of space do not admit of prefixing as Prolegomena a sketch of the birthplace and background of the Greek theology, and of the Apologists of the second century; but while this may be a desideratum from the point of view of the scientific student, the educated layman will probably count it no loss. Chapters XI.-XIV. form, so to speak, the epilogue, and indicate the nature and extent of Origen's influence upon subsequent theological thought.

I have deemed it advisable to devote a separate chapter to the life of Origen, instead of adopting the perhaps more scientific, but immensely more complicated plan of weaving in the biographical details with other matter in strict chronological sequence. Although in a monograph upon Origen more might, no doubt, be made of this aspect of the subject, I venture to hope that nothing very material has been omitted; but in any case it seems more important to make room for some adequate account of the writings and theology of one who did so much to "make Christianity a part of the civilisation of the world" than to tell with fuller detail the story of his life.

To those who may be inclined to question the utility

of studying the writings of an old-world personage like Origen, and to consider him as of little significance for those living in the twentieth century, it may be pointed out that the theme discussed seems likely to assume growing importance in relation to present-day problems in theology. There is a prevailing disposition to get back to the sources, and it is not to be forgotten that it was the Greek Fathers who laid the foundations of theological science. An American author, Professor A. V. G. Allen, in the Preface to a work the title of which is given below, says: "If I were revising my book I should try to enforce more than I have done the importance of the work of Origen. He was a true specimen of a great theologian, the study of whose life is of special value to-day, as a corrective against that tendency to underrate dogma in our reaction from outgrown dogmas, or the disposition to treat the feelings and instincts of our nature as if they were a final refuge from the reason, instead of a means to a larger use of the reason,—a process which, it is to be feared, in many is closely allied with the temper which leads men to seek shelter in an infallible Church."

In view of subsequent developments of theological thought, within the Greek Church and beyond it, it is equally important to note that while Origen valued dogma, he abjured dogmatism. He refused to make man's blessedness conditional upon the acceptance of certain shibboleths. Although speculative to the verge of audacity, he never failed to distinguish between his own opinions and the rule of faith as contained in Holy Scripture. If he himself was disposed to rate knowledge too highly, at all events he did not confuse it with faith, but was quite explicit in his declaration that the word of God is the sole source of absolute certitude, and the sole repository of essential truth. It would have been well for the Greek Church if she had clung to this position. As it was, she did not properly discriminate between the matter of revelation and the scientific handling of it, and ultimately succumbed under the incubus of a dead orthodoxy.

It only remains to mention the principal works consulted in the preparation of this volume. Apart from Origen's own writings, I have derived most help from Redepenning's *Origenes: Eine Darstellung seines Lebens und seiner Lehre*, 2 vols., Bonn, 1841–46; Pressensé's *The Early Years of Christianity*, 1879; Denis' *De La Philosophie d'Origène*, Paris, 1884; Bigg's *The Christian Platonists of Alexandria*, 1886; Harnack's *History of Dogma*, Eng. tr. 1894–1899; and the Church Histories of Mosheim, Neander, and Kurtz. The following works have also been useful: Schnitzer, *Origenes über die Grundlehren der Glaubenswissenschaft*, Stuttgart, 1835; Hagenbach's *History of Christian Doctrines*, Eng. tr. 1846; Allen, *The Continuity of Christian Thought*, 1884; Allin, *Race and Religion*, 1899; and the articles on Origen in Chambers's *Encyclopædia*, Smith and Wace's *Dictionary of Christian Biography*, Smith's *Dict. of Greek and Roman Biography*, and the *Encyclopædia Britannica*.

The translations of passages quoted from the writings of Origen are mostly taken from the two volumes published in *The Ante-Nicene Christian Library*, but sometimes they are those of Bigg or Pressensé, and in a few instances they are my own.

W. FAIRWEATHER.

KIRKCALDY, *September* 1901.

CONTENTS

PREFATORY NOTE vii

CHAPTER I

PRECURSORS OF ORIGEN

i. The Greek Theology	1
ii. The Catechetical School of Alexandria	8
iii. Pantænus and Clement	12
iv. Rights and Limits of Secular Learning	14
v. Clement's View of Holy Scripture, and his Distinction of Exoteric and Esoteric Doctrine	17
vi. Extant Writings of Clement: their *Apologetic* Drift	20
vii. Clement's Dogmatic	26

CHAPTER II

LIFE AND CHARACTER OF ORIGEN

i. Early Years in Alexandria	35
ii. The Persecution under Septimius Severus	37
iii. Ascetic and Philosopher	41
iv. Literary Labours and Foreign Travels	47
v. Collision with Demetrius	50
vi. Life at Cæsarea	54
vii. The Persecution under Maximinus Thrax	57
viii. Journeys into Greece and Arabia	58
ix. The End: Beauty of Character	62

CONTENTS

CHAPTER III

ORIGEN'S VIEW OF HOLY SCRIPTURE

		PAGE
i.	The Question of Canonicity	65
ii.	Inspiration and Unity of the Sacred Writings	67
iii.	The Twofold Object of Scripture	70
iv.	The Allegorical Method and the Threefold Sense	73
v.	Allegorism in relation to Apologetic	77
vi.	Economy or the Doctrine of Reserve	81
vii.	Radical Defect of Origen's Position	82

CHAPTER IV

RELIGIOUS PHILOSOPHY OF ORIGEN

i.	Relation of Christian Doctrine to Greek Philosophy	84
ii.	Gnostic and Neoplatonic Elements in Origen's System	87
iii.	Value of a scientific Conception of Christianity	89
iv.	Origen's Idealism and the religious Ideal	92
v.	Origen's Theory of Knowledge and its Relation to Faith	94
vi.	The Deification of Humanity	96

CHAPTER V

THE WRITINGS OF ORIGEN

i.	Contributions to Textual Criticism—the *Hexapla*	99
ii.	Apologetic Work of Origen—the *Contra Celsum*	105
iii.	Exegetical Writings	120
iv.	Dogmatic Works—the *De Principiis*	125
v.	Letters and Treatises on Practical Religion	133

CHAPTER VI

ORIGEN'S THEOLOGY: GOD AND HIS SELF-MANIFESTATIONS

i.	The Nature of God	142
ii.	The Doctrine of the Trinity	148

CONTENTS

CHAPTER VII

ORIGEN'S THEOLOGY: CREATION AND THE FALL

	PAGE
i. The World of created Spirits and the Conception of formal Freedom	161
ii. The Fall and the Creation of the Material World	168
iii. The Doctrine of Man	171

CHAPTER VIII

ORIGEN'S THEOLOGY: REDEMPTION AND RESTORATION

i. The Four Revelations	177
ii. The Incarnation	180
iii. The Sacrifice of Christ	185
iv. The Soul's Return to God	190
v. The Last Things	202

CHAPTER IX

SUCCESSORS OF ORIGEN

i. In Alexandria—
    (a) Presidents of the Catechetical School: Heraclas, Dionysius, Pierius, Theognostus, Peter the Martyr, Didymus, and Rhodon 214
    (b) Athanasius 220

ii. In Asia—
    (a) Friends and Correspondents: Theophilus of Cæsarea, Alexander of Jerusalem, Firmilian, and Julius Africanus 224
    (b) Gregory Thaumaturgus 225

CHAPTER X

HISTORICAL SERVICES, GENERAL CHARACTERISTICS, AND DISTINCTIVE DOCTRINAL COMPLEXION OF THE GREEK THEOLOGY

i. Services against Gnosticism and Montanism	228
ii. Characteristics: Allegorism, the Doctrine of Reserve, Intellectualism, Catholicity, Spirituality, Humanitarianism, Optimism	230
iii. Outline of the Hellenistic Position	233
iv. The Three Main Pillars of the Greek Theology	235

CONTENTS

CHAPTER XI

REACTION AGAINST ORIGENISM

		PAGE
i.	Dissatisfaction with Origen's Doctrinal Position	238
ii.	The Attack of Methodius	240
iii.	Defence by Pamphilus and Eusebius	241
iv.	Quarrels among the Egyptian Monks	243
v.	The Controversy in Palestine, Italy, Alexandria, and Constantinople	245
vi.	Interference of the Emperor Justinian	250
vii.	Condemnation of Origen's Tenets by the Fifth General Council at Constantinople in A.D. 553	251

CHAPTER XII

SUBSEQUENT HISTORY OF ORIGENISM

i.	Disappearance as a Scientific System	252
ii.	In the 7th Century represented by Maximus Confessor	253
iii.	In the West scarcely traceable during the Middle Ages	258
iv.	John Scotus Erigena	255
v.	Causes of the Neglect of Origen's Writings in East and West	257
vi.	The Latin Church more lenient than the Greek in its Judgment of Origen	258
vii.	Opinions concerning him in more recent Times	259
INDEX		263

ORIGEN AND GREEK PATRISTIC THEOLOGY

CHAPTER I

Precursors of Origen

CHRISTIANITY had introduced a new idea of God, which superseded not only the deities of classical mythology, but also the Hebraic Deism which regarded God merely as the God of the Jews, and as virtually separate from the world. The Greek patristic theology was the result of the application of the specific methods of Greek philosophy to the new material supplied by the Christian history, with the view of constructing a reasoned theory of God and the universe. As such it was "the last characteristic creation of the Greek genius." In the New Testament God is represented from a religious point of view; but for the Greek mind, which conceived God metaphysically as abstract Being, a scientific theology was indispensable. The facts of Christianity had to be so interpreted as to yield a conception of God which would at once conserve His unity, and yet admit of His organic connection with man as Lord and Saviour. Naturally this result was

2 ORIGEN AND GREEK THEOLOGY

reached only through a process of development. The speculations of the Gnostics and the labours of the Apologists, the constructive genius of Origen and the acute dialectic of Athanasius, all contributed towards the evolution of the matured scientific product of the Greek theology as defined by the Councils of Nicæa and Chalcedon.

Everything combined to mark out Alexandria as the place most likely to take the lead in any great intellectual movement. Many currents of thought met and mingled in this cosmopolitan city, which witnessed not only the first attempts at a scientific theology, but also the simultaneous rise of the last great system of ancient philosophy. As a result of the syncretism of the period, a remarkable spirit of toleration prevailed in the community; the adherents of different cults and creeds lived side by side in mutual goodwill. Jews and Samaritans, orthodox Christians and heretics, pagans and philosophers of all schools gathered under the same roof to listen to the prelections of Pantænus and Clement. Christian teachers in their turn, as we know from the examples of Heraclas and Origen, sat at the feet of some heathen professor of philosophy. In these circumstances, even where there was every disposition to be loyal to the faith they professed, it was impossible for any to remain unaffected by the general interchange of ideas. A certain mutual dependence of Christian and heathen speculation was thus one of the most pronounced features of the age. Men of diverse creeds unconsciously influenced one another both as regards the manner and the subject-matter of their thinking. From the standpoint of dogma the Church of Alexandria came thus to play a

PRECURSORS OF ORIGEN

foremost part, and to enjoy an unrivalled pre-eminence. The intellectual life of Antioch, where the new faith had first captured the Gentile heart, was feeble in comparison with that of Alexandria. Athens was too intimately associated with the faded glories of polytheism to dispute with her the supremacy. The genius of Rome lay in the direction not of lofty speculation, but of iron rule, and her Christian population naturally imbibed something of her spirit. The Church of Jerusalem was disqualified by its narrow Judaistic sympathies from taking the lead in theological discussion. This rôle fell therefore to the Alexandrian Church, and was nobly prosecuted and sustained, even during times of persecution.

Philo and his predecessors had to a great extent paved the way for a systematised expression, in terms of Greek philosophy, of the contents of Jewish-Christian tradition. Under the influence of philosophical and Oriental ideas the jagged edges of Judaism had been toned down, and elements of a metaphysical and mystical nature assumed. In the doctrine of the Logos a meeting-point had been found between Jewish monotheism and Gentile philosophy. "All the elements of Christian theology, except the history of Christ, were already prepared in the religious and philosophical eclecticism of Philo and other Jewish Hellenists: the absolute incomprehensibility of God, who, enclosed in the unfathomable abyss of His infinity, acts and manifests Himself only through His Son or the Word; the theory of the Word as necessary mediator between the Most High and rational creatures; that of the prophetic Spirit who sustains and animates the world of souls, and at the same time the entire universe; a morality

4 ORIGEN AND GREEK THEOLOGY

at once cosmopolitan and spiritualistic even to mysticism; the resurrection or the Zoroastrian-Jewish (*masdéo-juive*) doctrine of the future life, tending more and more to confound itself with that of the immortality of the soul, or with the form which the belief in a future life had assumed among the Platonists; in short, the very method that led to universal conciliation, and of which the principle was that 'the letter killeth and the spirit giveth life.'"[1] The *rapprochement* between Jew and Greek was further favoured by the general eclectic tendencies of the period, and by the fact that in their turn the Greeks allegorised their mythology with the view of showing that the various popular deities were merely crude expressions of the manifold activity of the one God.

The special task, then, to which the Christian theologians of Alexandria addressed themselves, was that of harmonising the apostolic tradition concerning Christ with the theological conclusions of the Jewish-Alexandrian philosophers—a task which necessarily involved considerable modification of absolute statement on the one side or the other. The problem had been already attempted by the Gnostics, whose wild speculation had on the one hand seriously endangered Christianity by nullifying both the divinity and the humanity of Christ, and on the other amounted to a gross abuse of the Greek philosophy, which was in consequence being widely put under the ban. It was the aim of the Alexandrian theologians to restore philosophy to its true place by substituting for the false gnosis of Basilides and Valentinus a true churchly gnosis which should do justice to the Old and New

[1] Denis, *De la Philosophie d'Origène*, p. 7.

Testaments alike. Certainly they were not hampered in the execution of their task by any narrow, intolerant, or particularistic view of the Christian tradition; their temptation, indeed, lay in the opposite direction. They were in danger of distorting it, and of destroying its essential character, by a too great readiness to concede the demands of philosophy. So far were they from consenting, with the fiery Tertullian, to denounce philosophy as the fruitful source of heresies, and so convinced were they of its possible value to the Christian faith, that they became themselves philosophers, and proceeded to define their position with regard to existing philosophical schemes of the universe. Not that they exhibited no originality in their thinking, or that it is impossible to decide with respect to fundamental doctrines whether they were derived from Christian or from heathen (Greek or Oriental) sources. But from the fact that many ideas were common to both, the line between philosophy and theology necessarily became very indistinct. Both were developed almost *pari passu*. There was an effort to enrich Christian doctrine by the assumption of elements from the schools, with the twofold result that Christian gnosis was made to include the sum total of knowledge, and that the distinction between scientific investigation and ecclesiastical orthodoxy was obscured. The points of resemblance between philosophy and Christianity were overestimated, and what was most characteristic of the latter was to a large extent lost sight of.

In order, then, to a right conception of the state of matters in Alexandria at the beginning of the third century, it must be recognised that there were growing and working on the same soil two twin schools, the heathen and the Christian. The history of the one is interwoven with that of the other. They existed side by side, opposed and yet indebted to each other in doctrine and teaching. In such circumstances it was clear that a new era must open for Christianity. Hitherto Christian writers had written only in the interests of practical religion. They had been eminently uncritical, and no system of theology had been elaborated. Now, however, the Alexandrian teachers were compelled to attempt something in this direction. The prevailing pagan philosophy had to be met on its own ground. To some degree the Gnostics may be said to have opposed it, but they gave no fair exposition of those Christian principles which they assimilated. The situation of the Alexandrian Christians was thus in many respects unique. They witnessed the fragments of the old systems gathered together to produce, through the introduction of Platonic ideas, a revived and spiritualised paganism in opposition to Christianity, for the ushering in of Neoplatonism by Ammonius constituted the last prop of the old world. If, however, we think to find in the writings of the Alexandrian teachers a systematic refutation of Neoplatonism in its various principles, we shall be disappointed. So, too, if we look for a definite position against Christianity in the works of Platonists. Neither system was as yet sufficiently developed to admit of this. But there was between the two systems an essential difference at bottom, and the real conflict for the Church lay in its being forced very much to leave its own standpoint and adopt that of its opponents. To combat Platonism it must needs accommodate itself to philosophy, and in submitting to this it became fettered with philosophical adjuncts to a dangerously suicidal extent. As in its conflict with Judaism, so also here, Christianity insensibly assimilated part of the error against which it strove. That errors, mystical, speculative, allegorical, and pagan, began to choke it like so many weeds, is clear from the works of the men who, from their position as prefects of the Catechetical School, necessarily became apologists for Christianity. All of them were more or less tinctured with Platonic views. They were themselves philosophers, and so could sympathise with their opponents, whose error they were disposed to view rather as one of defect than as a total perversion of truth. In this way they were led to overestimate the similarity between pagan and Christian wisdom. Prior to the latter part of the second century Christian teaching, with very few exceptions, had been true to apostolic example; but after philosophers embraced Christianity, and the new Platonism, which allied itself to Orientalism, began to exert its influence, the case was altered. The intellectual was frequently represented as the chief or only side of Christianity to be attended to; it was regarded not so much as a rule of life as a speculative scheme of doctrine. From this the transition was easy to "mysteries" similar to those of heathenism. Certain views were kept secret as a higher species of doctrine suitable only for the cultivated few. An attempt was made, in short, to provide the gospel with a philosophy, and to resolve it into such a system as philosophers would embrace.

Nor is the explanation of all this far to seek. It may at first sight seem strange that Christian teachers could embrace doctrines known to be Platonic, but we

8 ORIGEN AND GREEK THEOLOGY

must recollect that these same doctrines were supposed to have been borrowed from Holy Scripture, which they believed to be the revelation of God's wisdom to men. Speculative theologians, moreover, have always been influenced by contemporary philosophy, and these Alexandrian Fathers only sought to express the doctrines of the faith in a form adapted to the spirit of the times. Men like Justin and Clement had themselves passed over from heathen philosophy, and naturally carried with them much of its influence; but they had nevertheless an ardent desire to see Christian truth in its right place. It would be as unwarrantable to seek the main source of their theology in the philosophical speculation of the period as it would be to say that the Hebrew religion was essentially altered in the post-exilic period because it embellished itself somewhat with Persian angelology. After all, the Alexandrian Fathers "did not exchange the gospel for Neoplatonism."[1] They resolutely maintained the supreme authority of Holy Scripture; and with whatever distortions and incongruities it may have been associated, the assertion of this principle of an objective rule of faith was in itself of the utmost value in combating a philosophy of which the only standard lay in the subjective notions of its advocates.

The moulding of Christian theology according to the Greek type is specially identified with the Catechetical School of Alexandria. The origin of this famous school appears to have been as spontaneous as its growth was marked. It arose out of the necessities of the Alexandrian Church, but of its first beginnings we

[1] Redepenning, i. p. 98.

have no historical account. Owing, probably, to this circumstance it has been variously described as a school for catechumens, as a theological seminary, and as a philosophical institute. While it had elements represented by all of these names, it would be wrong to associate it with any one of them exclusively. It was a product of the gradual evolution of Church life in an educated community, and as such adapted itself to the changing necessities of the times. Apparently destined at first for the education of catechumens after the informal instruction of an earlier period no longer sufficed, it soon became a famous school of theology; and in view of its environment and of the intellectual bent of its most influential teachers, it is not wonderful that it became a school of philosophy as well. Contiguity to a great seat of learning has always an influence on Church life, and in a university town like Alexandria the Christian community as a whole, and the Catechetical School in particular, were inevitably affected in this way. The flower of their youth —students like Ambrosius and Heraclas—listened to the lectures of the Greek professors, while many of the latter, like Celsus and Porphyry, applied themselves to the critical study of the Scriptures. This mutual intercourse between the Church and the shrine of classical learning gave to the catechetical instruction in Alexandria a more systematic and scholastic form than it elsewhere assumed, and by the middle of the second century it had crystallised into a regular institution.

Although the catechist's office was not an ecclesiastical one in the sense of requiring any special consecration, his was not simply "the calling of a philosopher who held public lectures" (διατριβή).[1] No one could exercise this office without the consent of the bishop; and only in so far as it was carried on in his name and under his supervision was the instruction "public." Students were taught in the catechist's own house, not in a building set apart for the purpose. Although no salary was attached to the office, the catechetical teachers were virtually supported by their hearers. At first there may have been only one, but sometimes there were several, and they were free either to obtain an assistant or to vacate the post. Also, to begin with, there were no set hours for teaching, and no gradation of classes. Sometimes the teachers were in request the whole day long. The aim of the instruction given was the preparation of catechumens, especially those drawn from the learned heathen, for admission to Christian privileges and for the service of the Church. These cultured converts from paganism became in due time effective Christian teachers, and had among their pupils Christian youths and others who wished to gain a student's knowledge of Christianity. When the immediate disciples of the apostles no longer survived, a converted philosopher seemed to many the most reliable of guides. Thus in the second century we find multitudes gathered round Justin Martyr at Rome, Aristides at Athens, and Pantænus at Alexandria. The method of instruction was varied to suit pupils, who were of both sexes and of different ages. "We put the gospel before each one, as his character and disposition may fit him to receive it."[2]

[1] Schnitzer, *Origenes über die Grundlehren der Glaubenswissenschaft*, p. v.
[2] Origen, *Contra Celsum*, vi. 10.

PRECURSORS OF ORIGEN

If to some were imparted only the elementary facts of the Christian faith, others were introduced to more advanced studies in Christian doctrine, and trained in philosophy as well. What was embraced in a complete course of training is made clear from the detailed account given by Gregory Thaumaturgus of the course of study prescribed by Origen for his students.[1] "He took us in hand as a skilled husbandman may take in hand some field unwrought;" "he put us to the question, and made propositions to us, and listened to our replies;" he trained "that capacity of our minds which deals critically with words and reasonings." His pupils, Gregory tells us, were next introduced to natural science, geometry, and astronomy. To this was added the study of philosophy on the broad basis of a careful perusal of all the ancient poets and philosophers "except only the productions of the atheists." A programme like this would, of course, give ample scope for a suggestive comparison of pagan and Christian wisdom. The study of physical and mental science was a preparation for the still more important subjects of ethics and theology. Ethical problems lend themselves peculiarly to keen dialectic discussion after the Socratic method, and this was the method adopted in the Catechetical School for the expulsion of ignorance and error, and for the cultivation of a genuine love of truth. This Christian school, moreover, was honourably distinguished from the pagan schools of the period by making virtue a subject for practice, and not merely for definition and dis-

[1] Gregory is, indeed, here speaking of Origen's later work in Cæsarea; but the methods and subjects adopted by him there were doubtless those previously in use at Alexandria.

12 ORIGEN AND GREEK THEOLOGY

course. Says Gregory of Origen, "he stimulated us by the deeds he did more than by the doctrines he taught." But the grand distinctive feature of this school was its theology—its declaration regarding the incarnation, death, and resurrection of Jesus Christ as the Saviour of the world. To this all other topics and themes were reckoned subsidiary. It would be difficult to conceive a more enlightened scheme of Christian education than this, which the wisdom of the Alexandrian Fathers had already drawn up and put in force at the close of the second century. It fairly harnessed secular science to the chariot of Christian apologetics.

The Catechetical School first emerges from historic obscurity about A.D. 190. It was then under the mastership of Pantænus, a convert from Stoicism. Of his personal history little is known. According to Photius, his teachers were men who had seen the apostles. Jerome represents him as an extensive (allegorical) commentator, and as having discovered a Hebrew version of St. Matthew's Gospel during a missionary journey to the East; but, with the exception of a single remark about the use of the tenses in the prophetic writings, his works have perished. Ignorant as we are as to the particular nature of his teaching, we know that he was the first to give to the Alexandrian School its distinctive character as one that mingled philosophy with religious instruction. He was succeeded by his own pupil, the better known Titus Flavius Clemens.

Clement was born, probably at Athens, about the middle of the second century. His studies in religion led him to forsake paganism and embrace Christianity. The same inquiring spirit caused him afterwards to

PRECURSORS OF ORIGEN

travel through many lands in search of the most distinguished Christian teachers. Referring to this, he says: "The last of those whom I met was first in power. On falling in with him I found rest, having tracked him while he lay concealed in Egypt. He was, in truth, the Sicilian bee, and, plucking the flowers of the prophetic and apostolic meadow, he produced a wonderfully pure knowledge in the souls of the listeners."[1] The allusion here is obviously to Pantænus. Clement, who attained the rank of presbyter in the Church of Alexandria, discharged his catechetical duties with much distinction, and counted among his pupils Origen and Alexander, bishop of Jerusalem. In the year 202, during the persecution of Severus, he appears to have quitted Alexandria. Of his subsequent movements nothing is known except that in 211 he travelled to Antioch, and carried a letter of recommendation from Alexander of Jerusalem, who speaks highly of the service rendered by Clement to the Church of his own diocese.

In the great work of winning the Greek world for Christianity, Clement was the immediate precursor of Origen, the forerunner without whom Origen, as we know him, could not have been. His birth and training, as well as his temperament and scholarly acquirements, fitted him for the part he was destined to play. He knew the world both on its pagan and its Christian side. The Greek classics were as familiar to him as the Christian Scriptures. He was equally at home with the Greek philosophy and the Pauline theology. Essentially a literary man, he quotes—sometimes loosely, it must be confessed—from hun-

[1] *Stromateis*, i. 1.

14 ORIGEN AND GREEK THEOLOGY

dreds of authors, and evidently made good use of the library in the Sarapieion. He was neither an eloquent orator nor a bustling ecclesiastic, neither a public disputant nor a social reformer, but a genial man of letters, of a meditative cast of mind, and with a certain distaste for the strife and turmoil of everyday life.

The obscuration by the Gnostics, not only of the real nature of redemption, but also of the character of God, led Tertullian and others to pronounce Greek learning the invention of demons. Clement's whole teaching amounted to a strenuous denial of this position. Whatever its origin—and Clement still repeats the old charge of "theft" from the Pentateuch [1]—philosophy was in his estimation no work of darkness, but in each of its forms a ray of light from the Logos, and therefore belonging of right to the Christian. Strong as Gnosticism was in Alexandria, and strong as were the orthodox party in the Church who took their stand upon the creed *simpliciter*, " even in that age and place Clement saw and dared to proclaim that the cure of error is not less knowledge but more." [2] With an almost passionate conviction he asserted not only that there is in the Church a legitimate place and function for secular learning,—*e.g.* in the exposition of Scripture,—but also that such learning is ethically indispensable, inasmuch as it needs an intelligent Christian to act justly. Science, he contended, although it lends grace and clearness to the preacher, is no mere

---

[1] It is doubtful how far Clement was really convinced of this, although he speaks of philosophy having been "stolen as the fire by Prometheus," and allows that John x. 8 may be applicable to Greek philosophers (*Strom.* i. 17). He knew, at any rate, that their dialectic had not been borrowed by the Greeks.

[2] Bigg, *The Christian Platonists of Alexandria*, p. 50.

ornamental fringe to religion; it is necessary to right conduct. What philosophers of all schools had been aiming at was also the aim of Christianity, viz. a nobler life. The difference, according to Clement, was this: while the ancient philosophers had been unable to get more than glimpses of the truth, it was left to Christianity to make known in Christ the perfect truth. The various epochs in the history of the world all pointed forward to this final revelation; and just as the law prepared the Jews, so also philosophy prepared the Greeks for Christ. Clement believed in a similar evolution in the Christian life. As the world must needs go through several stages preparatory to the coming of Christ, so must a man advance by degrees from faith ($\pi\iota\sigma\tau\iota\varsigma$) to love, and from love to knowledge ($\gamma\nu\tilde{\omega}\sigma\iota\varsigma$), to the position of a perfect Christian. What he and his fellow-teachers set themselves to do, therefore, was to educate philosophers up to the point of accepting Christianity, which they represented as only a higher development and further advance on the same line as that along which they had themselves been travelling.[1] The same God had been recognised by Greek, Jew, and Christian alike, but to the last only had there been given a truly spiritual knowledge of Him. Christianity was the ultimate goal for all philosophy. Whatever was good in the latter was (as Justin had already taught) the result of the teaching of the same Logos who in Christianity had revealed the totality of truth. While, therefore, Clement admires, and within proper limits defends, philosophy,

[1] "There is in philosophy . . . a slender spark capable of being fanned into flame, a trace of wisdom and an impulse from God" (*Strom.* i. 17).

he maintains its inadequacy as a guide to the knowledge of God.[1] Although viewing it as good in itself, as a useful weapon for the defence of Christian truth, and as an invaluable aid in the education of the enlightened man—the true Gnostic, he clearly sees its limits, and refuses to set it in the seat of Christ, the one Physician of the soul. If on its intellectual side Clement's theology is coloured by Greek philosophy, on its religious side it is derived directly from Christianity. If he thinks as a Platonist, he feels as a Christian. The two sources from which he drew—Greek philosophy and literature on the one hand, and the Bible and Christianity on the other—are no doubt at many points imperfectly fused; instead of an intimate blending of philosophy and tradition, we have them set merely in juxtaposition. For instance, at one time, in characteristic philosophic fashion, he strips God of all His attributes and conceives Him as the pure Monad; at another he abandons this transcendental position and apprehends God as the loving Father of His creatures. But in the circumstances this defect is not surprising; it arose from his being at once an advocate and an opponent of philosophy.

Clement further maintained that, in order to a fullgrown Christian manhood, practical piety must be combined with intellectual freedom. There must, he held, be scope for reason as well as for faith, for knowledge as well as for love. This led him, in common with others of the Alexandrian school, to attach less importance to mere historical facts than to the underlying ideas. The letter of revelation he brought under the judgment of reason. But not so as to make reason

[1] See *Strom.* i. 20.

independent of faith, which he declared to be as necessary for spiritual as breath for physical life.[1] It was his endeavour to do justice to both, and to represent both as essential to a healthy piety. In this way Clement at once anticipated the great principle of Protestantism, and showed sympathy with the standpoint of the Mystics, although with him the mystical has always its roots in the rational.

In his view of Holy Scripture Clement stands midway between Justin and theologians like Irenæus and Tertullian. On the one hand he makes use of sacred Christian writings as well as of the Old Testament. But on the other hand he does not educe from the Christian tradition a series of propositions purporting to embrace the whole content of Christianity, and represent these as an apostolic rule of faith. The *regula fidei* of the Churches of Rome and Carthage had not yet been established in the Alexandrian Church. In Clement's view the enlightened man is able to decide as to the truth of Christian doctrine. Apart from the appearance of the Logos in flesh, the most perfect revelation given to men in this life is that contained in the Old and New Testaments, which are throughout verbally inspired. Its simplicity of language is intended to make it comprehensible to all; and as it affords everything needful for the soul's peace and happiness, and is the best guide to holiness, it should be read daily. While treating the law as inferior to the gospel in respect of its teaching being more negative and more obscure, and based upon fear instead of love, he yet asserts the unity of all scripture as emanating from the Most High; "for faith in

[1] *Strom.* ii. 6.

18 ORIGEN AND GREEK THEOLOGY

Christ and the knowledge of the gospel are the explanation and fulfilment of the law." In defending the unity of Holy Scripture against the Gnostics, who strongly impeached the morality of the Old Testament in connection with such things, *e.g.* as the approval of wars of extermination, Clement is content to maintain that justice (severity) is not incompatible with goodness, being indeed but its obverse side. It was left for Origen to attempt a systematic refutation of the charges of immorality thus brought against Jehovah. Assuming that whatever fragments of truth may be in the possession of heathen authors must be contained in the source from which they were all originally borrowed, Clement further seeks through inspired Scripture to arrive at the solution of the speculative questions canvassed in his time.

Corresponding to the twofold nature of the incarnate Logos is the double sense of Scripture—the outward or literal, and the inner or allegorical.[1] The "method of concealment," or the wrapping-up of truth in figures, is both necessary and universal,—necessary, because the inexpressible God of the universe can never be committed to writing; universal, because common to men of different nationalities and to sacred and profane writers alike.[2] In support of the latter statement,

[1] According to Clement (*Strom.* i. 28), Scripture has even a fourfold sense—the literal, the mystic, the moral, and the prophetic. For τετραχῶς some would read τριχῶς, as the three last senses only are specified, but the literal may be omitted as self-evident. Clement also classifies "the Mosaic philosophy" as—(1) History, (2) Legislation (=Ethics), (3) Sacrifice (=Physics), (4) Theology or Epopteia (=Metaphysics or Dialectics). This identification of the sacrificial with physical science is certainly very forced. Epopteia or vision was the term used of the highest stage of initiation into the mysteries.

[2] *Strom.* v. 4.

Clement points to the mystic meaning of the Mosaic Tabernacle and its furniture, to the Egyptian hieroglyphics and sphinxes, and to the Greek oracles, poets, and philosophers.

The practical outcome of these views is seen in the distinction drawn between the true Gnostic or fully enlightened Christian and the ordinary unsophisticated disciple. The belief of the former is elevated into a mystery which may not be revealed to the latter any more than to the profane. When truth is veiled in symbols, the true Gnostic apprehends where the ignorrant man fails; hence the inadvisability of exposing the benefits of wisdom to all and sundry (*Strom.* v. 9). Founding on Col. i. 25 ff., Clement holds that hidden mysteries received by the apostles from the Lord had been handed down in direct succession until those who possessed the tradition of the blessed doctrine "came by God's will to us also to deposit those ancestral and apostolic seeds" (*Strom.* i. 1, vi. 8). These Christian mysteries were not disclosed to the general body of the pupils attending the Catechetical School. Their proper diet was "milk" or catechetical instruction, and not "meat" or mystic contemplation. On this principle the lower grades among the catechumens were not introduced to anything which he reckoned as *Gnosis*. They had the fundamental dogmas of the Church expounded to them, but not the abstruser speculations about "the being of God, the origin of the world, the last things, the relation of reason to revelation, of philosophy to Christianity, of faith to knowledge," which were reserved for the enlightened. It is clear, however, from some extant passages of works written by Clement for general use, that he took note of heresies with the view of fortifying the catechumens against apostasy.[1] All were taught the gospel from the standpoint of one who acknowledged that even in paganism there were finger-posts pointing to Christ; all were instructed, probably with much minuteness, in Christian ethics, both individual and social; but only the specially devoted were taken as it were into the Holy of holies and secretly schooled in the deeper mysteries.

Although his teaching does not seem to have been characterised by orderliness, his daring flights of thought, his lively speech, with its wealth of figure and literary allusion, and his spiritual depth, must have profoundly impressed his hearers, and probably Origen among the rest. It seems more than likely that the latter became orally acquainted with his views, and imbibed from him the distinction of exoteric and esoteric doctrine. At any rate his influence on Origen is undoubted. That writer never, indeed, quotes Clement by name, but his works show how much he was indebted to his genial and erudite predecessor in the Catechetical School.

With the exception of the treatise *Quis Dives Salvetur* (" Who is the rich man that is saved?"), Clement's extant writings are limited to three great works which form a connected and graduated series. The idea underlying the whole of this tripartite work is that of the activity of the Logos, the reason of the world, and the divine teacher of the human race. As such he "first conducts the rude heathen, sunk in sin and idolatry, to the faith; then progressively reforms their lives by moral precepts; and finally elevates those who have undergone this moral purification to the profounder knowledge

[1] His own phrase is that he drew round them "a hedge" of learning.

PRECURSORS OF ORIGEN 21

of divine things, which he calls *Gnosis*."[1] Clement's one great theme was this divinely wrought development in the spiritual life of men. The *Protreptikos* ("Exhortation to the Heathen") is an appeal to his pagan hearers to rise above the slavery of custom; to abandon a worship not only irrational in itself, but associated with immorality and cruelty, and to take on them the yoke of Christ. Brimful of classical lore, it is written throughout in a cultured and Christian spirit, and contains many passages of great beauty. The *Pœdagogos* ("Instructor") is addressed to neophytes, and is designed to train them in the art of Christian living as "an indispensable preparation for the contemplative knowledge of God." In the first of the three books into which it is divided Clement exhibits Christ as the great *Pœdagogus*, dealing, however, more with the method than with the substance of His teaching. The second and third books contain very minute regulations as to the behaviour required of a Christian in the different experiences, relations, and circumstances of life. Although no longer necessary, such an encyclopædia of conduct may well have served a useful purpose among those just emerging from heathenism and beset with great temptations and difficulties. At the close of the third book Clement gives a bird's-eye view of the ethical side of Christian life; and appended to the "Instructor" are two hymns ascribed to his pen. *Stromateis* ("Miscellanies," lit. coverlets made out of odd pieces of cloth) is the fitting title given by Clement to his largest work. It is a miscellaneous collection of materials drawn partly from Greek philosophy and literature, and partly from Scripture, without any

[1] Neander, *Church History*, ii. p. 486.

definite plan or arrangement, and designed to enable those already familiar with the discipline of the Instructor to advance to a higher Christian gnosis founded upon faith. It seeks to exhibit the attitude of the true Christian Gnostic to philosophy. Of the eight books of which it was composed the last appears to have been lost, its place having been taken by a fragmentary treatise upon Logic which had originally no connection with the work.

According to some writers,[1] it was Clement's intention to publish a further treatise suitable for more matured Christians, somewhat on the lines of Origen's *De Principiis*, with the view of leading them, through the help of philosophy, to a more recondite knowledge of Christian truth. However this may be, it is at any rate permissible to discount liberally Clement's statement that he did not impart all he knew. He was aware, of course, that his work would be misused by the heathen, and by some Christians as well, but he was anxious to counteract Hellenic and heretical literature, and to protect esoteric doctrine from falsification and destruction. For these reasons, and also to assist his own memory in old age, he felt constrained to write the above-mentioned works in which nothing essential has been withheld. At the same time, he appears to have resolved in all the circumstances not to treat the esoteric doctrine systematically, but to weave it in with his lectures in the form of hints to those who could profit by them. Nor is Clement to be taken too seriously when he represents the whole contents of the *Stromateis* as tradition, for there was in his day a strong desire to emulate the antiquity of

[1] Eugene de Faye, *Clement d'Alexandrie*.

philosophical systems, and to regard the form of truth arrived at as permanently fixed. Even then, it would seem, there were advocates of what has been wittily termed "tinned theology."

From the necessity of the situation Clement's teaching assumed a generally *apologetic* aspect, and accordingly it is from the standpoint of apologetics, and not from that of dogma, that it must be judged.[1] By the light which it threw upon the great problems raised by philosophy regarding God, the world, and the human soul, Christianity had awakened the dormant spiritual sense in vast multitudes of men. But in the matter of satisfying the spiritual needs of humanity it found a rival claimant in Neoplatonism, which took for its religious ideal the direct apprehension of the divine essence. Thus, it was believed, would the traditional worship receive a new impetus, and the desideratum, for want of which men were seceding to Christianity, be supplied. The promoters of Neoplatonism saw that if heathenism was to prevail, it must both get rid of its more glaring absurdities, and also strengthen itself by a large accession of ideas, principles, and rites. Thus they borrowed whatever appeared to them good from every available source. They contemplated nothing less than the introduction of a universal religion, constructed on principles so broad that the wise of all the earth could adhere to it. It was their aim to set matters right between philosophy and theology, between doctrine and life, and to satisfy the needs of the soul on a scale to which Christianity could make no pretension. Such, then, was the situation which Clement had to meet, and it fully explains the apolo-

[1] Dods, *Erasmus and other Essays*, p. 129.

getic drift of his writings as well as his constant references to philosophy.

Before pronouncing a hasty judgment on the extent to which Clement has allowed his philosophic bent to influence his theology, we must take into account the character of his environment. One of the dangers of the prevailing eclecticism was that it tended too much to speculation. Possibly for a Christian teacher in Alexandria there was no choice; either the gospel had to be presented in the light in which it was presented by Clement, or it could have obtained no hearing at all. At any rate he deliberately chose his method of stating the truth, and there is no reason to doubt that he honestly tried to serve Christ by pleading His cause in terms fitted to appeal to the cultured Greeks of his time.

Although no systematic theologian in the modern sense, Clement may be said to have laid the foundation of a true scientific Christian dogmatic. His position marks a great advance upon that of Justin, who to some extent anticipated him. Departing from the purely apologetic aim of that writer, Clement conceived his task to include a certain positive presentation of Christian truth as well. To the idea of the Logos in particular he gave a much fuller and more definite content than Justin did, and made it the keystone of his religious philosophy, and of his interpretation of Christianity. The gospel is the highest revelation of the Logos, who has given indication of his presence wherever men rise above the level of the beasts and of the uncivilised savage. All truth and goodness are traced to the Light that lighteneth every man that cometh into the world. This " bold and joyous thinker " constructed in this way an optimistic theory of human history of a singularly attractive kind, in which the Saviour is represented as smiling upon and nurturing every root of beauty and nobleness, of piety and worth, which has at any time and in any place sprung up on the soil of humanity. A place was thus found within the pale of Christianity for the whole of Hellenic culture as a stage in the education of mankind. But while the Logos is the moral and rational in every degree of evolution, it is only from revelation that a reliable knowledge of him can be gained. "In Christ he is the officiating high priest, and the blessings he bestows are a series of holy initiations which alone contain the possibility of man's raising himself to the divine life."[1] Christianity is thus, according to Clement, the doctrine of the Logos, the creator, teacher, and redeemer of men, whose finished product is found in the man of true knowledge, the perfect gnostic. "His great work, which has rightly been called the boldest literary undertaking in the history of the Church, is the first attempt to use Holy Scripture and the Church tradition together with the assumption that Christ as the Reason of the world is the source of all truth, as the basis of a presentation of Christianity which at once addresses itself to the cultured by satisfying the scientific demand for a philosophical ethic and theory of the world, and at the same time reveals to the believer the rich content of his faith."[2]

It is impossible here to enter minutely on the subject of Clement's dogmatic, which he made no attempt to construct into a regular system. On the basis of the

---

[1] Harnack, *History of Dogma*, ii. p. 324.
[2] Harnack, *loc. cit.*

materials scattered throughout his pages its main lines may, however, be briefly indicated.

One of his merits is that he grasps so firmly the doctrine of the Trinity. A writer who pronounces his scheme of doctrine "very meagre and latitudinarian" certifies his soundness on this point.[1] Distinctly as he affirms the doctrine of the Trinity, it can scarcely be said, however, that in his writings this doctrine appears in a more advanced form of development than in those of his predecessors. God is inexpressible, having neither parts, qualities, nor relations. "He is formless and nameless, though we sometimes give Him titles which are not to be taken in their proper sense,—the One, the Good, Intelligence or Existence, or Father, or God, or Creator, or Lord" (*Strom.* v. 12). This idea of God, whom he further speaks of as the great "depth" or "abyss," would hardly be distinguishable from the empty abstraction of Philo and the Alexandrian Platonists, were it not for the qualifying declaration that to the Son of God there is nothing incomprehensible. God is therefore not absolutely, but only relatively, incomprehensible. It is owing to our limitations as human beings that He is to us inscrutable. Clement summons an old poet to express his meaning—

"Him see I not, for round about, a cloud
Has settled ; for in mortal eyes are small,
And mortal pupils—only flesh and bones grow there."

God is manifested through the Son, by whose grace as Logos He has in some degree been known to the nobler spirits of every age and country. In the New Testament, however, He is revealed as a Trinity—Father, Son, and

[1] Cunningham, *Hist. Theol.* i. p. 150.

PRECURSORS OF ORIGEN

Holy Spirit. While the Father is not knowable, the Son as the mind or consciousness of the Father may become the object of knowledge. After Philo, he speaks of the Son as the Name, Energy, Face, etc., of God; but between the Father and the Son there is an essential unity, and prayer may be offered to the Son. Clement is not less explicit as to the coequality and coeternity of the First and Second Persons in the Godhead. While his view of the relations of the Third Person to the First and Second Persons is nowhere clearly stated, he undoubtedly accepts the distinct personality of the Holy Spirit. "O mystic marvel," he exclaims, "the universal Father is One, and One the universal Word, and the Holy Spirit is one and the same everywhere."[1] The Spirit he also represents as speaking by the prophets,[2] and as the Sanctifier of soul and body.[3] It is, however, as Clement is careful to explain in a quotation from the apostolic Barnabas, not in essence, but in power, that the Holy Spirit dwells in the heart, which from having been "the house of demons" has become through faith the temple of God.[4]

Clement's general view of the creation is based upon that of Philo, although he denies the pre-existence of matter and of the soul. The creation of the world through the Word is the outcome and the manifestation of God's eternal goodness. It was this that prompted Him to become Creator and Father. Man was the special object of His love, and as such, in an important sense, the end of creation. God communicated to man what was peculiar to Himself, and made him a beauti-

[1] *Pæd.* i. 6.   [2] *Protrept.* i. 8.
[3] *Strom.* iv. 2, 6.   [4] *Strom.* v. 20.

28 ORIGEN AND GREEK THEOLOGY

ful breathing instrument of music. "The Word of God, despising the lyre and harp, which are but lifeless instruments, and having tuned by the Holy Spirit the universe, and especially man,—who, composed of body and soul, is a universe in miniature,—makes melody to God on this instrument of many tones."[1] This divine element, imparted to man by the Word, constitutes between him and God an essential spiritual affinity which has not been totally destroyed even by the Fall.

The existence of sin Clement holds to be sufficiently explained by the freedom of the human will.[2] Although God foresaw who would prove rebellious, they were not predestinated to evil; obedience is possible to us. There is no incompatibility between grace and freewill, for "God's greatest gift is self-restraint."[3] Clement repudiates the claim of the disciples of Basilides and Valentinus with respect to their enjoyment of a natural advantage in the shape of a germ of superior excellence, —a claim which based the salvation of the complete Christian, not upon faith as the result of free choice, but upon an arbitrary supramundane selection on the part of God. Such necessitarianism would, he points out, at once cancel the guilt of unbelief by freeing man from responsibility, and leave no room for repentance, or forgiveness, or baptism. Evil is the deliberate act of man, and is not to be ascribed to any hereditary taint in human nature. The soul is not begotten. We fall as Adam fell, not because of his sin, but

---

[1] *Protrept.* chap. i.

[2] The phrase *liberum arbitrium* is Tertullian's, but it exactly expresses Clement's meaning.

[3] *Strom.* ii. 20.

PRECURSORS OF ORIGEN

through our own lust. Clement refuses to believe that the newborn babe, who has done nothing, can rest under any condemnation. It is only wilful sin that God punishes.

While denying "original sin," Clement admits that fallen man is powerless to restore himself to good. Here we need the help of Christ. The eternal Word has appeared as man in order to become our Teacher and Saviour. "Lost as we already were, He accomplished our salvation."[1] It was the object of His incarnation and death to deliver us from the guilt, and from the ignorance which constitutes the power, of sin. Like the Alexandrians generally, Clement lays more stress upon the latter aspect of redemption than upon the former. The ideas of atonement and forgiveness did not fit in well with their favourite belief as to the unchanging God. Yet, in view of certain statements contained in his own writings, it would be a mistake to say that he entirely ignores the sacrificial character of Christ's work. No doubt the term "Lamb of God" is applied to Him only in respect of His innocence. It is also true that Clement fails to grasp the expiatory significance of the Mosaic sacrifices. For him they simply express devotion to God and the return to holiness. And the raison d'être of Christ's sacrifice upon the cross is in like manner to lead us back to the practice of the good. Nevertheless — whether consistently or not is another question — he speaks of the Lord being immolated and bearing the wood of the cross;[2] of the Word as Mediator;[3] and of Christ as giving Himself in sacrifice for us,[4] as the expiator of

---
[1] Pæd. i. 4. [2] Pæd. i. 5. [3] Pæd. iii. 1.
[4] Strom. v. 11, vii. 3; Pæd. i. 11.

sin, the Saviour, the Reconciler, the giver of peace.[1] He further writes: "And He is the propitiator for our sins, as John says; Jesus who heals both our body and soul,"[2] and represents Jesus as addressing the sinner in these terms: "I am the master of heavenly wisdom; I have wrestled with death for thee. I have abolished that death which was thy due, on account of thy sins and unbelief."[3] When all is said, however, there is no doubt that, in the general view of Clement, salvation hangs not upon atonement, but upon moral amendment; not upon Christ's finished work as a sacrificial victim for the sins of men, but merely upon the fact of a spiritual transformation wrought in us by the Word as the world's Instructor. He fails, though, to find in such a position a solid basis for man's restoration to goodness, and is obliged to fall back upon the distinction of "First and Second Repentance." Only for pre-baptismal sins, *i.e.* sins committed in the darkness of ignorance, is there a free pardon in consideration of the work of Christ. He who has received forgiveness ought to sin no more. Yet God in his mercy has vouchsafed a second repentance for the transgressions of believers. These must be purged by corrective discipline, which may not end with the present life, in order that at length we may be raised to the highest degree of heavenly glory. Meanwhile, those who have entered on the distinctive Christian life must look upon "the risen Lord, the fountain not of pardon, but of life." As God, Christ forgives our sins, and as Man trains us not to sin.[4] In Clement's view redemption is not so much the restoration of what man lost by the

---

[1] *Protrept.* x.   [2] *Pæd.* iii. 12.
[3] *Quis div. salv.* xxiii.   [4] *Pæd.* i. 3.

Fall as it is the grand climax of human destiny. "The Word of God became man, that thou mayest learn from man how man may become God."[1]

As given to us at the first our reason is pure and uncontaminated. But we need more than reason and freewill in order to attain vital fellowship with God. These afford adequate guidance for our earthly life, but can lead us no higher. The true Gnostic builds up his spiritual life on his faith, which is "a sort of natural art," and contributes to the process of learning as the earth's productive power co-operates with the seed cast into it. In the higher life the faith of the ordinary believer becomes knowledge, the hope and fear of the lower life are supplanted by love, while holiness, or the negative virtue of abstinence from what is evil, is transmuted into righteousness. Man's salvation is thus a gradual process. Beginning with faith, it rises into love, and finally to perfect knowledge. We are fed by Christ's body and blood in the Eucharist, He becomes our Light and our Life, and we are led to "the mountain beloved of God, not the subject of tragedies like Cithæron, but consecrated to dramas of the truth,—a mount of sobriety, shaded with forests of purity."[2]

The Christian must advance from faith to knowledge by the path of simple obedience and rectitude. In spite of his inadequate conception of the doctrine of redemption, Clement's writings are pervaded by the highest spirituality of tone and feeling, and embody the noblest moral ideals. This is due to his having made the love of God the fundamental principle of his doctrine. If he fails to harmonise the divine love and holiness, he nevertheless reaches by a path of his own

[1] *Protrept.* i. 8.   [2] *Protrept.* xii.

the great gospel truth of man's reconciliation to God through the Word made flesh, and with masterly ability sums up its logical and practical results. For Clement, Christian morality means the imitation of God. This is the one great principle running through his often very detailed treatment of Christian ethics. By the aid of the incarnate Word we are enabled to become imitators of God. The true Christian may engage in any honourable occupation, or take part in public affairs, without injury to the higher life. There is no exceptional virtue in poverty, celibacy, or martyrdom as such; for Christian morality is not a matter of outward distinctions or circumstances, but of inner love to God.

When at length the Christian attains to *gnosis*, he no longer does anything evil, but has freed himself from the dominion of passion, and lives according to reason. Here we reach what is most characteristic in Clement's teaching. The now familiar distinction between the Church visible and invisible was not yet clearly drawn, and Clement, from what he saw of the lives of many who were flocking into the Church, was driven back upon Philo's distinction of the two lives, for which he found corroboration in St. Paul's antithesis between milk and meat as the food suited respectively for babes and full-grown men. In the acquisition of this saving knowledge Clement leaves more to man's unaided powers than is warranted by Scripture, but he was probably led into overstatement here by the denial on the part of the false Gnostics that the spiritual destiny of man is in any way contingent upon his own will.

The Church is the city of God, a decorous body

PRECURSORS OF ORIGEN

and assemblage of men regulated by the Word.[1] She is the Bride of Christ,[2] and the Virgin Mother.[3] She is one, true, ancient, catholic, apostolic.[4] We are bound in no way to transgress the canon of the Church.[5] There is a wide difference between the Church and "a school" set up by heretical sophists and supported by human arts of their own invention.[6] Although Clement distinguishes between bishops and presbyters,[7] and calls Peter the first of the apostles,[8] he knows nothing of the claims of Rome to the power of the keys. He is not concerned about the different orders of clergy, his references to this subject being of the most casual description. In particular, he never alludes to it in connection with the Sacraments. For Clement the real antitype of the Old Testament priest is the Christian Gnostic, who offers with a pure mind and unswerving abstraction from the body and its passions the sacrifice of praise, and the incense of prayer, upon the altar of the congregation of the saints. Nor does he attach importance to consecrated buildings. "For it is not the place, but the company of the elect, that I call the Church."[9]

For the rest, Clement held that after death perfect blessedness will be reached through a further process of spiritual development, accepted the Pauline doctrine of a glorified resurrection body, and allowed the possibility of repentance and reformation until the last day, when probation would cease.[10] He adhered to

[1] *Strom.* iv. 26.
[2] *Strom.* iii. 6.
[3] *Pæd.* i. 6.
[4] *Strom.* vii. 17.
[5] *Strom.* vii. 7.
[6] *Strom.* vii. 15.
[7] *Pæd.* iii. 12 ; *Strom.* vi. 13.
[8] *Quis div. salv.* 21.
[9] *Strom.* vii. 5.
[10] *Strom.* vii. 2, 16.

34   ORIGEN AND GREEK THEOLOGY

the Platonic theory that the sole object of punishment is amendment,—a theory which logically carries with it the final restoration of all. The latter doctrine, however, was not formulated by Clement, although sometimes he makes a close approach to it, as when he says: "For all things are arranged with a view to the salvation of the universe, both generally and particularly."[1] But it was soon to receive full and bold expression in the writings of Origen, his great successsor, whose master-thought was the unity underlying all phenomena and making steadily for the removal of all discord and evil.

[1] *Strom.* vii. 2.

CHAPTER II

LIFE AND CHARACTER OF ORIGEN

ORIGEN was born in Egypt, probably at Alexandria, in or about the year 185. He bore the surname Adamantios,[1] which has been supposed by some to point to the irresistible force of his arguments, and by others to his own diligence. The latter idea found further expression in the epithets Chalcenteros (*Man of brass*), applied to him by Jerome, and Syntactes (*Composer*), given him by others. It cannot be inferred from the name Origen (*i.e.* son of Or or Horus, the Egyptian sun-god) that his parents became Christians only after his birth, for such names as Diotrephes, Hermas, Apollinaris, etc., continued for long to be quite customary among Greek Christians.

His father Leonides was a prominent member of the Christian community at Alexandria, although the statement of Suidas that he was "bishop" is not otherwise corroborated. A man of means and culture, and, perhaps, a professor of Greek language and literature, Leonides was in a position personally to

---

[1] That this surname was self-assumed (Epiphanius, *Hær.* lxiv. 74) is, in view of his whole character, highly improbable; it is much more likely that it was given to him from his birth (Eusebius, *H. E.* vi. 14); but it is possible that it was applied to him only after his death.

superintend the education of his son. At an early age the boy showed unusual talent, and his training both on the scientific and on the Christian side was to his father a matter of conscientious care. Drilled in every branch of Greek learning as then practised in the city which had virtually succeeded Athens as "mother of arts and eloquence," his naturally acute mind was disciplined and developed to the best advantage. To the good Leonides the moral and spiritual welfare of his son was an object of equal and even greater solicitude. From his childhood Origen, like Timothy, learned to know the Holy Scriptures, and imbibed the fundamental truths of Christianity so thoroughly that none of his later speculations could ever efface them from his heart. Daily his father selected a portion of the Bible for him to commit to memory, and heard him repeat it. This was to the youthful Origen no uncongenial or mechanical task. Already he began to exercise that passionate eagerness to discover the deepest meaning of the record of revelation which distinguished his riper years. Leonides was frequently puzzled by his demands for a fuller exposition of passages of which the literal meaning only had been communicated, and had even to pretend to chide his over-inquisitiveness as not befitting his years, while secretly thanking God for having given him such a son. He formed the habit, it is said, of reverentially kissing the bosom of the sleeping boy, in the firm conviction that the Holy Spirit had marked it for His dwelling-place.

Few further particulars are known with reference to Origen's early training. That he came under the influence of Pantænus, after the return of the latter

LIFE AND CHARACTER OF ORIGEN 37

from his missionary enterprise in India, appears from a letter written to Origen by Alexander, bishop of Jerusalem, in which he alludes to the early friendship existing between them as fellow-students. It is not, however, anywhere distinctly affirmed that Origen was the pupil of Pantænus, as he certainly was of Clement, the catechist of the Alexandrian Church. In the cultured Christian circles of which these men were the leading ornaments Origen formed an acquaintance with Alexander, which was in a very marked degree to affect his future. Meanwhile he continued to slake his thirst at the fountains of knowledge. The instruction imparted to him by his father Leonides was now supplemented by the prelections of Clement. If these did not amount to systematic training in theology, they at least discussed the claims of Christianity as opposed to paganism, and cleared up the relation of the current philosophies to revealed religion. As he listened to such a teacher Origen's splendid thinking faculties must have been greatly stimulated, and his mental horizon vastly enlarged.

The terrible persecution of Christians which arose in the tenth year of Septimius Severus (A.D. 202) bore with special severity upon the Egyptian Church. One of the first victims was Leonides, who was arrested and thrown into prison. Although Origen had not then completed his seventeenth year, he ardently desired the martyr's crown,[1] and was minded to appear before the authorities as an avowed Christian in order that he might die along with his father. As no entreaties could dissuade him from his purpose, his

[1] In view of Matt. x. 23 he soon afterwards relinquished this ambition, which was nevertheless in the end virtually to be realised.

mother contrived effectually to defeat it by the simple stratagem of hiding his clothes. Finding himself thus thwarted, he wrote to his father imploring him to stand firm, and not to change his mind out of consideration for his family. Leonides did not disappoint the hopes of his son—he died a martyr; but, as his property was confiscated to the State, his widow and family were left destitute.

The eldest of seven children, Origen was at this time hospitably received into the house of a noble and philanthropic lady of Alexandria who had embraced Christianity, although, as it appeared, she had allowed herself to be moved away from the simplicity of the gospel. A certain false teacher, Paul of Antioch, had so captivated the lady by his eloquence that she adopted him as her son, and gave him permission to propagate his Gnostic heresies by means of lectures held in her house. To these lectures many of the orthodox, as well as of the heretics, of the city resorted; but Origen held steadily aloof from them, positively declining to hold fellowship with the Syrian Gnostic by joining in his prayers. To have done so would have been in his estimation a betrayal of Christ and His Church. Origen's action in this matter has often been thought to indicate a youthful intolerance in marked contrast to the gentleness and liberal-mindedness of his later years. But in view of his lifelong uncompromising opposition to the fundamental doctrines of Gnosticism, this seems a wrong construction to put upon it. Rather is it important to note that this steadfastness in clinging to ascertained truth was a very real trait in his character, and proved his anchor in the wild sea of speculation on which he

LIFE AND CHARACTER OF ORIGEN 39

was himself afterwards to embark. The environment in which Origen thus found himself, however, necessarily proved irksome to him. He keenly felt

> "How salt the savour is of others' bread,
> How hard the passage, to descend and climb
> By others' stairs."[1]

To live in the same house with this Gnostic teacher, and to come into daily contact with him, while constrained to repudiate his views and share his fellowship, constituted for the high-minded youth a heavy cross, and he resolved to carry it no longer than he could help. He continued to prosecute with most praiseworthy zeal the studies which he had begun under the direction of his father, and his proficiency in grammar, philology, and Greek literature soon became a ladder to independence. He now stood on the threshold of his great career.

Origen quickly made his mark as a teacher. At first he gave instruction only in "grammar" and ancient literature, but, like Christ Himself, His servant's faith "could not be hid." It found expression so often as he had occasion to refer to the theological position of pagan writers. One result of this was that certain of the heathen applied to him for instruction in Christianity,— among others, two brothers, Plutarch and Heraclas, of whom the former was destined to die a martyr's death, while the latter was yet to hold the bishopric of Alexandria. That Origen should have made two such converts, and that many others of his pupils should have been ready to follow Plutarch's example and seal their testimony

[1] Dante, *Paradiso*, xvii. 58-60.

40 ORIGEN AND GREEK THEOLOGY

with their blood, speaks volumes for his tact and zeal.[1]

But if Origen's fame as a teacher brought him into notice, so also did his pronounced sympathy with those who for Christ's sake suffered martyrdom. The persecution had become hotter under Aquila, who succeeded Lætus as proconsul of Egypt. But apparently nothing could damp the ardour of the youthful Christian teacher. By attending and encouraging the martyrs in their last moments he exposed himself to repeated and serious peril. He was pelted with stones and hunted from house to house. It is related[2] that on one occasion he fell into the hands of a heathen crowd, who arrayed him in the vestments of a priest of Serapis, compelled him to stand with shorn head upon the steps of the temple, and ordered him to distribute palm-twigs, according to use and wont, to those who entered, in order that they might lay them upon the altar of the god. But while doing what was so imperiously required of him, Origen cried out in clear and resolute tones: "Receive not the idol's palm, but the palm of Christ." Nevertheless in God's great providence he was marvellously preserved from hurt.

The persecution had practically obliterated the Catechetical School, whose teachers, Clement included, had sought safety in flight, although their action appears to have been dictated by a sense of duty, and not by cowardly fear. Meanwhile Origen's intrepid devotion on behalf of the martyrs drew forth the admiration of his pupils, and attracted to his lectures some even of

---

[1] Eusebius mentions by name six of his converts who died a martyr's death.

[2] Epiphanius, *Hær.* lxiv. 1.

LIFE AND CHARACTER OF ORIGEN 41

the philosophically cultured heathen. Although but a stripling of seventeen, he had by reason of his literary attainments and his Christian zeal already won for himself a front-rank place in the Egyptian Church. This was recognised by Demetrius, bishop of Alexandria, who now appointed him to the office of teacher in the Catechetical School. Nor did Origen shrink from filling the post of eminence in the hour of danger. Menaced at every turn by the emissaries of a now intolerant paganism, he calmly pursued his course, gathering and imparting knowledge with a zeal that knew no respite, and inspiring the hearts of his hearers, who were older than himself, with his own unconquerable devotion to truth.

That Demetrius had made a wise choice the result showed. In spite of the persecution, students flocked in increasing numbers to sit at the feet of Origen; and so important did he deem his new work of catechetical instruction that he discontinued his literary classes in order to give his whole time and strength to it. He insisted also on making it a labour of love, declining to take fees as formerly. Resolved to maintain his independence, and to keep himself free from all worldly distractions, he fell upon an ingenious scheme of self-endowment. By selling to a literary collector his manuscripts of the Greek classics—many of them carefully transcribed by his own hand—in consideration of a pension of four obols (about fivepence) a day, he solved the problem of his maintenance. It was a miserable pittance, but he made it suffice. Even so he trembled as he repeated the words: "He that forsaketh not all that he hath, cannot be My disciple." The very existence of such a man was a tower of strength to Christianity; for of him it was literally true, as Eusebius says, that "he taught as he lived, and lived as he taught."

At this period the Græco-Roman world, weary of an enervating self-indulgence, turned wistfully from the refinements of Epicureanism to the stern renunciations of Stoicism, with the remarkable result that Jewish theosophy, the later Platonism, and Christianity were all looking in the direction of self-denial as the key to the deepest philosophy of life. Thus early, through the high value set upon outward privations as a means of sanctification, was the germ of monasticism planted in the Church. And in this respect Origen fully imbibed the spirit of the age. By the mortification of the flesh he earnestly endeavoured to realise the Christian ideal. Than his a life of more rigid asceticism, combined with severe application to study, was probably never lived. Wine and luxuries in general he abjured. He allowed himself but little food, and practised frequent fasting. After toiling in the school by day, he gave himself to the investigation of the Scriptures by night, sleeping but for a short time, and that upon the bare ground. Only his "brazen" constitution prevented his health from being entirely undermined, and even as it was he had sown the seeds of future bodily trouble.

But Origen's deepest motive for self-sacrifice probably lay in the literalistic interpretation of Holy Scripture which at this period commended itself to him. In view of the Saviour's precept not to have two coats or to wear shoes, he restricted himself to a single garment, and went barefooted for years. Eager to mortify the flesh, to raise himself above suspicion in his relations with youthful catechumens of the other sex, and to carry out what in common with many Christians of his time he mistakenly considered to be the injunction of our Lord (Matt. xix. 12), he also rashly perpetrated an act of self-mutilation, which he afterwards regretted, and which was yet adversely to influence his future. That he could have done this has been declared incredible,[1] although upon insufficient grounds. The fact is well attested. Moreover, the practice in question was far from uncommon in the ancient world. Origen seems to have been much disconcerted when his indiscretion became publicly known, possibly because, wittingly or unwittingly, he had run counter to the conscience, if not even to the rule, of the Church. Bishop Demetrius, however, recognising the purity of his motives, treated him sympathetically, and encouraged him to throw himself heartily into the work of the Catechetical School. But this did not, apparently, prevent him from subsequently using this act of undisciplined zeal as a handle against Origen.

From this period, and in connection perchance with this *faux pas*, some would date the influence of the Platonic philosophy upon Origen's thought. But there is no evidence of his having undergone a sudden conversion of this sort, although some uncertainty does obtain as to the precise circumstances under which he became indoctrinated with the spirit of the Greek master. His own account of the matter is interesting so far as it goes, but it does not clear up everything. In a letter written in defence of his position as a student of Greek philosophy, he says: "When I had devoted

[1] *E.g.* by Schnitzer and Baur.

44 ORIGEN AND GREEK THEOLOGY

myself entirely to theology, and the fame of my skill in that department began to be noised abroad, and sometimes heretics, sometimes those who had studied the Greek sciences, and philosophy in particular, came to visit me, I deemed it advisable to investigate both the doctrinal views of the heretics and what the philosophers claimed to know of the truth." He then goes on to say that Pantænus and Heraclas were his precursors in this field, and that the latter had already been five years in attendance upon "the teacher" of the philosophical sciences before he himself began to hear his lectures. There can be little doubt that the reference is to Ammonius Saccas,[1] the founder of Neoplatonism, who was then a professor at Alexandria, and at the zenith of his reputation. Porphyry, indeed, definitely calls Origen a pupil of Ammonius,[2] and it is reasonable to suppose that under the guidance of this teacher his philosophical studies were perfected and matured. The elements of such knowledge may well have been already acquired by him under the tuition of Clement, and the widening horizon and fellowship of life in a learned centre such as Alex-

---

[1] Euseb. *H. E.* vi. 19. When Origen says he found Heraclas παρὰ "τῷ διδασκάλῳ" τῶν φιλοσόφων μαθημάτων, this is virtually to name Ammonius, whose pre-eminence among the then philosophers of Alexandria was acknowledged.

[2] Ἀκροάτης Ἀμμωνίου (*ap.* Euseb. *H. E.* vi. 19). It is certainly strange that Porphyry should represent Origen as being of heathen extraction, and many have concluded that it is not the Christian Origen at all that he refers to. So, *e.g.*, Bigg, *The Christian Platonists*, etc., p. 120, and Denis, who thinks this hypothesis has been adopted "sans raisons suffisantes" (*De la Philos. d'Origène*, p. 3). But if Porphyry was born *c.* 233, and Origen died *c.* 254, the possibility of their being acquainted must be admitted. According to Porphyry, they met in Tyre. This witness is accepted by Redepenning and Neander.

LIFE AND CHARACTER OF ORIGEN 45

andria must have led him to desire deeper draughts from this well. The necessity of meeting on their own ground the philosophers and heretics whom he mentions, was only the outward occasion for devoting himself to a more thorough prosecution of a line of study that must all along have had for him a peculiar charm. Even before he attached himself to the Philosophical School, he had read the works of such celebrated philosophers as Kronius and Numenius, Moderatus and Nicomachus. And although for a time, owing to absorption in his duties as catechist, and also, perhaps, to the advisability of refraining from openly receiving instruction from a heathen philosopher until the example of Heraclas and others had shown that even a Christian might profit by the teaching of a non-Christian, his philosophical studies had been to a great extent suspended, he naturally availed himself of the opportunity which at length presented itself. But in all this there is nothing to justify the assumption that about the time when he began to attend the Philosophical School, *i.e.* when nearly thirty years of age, his whole theological standpoint underwent a complete change.[1] Equally unfounded is the opinion, already rejected by Eusebius, that he was thoroughly versed in the various branches of secular learning prior to the commencement of his studies in the Sacred Scriptures.[2] If he now graduated, so to speak, in Greek philosophy and culture, this was simply the logical outcome of his early education, his natural bent, his position as a Christian teacher and apologist, and his environment. Of all the different philosophical systems with which he

[1] Neander, *Church Hist.* ii. p. 496.   [2] Schnitzer, Baur.

must have become acquainted, it was Platonism, in the new form which it had assumed, that alone exercised a deep and lasting influence on his general standpoint and mode of thought. He was attracted to it partly by his natural affinities for its mystic and ascetic trend, and partly by the many approximately Christian elements by which it was characterised. Needless to say, his familiarity with the speculations of philosophy was the root from which sprang most of the "heresies" which continued to agitate the Church for quite two centuries after his death.

On the death of Severus in 211 the persecution ceased, and Origen, who valued Church fellowship, took advantage of the opportunity thus offered of visiting Rome, in order to make the acquaintance of the members and teachers of the metropolitan Church. This journey was made during the papacy of Zephyrinus (201–218), probably in the first year of the reign of Caracalla, and certainly before Origen was thirty years of age. Very soon he returned to Alexandria, apparently with the intention of devoting himself absolutely to study; but at the urgent request of Demetrius he resumed his catechetical duties. As, however, the number of his students, pagan as well as Christian, continued largely to increase, he handed over the juniors to his accomplished friend Heraclas, and charged himself with the instruction of the more advanced pupils. Relieved thus of a part of his labours in the Catechetical School, Origen now applied himself with indomitable energy to the exegesis of Scripture, and at the same time endeavoured to acquire a competent knowledge of Hebrew so as to qualify himself for reading the Old Testament in the

LIFE AND CHARACTER OF ORIGEN 47

original. His proficiency in this language appears, however, until recently, to have been overrated. Nowhere does he himself claim to have a profound comprehension of it; on the contrary, he confesses his ignorance upon some points, and states that he was in the habit of referring his difficulties to Jewish proselytes.[1] At the same time the extant fragments of his great work, the *Hexapla*, show that he had no mean acquaintance with the traditional usage of the language, and beyond this Hebrew scholarship then scarcely went.

About this time Origen formed a fast friendship with Ambrosius, a rich and intelligent Alexandrian who had previously attached himself to one of the Gnostic sects, but who now through Origen's teaching embraced the orthodox faith, and found the true *gnosis* which he had earnestly been seeking. The formation of this tie was a fortunate thing for Origen, and still more so for biblical science. The estimation in which Ambrosius held the ability and scholarship of his friend was equalled only by the persistent zeal with which he spurred him on to the exercise of his literary gifts, and by the generosity with which he defrayed the costs of purchasing manuscripts for collation, as well as of the transcription and publication of his own exegetical and theological writings. He also furnished him with seven (or more if necessary) expert scribes, who wrote by turn to his dictation, and with an equal number of skilled caligraphists, who multiplied copies of his works. From this time his literary labours assumed Herculean proportions. In a letter to a friend he says: "The work of correction leaves us no time for supper, or

[1] *De Principiis*, i. 5.

48 ORIGEN AND GREEK THEOLOGY

after supper for exercise and repose. Even at these times we are compelled to debate questions of interpretation and to emend MSS. Even the night cannot be given up altogether to the needful refreshment of sleep, for our discussions extend far into the evening. I say nothing about our morning labour, continued from dawn to the ninth or tenth hour, for all earnest students devote this time to the study of the Scriptures and reading." Small wonder that Origen called Ambrosius his "taskmaster."[1] Yet for one of his scholarly instincts and Christian devotion those must have been crowded years of glorious life, perhaps the happiest he ever knew.[2] The literary output secured was enormous, although its quality must necessarily have suffered. That Origen should have produced such workmanship as he did under conditions so adverse, leads one to wonder what he might have accomplished if, instead of composing under this high-pressure system, he had been able to command adequate leisure. The object, however, which his "taskmaster" and himself had in view in publishing the results of his exegetical and theological studies was not fine writing, but the checkmating of the Gnostics, who "under cover of the *gnosis* set themselves against God's holy Church."[3]

---

[1] Ἐργοδιώκτης.

[2] "There was something beautiful and noble in the association of these two men, of whom the one placed all his fortune and all his interest at the service of truth, and the other consecrated to it all his genius. The house of Ambrose became a sort of scientific and Christian monastery, where zeal alone imposed severe regulations, which were freely accepted and joyfully observed. It was a sort of foreshadowing of Port-Royal" (Pressensé, *Early Years*, etc., ii. p. 305).

[3] *In Joann.* tom. v.

LIFE AND CHARACTER OF ORIGEN   49

By this time Origen had made a name for himself far beyond the confines of his native city. The governor of the Roman province of Arabia wrote to Bishop Demetrius and to the prefect of Egypt, requesting that the great Alexandrian teacher should be sent to confer with him, presumably on matters spiritual. It was perhaps on this journey, which involved only a short absence from the scene of his literary activities, that he heard Hippolytus preach.[1] An even more flattering invitation came to him from Julia Mammæa, mother of the emperor Alexander Severus, who was then at Antioch. This noble lady, of Syrian extraction, and interested perhaps in Christianity from her early days, desired to become acquainted with the religious philosophy of the most celebrated Christian teacher of the age. A military escort was sent to conduct Origen from Alexandria to Antioch. Here he found himself at a court where, if there was no disposition to proscribe, there was just as little to espouse, any particular form of religious belief. According to Eusebius, he abode for some time at the royal palace, and "after bearing powerful testimony to the glory of the Lord and the worth of divine instruction, hastened back to his accustomed studies."

In A.D. 216 Origen appears again to have left Egypt, not for scientific or religious objects, but to escape the fury of the emperor Caracalla, who, stung by some sarcastic stanzas respecting the base murder of his brother Geta, and believing them to have emanated from Alexandria, arrived there in that year with an army, and massacred thousands of the inhabitants. As a prominent figure in the literary life of the city,

[1] Jerome, *Catal.* c. 61.

50 ORIGEN AND GREEK THEOLOGY

Origen deemed it prudent to remove to safer quarters in Palestine. There he was cordially welcomed by his old friend Alexander, bishop of Jerusalem, and subsequently by Theoktistus, bishop of Cæsarea, who jointly invited him to give expository lectures in their churches. In this proposal, although as yet a layman, Origen acquiesced, to the no small displeasure, however, of his own bishop Demetrius, who, besides being a "high" Churchman, was growing jealous of his gifted catechist. The Palestinian bishops were able to plead precedents for what they had done; but the usage of the Egyptian Church differed from that of the Palestinian with respect to the point at issue, and Demetrius, declaring it to be an unheard of innovation "that laymen should deliver discourses in the presence of the bishops," ordered the immediate return of Origen to Alexandria. The latter loyally obeyed the summons, and once more took up with zeal his labours as teacher and student. During this journey to Palestine he is said to have discovered in a wine jar at Jericho a translation of the Old Testament, which he embodied in his *Hexapla*.[1]

Origen's next journey was into Greece, and involved two years' absence from Alexandria (228–230). He went in response to the call of the heresy-distressed Church of Achaia, apparently to act the part of peacemaker, and armed with written credentials from his bishop. His route lay through Palestine, and at Cæsarea he was ordained a presbyter by the friendly bishops of those parts. It is probable that he desired presbyterial status in view of the difficult task awaiting him in Greece, while on their part they may have thought it well to obviate all risk of further rebukes

[1] Presumably the *Editio Quinta*.

from Demetrius by licensing him to preach. But if their former attitude towards Origen had caused some coolness between the latter and his own bishop Demetrius, the step now taken was yet to bring about an open rupture. Meanwhile Origen pursued his journey, carried off the honours at a public disputation in Athens, and travelled back to Alexandria by way of Ephesus and Antioch. At Ephesus he appears to have taken part in a conference with a view to settling disputed points of doctrine, and wherever he went he evidently exercised a "sort of moral episcopacy."

To this latter circumstance, far more than to the fact of his supremacy as a theologian, is to be ascribed the jealousy of Bishop Demetrius, which, in conjunction with the long-cherished dislike of the more narrow-minded section of the Church, was now to drive him from Alexandria. In that capital of learning he had for nearly a generation been a popular favourite, but on returning from this tour he found himself in a changed atmosphere. "Had Origen been transported from his study in Alexandria to the deck of a trireme in the Bay of Biscay, the contrast could not have been more complete. So effectually had the thorns been fixed in his nest during his absence, that a residence in his native city was no longer possible."[1] Demetrius had "nursed his wrath to keep it warm" against his return, and Origen, fully gauging the situation, voluntarily left the city (231). With such a record as he had behind him, with his unequalled ability, and with such powerful friends as the bishops who had ordained him, Origen might have become the leader of a great party, and fought Demetrius on equal terms, had he so

[1] R. A. Vaughan, *Essays and Remains*, i. p. 17.

chosen. But he abhorred schism, and with noble Christian unselfishness counted no sacrifice too great in order to maintain the unity of Christ's Church. Not waiting for any formal sentence of deprivation, he quietly took leave of the place that was dearer to him than any other on earth, never, as it chanced, to set foot in it again. "Great even from his cradle," as Jerome says, Origen never showed himself greater than at this critical juncture in his career.

This conciliatory action did not prevent Demetrius from pressing matters to the quick as regards his quondam catechist. In hot haste he convened a synod of Egyptian bishops and presbyters, at which it was resolved to exclude him from the Alexandrian Church as one unworthy to fill the teacher's office. Origen was perhaps the first illustrious teacher—alas! that he should not also have been the last—to be cast off by the Church he loved, in order "to teach the world how much it costs to serve steadfastly the cause of liberty." But even so the wounded vanity and hierarchical pride of the Alexandrian bishop were not sufficiently appeased, and at a second synod, attended by bishops only, Origen's deposition from the rank of presbyter was decreed. This decision, which appears to have been based on his alleged promulgation of heretical doctrines,[1]

---

[1] According to Jerome (*in Rufin.* ii. 18), his writings were much corrupted even during his lifetime, while the zeal of Ambrosius had outrun his discretion in the matter of publishing certain things which were never meant to be given to the world (Jer. *Epist.* 65). But even in his (already published) *De Principiis* heterodox teaching might have been detected, and there may have been some justification in fact for the old monkish epitaph upon Origen—

"Sola mihi casum $\pi\epsilon\rho\grave{\iota}\ \dot{\alpha}\rho\chi\hat{\omega}\nu$ dicta dederunt,
His me collectis undique tela premunt."

LIFE AND CHARACTER OF ORIGEN 53

and possibly also on his self-mutilation, was intimated by circular letter to the foreign Churches, and homologated—so influential was the Alexandrian See—by all of them except those in Palestine, Phœnicia, Arabia, Greece, and perhaps Cappadocia. Rome, in particular, was ready to join in the condemnation; and though, according to some accounts, Origen afterwards wrote to the Roman bishop Fabian, he met with no favourable response. His old friend Heraclas is said to have opposed him. Even a rumour that he had become an apostate found currency. This would seem to indicate that the only real charge against Origen was the irregularity of his ordination, and that everything in his life or writings that was fitted to damage him was raked up to justify the severe measures taken against him. Unfortunately, owing to the loss in great part of a treatise written by Pamphilus and Eusebius in defence of Origen, and containing full details of all these proceedings, our information on the subject is meagre. This circumstance, and the somewhat fluid condition of Church law and discipline that then obtained, render it difficult to adjudicate in this quarrel. Very possibly, as Redepenning suggests, Origen may have believed himself within his rights, while Demetrius may also have considered it his duty to interfere. But if both were to some extent in the right, both were also in the wrong. For Origen's ordination was "undoubtedly an infringement of the rights of the Alexandrian bishop; at the same time it was simply a piece of spite on the part of the latter that had kept Origen so long without any ecclesiastical consecration."[1]

[1] Harnack, art. "Origen" in *Ency. Brit.*

This episode, it may further be noted, synchronises with Origen's final emancipation from the bondage of the letter, and was followed within a year by the death of Demetrius and the appointment of Heraclas as his successor. That Heraclas took an active part in the banishment of Origen is stated by Gennadius and others, but may really have been an inference from the fact that he succeeded Demetrius. On the other hand, it does seem strange that under the *régime* of his former friend, pupil, and colleague, nothing should have been done to revoke the sentence against Origen; but the Egyptian prelates had probably gone too far to think of rescinding their former resolution.

Origen made his new home at Cæsarea, in Palestine. From several points of view this was a happy choice. It brought him within easy reach of the scenes associated with Jesus, His disciples, and the prophets. It was the centre of the civilised world, and therefore a vantage-ground from which his influence could be widely felt. In some respects also this new field of activity closely resembled that which he had left. As the highly favoured embodiment of the splendid conceptions of Herod the Great, Cæsarea was exceptionally rich in all the adjuncts of culture. Although no change of circumstances could have seriously affected Origen's innate love of scientific investigation, or his indefatigable devotion to literature, we may believe that such congenial surroundings were helpful to him. It had been a great wrench for him to sever the ties that bound him to Alexandria, and his work had been rendered almost impossible by the tumult of conflicting emotions thereby occasioned. "I have been enabled," he says, "to reach my fifth volume on the Gospel of

LIFE AND CHARACTER OF ORIGEN 55

John, although the storm raised against me at Alexandria threatened to hinder; but Jesus spoke with authority to the floods and to the sea."[1] At Cæsarea he found a haven of rest, or at least a quiet anchorage; but it furnished him with more than shelter. Troops of steadfast friends gathered round him, and showered upon him every token of veneration and honour. In the warm glow of this friendly sunshine his energies revived. Besides preaching daily, he continued to toil at his *Hexapla*, and at his exegetical commentaries on the books of the Bible. The greatest hindrance he had to contend with was the temporary lack of shorthand writers. His attainments enabled him to give systematic instruction in all branches of knowledge; and such was his reputation in the literary, scientific, and theological world, that in a short time, and more by the sheer force of his own personality than by the countenance he received from the emperor Philip the Arabian, he established in Cæsarea a theological school whose fame rivalled that of Alexandria itself.

As Demetrius attempted by letter to obtain recognition in Cæsarea for Origen's degradation from the office of presbyter, and set in motion against him "all the winds of malice in Egypt," the latter wrote to friends in Alexandria in vindication of his orthodoxy, which seems also to have been impugned. In particular, he exposes the falsification of the record of his disputation with Candidus the Valentinian, denies having ever asserted the future salvation of the devil,[2] and

---

[1] *In Joann.* vi. 1.

[2] Although the ultimate salvation of the devil is undoubtedly an article in the Christian philosophy of Origen, he was entitled to deny the statement in the form in which it was quoted against him. Candidus

56   ORIGEN AND GREEK THEOLOGY

complains of a forged document purporting to give an account of a disputation of his with a heretic which never came off at all. He also quotes certain passages from the prophets which deprecate too much confidence in leaders (Mic. vii. 5; Jer. iv. 22 [LXX]), and declares such antagonists as his to be fit subjects, not for hatred and cursing, but for pity and prayer. According to Jerome (*in Rufin.* ii. 18), indeed, Origen brought railing accusations against Demetrius and bishops in general; but it is to be feared that, in his anxiety to represent Origen as having shown animosity to Demetrius, he has only succeeded in giving vent to his own.

In spite of all efforts to damage him, Origen's career continued to be brilliant and prosperous. Among foreign Churches his counsel was greatly valued and in much request. Leading theologians in Cappadocia and Arabia corresponded with him. The Palestinian bishops Alexander and Theoktistus were among those who gladly sat at his feet. His fame, together with the magnetic influence of his personality, attracted to him a band of earnest-minded youths, who under his tuition received a thorough training in theology. To this class belonged Gregory, surnamed Thaumaturgus (*Wonder-worker*), who having come to Cæsarea along with his brother Athenodorus on a visit to a relative, met in with Origen and felt constrained to attend his lectures, although it had been his intention to proceed to Berytus in order to study Roman law. "We could

represented the *nature* of the devil as incapable of salvation, and Origen replied that he fell by his own will, and can be saved. This was wrested to mean that the *nature* of the devil is to be saved. Origen taught, of course, not that the evil in him will be saved, but that he will be saved when he ceases to be evil.

LIFE AND CHARACTER OF ORIGEN

not loose ourselves from his bonds;"—so he declares in his *Panegyric* upon Origen. In this address, delivered by him, in accordance with ancient custom, on his departure from Cæsarea, after a pupilage of five years, he bears emphatic and loving testimony to Origen's attaiments as a scholar, to his abilities as a teacher, to his lovableness as a man, and to his piety as a Christian. If written in a somewhat rhetorical strain, it nevertheless throws most valuable light upon the nature and method of Origen's academical labours, explains the kind of curriculum through which his students were conducted, and helps us to understand the extraordinary charm of his personal character. If Gregory and his brother were fascinated by his discourses, which are described in the *Panegyric* as "unspeakably winning, hallowed, and passing lovely," they were not less so by the man himself, towards whom they soon came to cherish an ardent affection.

During the persecution initiated by Maximin the Thracian, who seated himself on the throne by murdering his benefactor Alexander Severus (235), Origen took refuge in the Cappadocian Cæsarea under the wing of his friend and correspondent Firmilian, bishop of that city. But as the persecution broke out there also, he was forced to withdraw to the house of a Christian lady named Juliana, where for two years he lived in strict concealment. It so happened that this lady had inherited the library and writings of Symmachus, the Ebionitic Greek translator of the Old Testament, and the use of these MSS. proved a welcome windfall to Origen, who was quietly working at his critical recension of the Bible. But although he himself passed unscathed through this time of persecution,

58 ORIGEN AND GREEK THEOLOGY

some of his associates were not so fortunate. His old friend Ambrosius, and Protoktetus, a presbyter of Cæsarea, were seized and thrown into prison. While their fate still hung in the balance, he wrote and dedicated to them his treatise *On Martyrdom*, in which he exhorts them to emulate the heroism displayed by the Jewish martyrs of the Maccábæan age, to show their love to God by rising above the love of the visible, and to sacrifice their lives if need be for the truth. It fell out, however, that the murder of Maximin in his tent at Aquileia in the year 238 relieved the Church from persecution. Ambrosius and Protoktetus were set at libery, and Origen returned to Cæsarea in Palestine, where he resumed his former activities. Besides lecturing daily, he zealously prosecuted his exegetical and critical labours. The commentaries upon which he was at this time chiefly engaged were those upon Isaiah and Ezekiel, of which only fragments have been preserved. A portion of his time was also devoted to the monumental *Hexapla*.

Years before, Origen had intermitted his labours at Alexandria in order to visit the Church in Greece, and now we find him again in that country, where he seems to have sojourned for a while. The precise date and the occasion of this visit are, however, uncertain; we do not even know whether it was ecclesiastical or private business that took him once more to Athens. Travelling through Bithynia, he spent several days at Nicomedia with Ambrosius, who had meanwhile become deacon. While there he received a letter from Julius Africanus, a scholarly Christian resident at Emmaus (Nicopolis) in Palestine,

LIFE AND CHARACTER OF ORIGEN 59

who had been present at a discussion in which Origen quoted the story of Susanna as an authentic portion of the Book of Daniel, and who now wrote disputing this position, and requesting a further statement of his views. Origen replied in a lengthy letter from Nicomedia; but no ingenuity could undermine the arguments adduced by Africanus, to whom the laurels must be adjudged. It was the victory of the unbiassed critic over the champion of Church tradition. It seems odd that Origen should in this instance have allowed his judgment to be so warped by prejudice; possibly he had taken alarm at the commotions which, with no desire on his part, he had been instrumental in raising within the Church. To this period also should probably be ascribed Origen's letter to Gregory, in which he declares that Greek philosophy has its true function as a preparation for Christianity, and that all scientific learning is rightly viewed as the handmaid of Scripture. During his stay at Athens Origen finished his commentary on Ezekiel, and began that on the Song of Songs. His important work on St. John's Gospel seems to have been completed before his sixtieth year, when he wrote his exposition of St. Matthew, since in the latter work are quoted passages from the former which must have been written towards the close of it. The bulk of his exegetical work seems to have been done during the Cæsarean period of his life (231–249).

In the year 244 an Arabian synod was convened to discuss the Christological views of Beryllus, bishop of Bostra. Presumably in opposition to the peculiar tenets of the Elkesaites, who inhabited the region to the east of the Dead Sea, and whose leanings appear to have been in the direction of a rude Tritheism, Beryllus had given expression to Patripassian views about the divinity of Christ. His object was to conserve the unity of God without impairing the divine worth of the Redeemer, and apparently he saw no other way of doing this than that of adopting the Unitarian position that there is only one Person in the Godhead. The divinity of Christ he held to be merely a new form of manifestation on the part of God,—not a θεότης ἰδία, but only a θεότης πατρική. The synod, which was largely attended, condemned Beryllus, and vainly tried to bring him round to the orthodox position. The mediation of Origen and others was then called in. The "homeless presbyter," who was an adept in the art of becoming all things to all men, went to Bostra, interviewed the recalcitrant bishop in private, and subsequently at a synodical disputation succeeded in convincing him of his error. Beryllus not only frankly recanted,[1] but seems even to have written a letter of thanks to Origen.[2] The wonder is that even Demetrius did not capitulate before the strange power wielded by this remarkable man.

Another question which agitated the Arabian Church about this time, and which Origen was called in to clear up, was that of the natural immortality of the soul. According to Eusebius, one party maintained that the soul dies with the body, and is to be revived with it at the resurrection — a doctrine probably derived from Jewish sources, and which has been mooted oftener than once in the subsequent history of the Church. Through Origen's influence those who held this erroneous view were led to renounce it. On

Euseb. *H. E.* vi. 33.   [2] Jerome, *Catal.* c. 60.

LIFE AND CHARACTER OF ORIGEN 61

this third visit to Arabia he seems also to have succeeded in repressing the Elkesaitic heresy, based upon a pretended revelation from heaven, that no moral quality attached to the act of denying the faith in time of persecution.

As he had formerly entered into intimate relations with the household of Alexander Severus, so now Origen, presumably by request, corresponded with the emperor Philip the Arabian and his wife Severa, who were favourable to Christianity. During Philip's reign (244–249) he wrote his famous work against Celsus, and his commentaries on Matthew's Gospel and the Twelve Prophets. It was at this period also, when he had completed his sixtieth year, that he first sanctioned the taking down of his discourses by shorthand reporters.

Origen's life was not to have a peaceful sunset. The storm-clouds of persecution rose darkly under the reign of Decius (249–251), a lover of paganism, who sought to extirpate Christianity as dangerous to the State. Alike in extent and in severity, this was the most serious persecution yet experienced by the Church. The civil authorities were everywhere required to leave no stone unturned in order to reclaim Christians for the service of the gods. Gentler measures were resorted to at first, and where these proved insufficient, a gradual scale of increasing tortures was brought to bear upon recusants. It was also part of the *modus operandi* to strike at the men of mark among the Christians. Those distinguished for their zeal, rank, scholarship, or wealth were singled out as special victims of this calculated cruelty. In these circumstances it was impossible for Origen to escape. After

62 ORIGEN AND GREEK THEOLOGY

an unflinching confession, he was imprisoned and maltreated in the fiendish fashion prescribed. Eusebius tells us that he was thrust into the innermost den of the prison, wearing a heavy iron collar; that his feet were for days together strained on the rack; and that he was threatened with being burned at the stake. But no pains or threats could move him to recant, and although the cruelties to which he had been subjected had shattered a frame already weakened by a toilsome and ascetic life, he survived the persecution, which ceased with the death of Decius in 251. Not, however, for long did he survive it. The three years that remained to him he spent mostly in writing consolatory letters to sufferers, and in brotherly fellowship with his friends. About this time Dionysius of Alexandria, who had succeeded Heraclas as bishop, sent him a letter on martyrdom. The communication came too late, however, to lead to any renewal of Origen's old relations with the Alexandrian Church. Now a worn out old man, and reduced to poverty by the death of his benefactor Ambrosius, he died, probably in A.D. 254, in the seventieth year of his age, at Tyre, where a marble monument continued to mark his grave until the end of the thirteenth century.

The personality and character of Origen are invested with a rare charm. He was at once a great man and a good. His was a rich and well-balanced nature, in which the intellectual did not dwarf the moral, nor the speculative the emotional. In the highest sense he was "every inch a man." The resolute firmness which already showed itself in his youthful repudiation of Paul the Gnostic teacher from Antioch distinguished him throughout, and carried him triumphantly through the

LIFE AND CHARACTER OF ORIGEN

persecution that clouded his latter years. That he was brave to the point of absolute fearlessness is demonstrated by his effusive sympathy with the martyrs, openly extended up to the hour of their death. His diligence as a student, catechist, and scientific theologian was phenomenal, and has certainly never been surpassed. In his behaviour under the hard treatment meted out to him by the Egyptian Church at the instigation of Bishop Demetrius, he has given an object lesson in Christian meekness and forbearance which is difficult to match in ecclesiastical history. His lifelong self-denial brightly contrasts with the sin-stained youth of Augustine, the only one among the Fathers whose distinction and influence are comparable to his own. Other noteworthy elements in his character were his holy earnestness, his love of truth, his deep devotional feeling, and his unfaltering faith. Nothing could exceed his scrupulous conscientiousness. On one occasion, being at a loss to know the Hebrew name of a tree mentioned in Scripture, he handed several twigs to a company of Jews so as to ascertain definitely the facts of the case. The same punctilious care for accuracy in all his investigations appears also in the deference with which he consulted Jewish acquaintances upon other difficulties connected with their language. What he was as a friend may be gathered from the princely liberality of Ambrosius, kept up while he lived, in giving him every facility for research that money could provide, as well as from the happy relations maintained from youth to old age with Alexander, bishop of Jerusalem. To say that his qualities as a teacher were of the highest order of excellence would be to underrate them. In this department he was a master genius, a professor whom his students almost worshipped. From the *Panegyric* of his pupil Gregory we learn how he inspired them with his own spirit, and drew out their affection till they were joined to him "as the soul of Jonathan was knit to the soul of David." We could have no better proof that, great as he was in intellect, he was equally so in heart. In point of gentleness and winsomeness of disposition Origen may be fitly compared with Melanchthon. He exercised an irresistible personal magnetism over those with whom he came into close contact. This accounts for his having been so frequently employed as arbiter in matters of dispute, and for his success in gaining over "heretics" to the side of the Church. But he resembled the Reformation theologian in saintliness also. In the purity and loftiness of his Christian character, in the sincerity, depth, and earnestness of his piety, we have the perfect counterpoise to his extraordinary attainments as a scholar, his singular acuteness as a thinker, and his constructive powers as a theologian. His eye was single, and therefore his whole body was full of light. A character like this, so rich and so noble, so rounded and complete, is a possession to the Christian Church for all time, and one in view of which Origen is rightly ranked as at once "the greatest of the Fathers," and "the finest genius of Christian theology."

CHAPTER III

ORIGEN'S VIEW OF HOLY SCRIPTURE

ALTHOUGH in his great work on the fundamental principles of Christianity Origen reserves his discussion of Holy Scripture for the closing chapter, his whole system of doctrine is necessarily based upon his views regarding this subject, and in any review of his theology it seems proper to give it precedence.

The pronouncement of Melito, bishop of Sardis, limiting the Old Testament Canon, apparently remained without influence in the Church. Christians regarded with veneration the whole body of Jewish-Greek literature, without drawing any hard and fast line in respect of authority. That many books, such as those of Solomon, had been lost, was held to be entirely consonant with the divine purpose, and the importance of tradition, as pointing to those which had met with universal acceptance, was frankly recognised. But in the third century no definite choice between the Hebrew Canon and the Septuagint had been made; and the uncertainty is not dissipated by Origen. Indeed "the most striking features in the mass of facts furnished by him are the uncertainty of the results, the want of precision in his point of view, and the facility with which he passes in turn from scientific discussion to

66 ORIGEN AND GREEK THEOLOGY

popular usages. That is already visible in what he says of the Old Testament."[1] While Origen was evidently acquainted with the Jewish Canon, and gave a mystical signification to the number of its books, there is no reason to suppose that he accepted it as his own. His list of Old Testament books given by Eusebius (*H. E.* vi. 25) agrees, indeed, in respect of number, though not of order, with the Hebrew Canon, yet in common with the Greek Fathers generally he frequently quotes the Apocrypha as inspired Scripture. Although used by his translator, the word *canonical* is unknown to himself. With Origen *apocryphal* means *secret* or *hidden*, and the pseudepigrapha as represented by the *Book of Enoch*, etc., are not included by him among the sacred writings. Books which might claim to serve as a rule for the Church he classifies as authentic, spurious, and mixed. To the first category belong all those which rank as sources of dogma; to the second, those which contain heretical additions; and to the third, those which, along with much that is excellent, embody also elements either uncertain or false. The genuineness of the separate books of Scripture was accepted by him without critical inquiry. Thus he never seems to have doubted that Moses wrote the Pentateuch, or David the Psalms, or that the Book of Job was actual history.

With Origen the New Testament was still less of a fixed quantity than the Old. In admitting books to canonical rank he was careful, however, to exclude such as could not lay claim to general ecclesiastical recognition, even although he himself believed them to be genuine apostolic records. The Gospel of the

---
[1] Reuss, *History of the Canon*, etc., p. 129.

ORIGEN'S VIEW OF HOLY SCRIPTURE

Hebrews he prized highly because it teaches that the Holy Ghost is the mother of the Lord, but he attached canonical value to none but our Four Gospels. St. Paul's Epistles he reckoned as fourteen in number, ascribing as he did to that apostle the thoughts, although not the language, of the Epistle to the Hebrews. The Book of Revelation, which he interpreted allegorically, he attributed to John the son of Zebedee. He doubted the canonicity of 2 Peter, and of 2 and 3 John, and was less clear about the Epistle of James than he was about that of Jude. Writings bearing the marks of non-inspiration he at once relegated to the category of ordinary profane literature. Certain other records, either on account of their apostolic origin, or because of the valuable character of their contents, he designated as "mixed," these last forming, as Redepenning happily observes, "the spacious forecourts around the sanctuary of the covenant record." This corresponded to Origen's view of the relation of the books of Scripture to one another, according to which some possessed a higher degree of sanctity than others. Thus in the Old Testament he ranked Ecclesiastes before Proverbs, and Canticles before Ecclesiastes, while in the New he gave precedence to the Four Gospels, and among these again to the Gospel according to St. John. In this we may trace the first beginnings of that distinction between Scripture and the word of God which has bulked so largely in modern theology.

Origen firmly believed in the inspiration of the Scriptures. To him they are "divine writings," "the word of God," and not "the compositions of men." They are throughout pervaded by the fulness of the divine majesty, having been "composed by inspiration

68 ORIGEN AND GREEK THEOLOGY

of the Holy Spirit, agreeably to the will of the Father of all things through Jesus Christ." The inspiration extends to all biblical books, and to every word in them, so that errors are impossible. Apparent discrepancies he explains either by assuming that two separate events are recorded, or by resorting to the allegorical method. In the case of solecisms and grammatical defects he distinguishes between the external word in regard to which the writers were conscious of their liability to err, and its contents, which are uniformly and absolutely devoid of error. The medium of inspiration is the Holy Ghost, who transmits the self-revelation of God in the Son to those whose special sanctity has fitted them to be the organs of its communication to others. This spiritual elevation, to which alone such illumination has been granted, has nothing in common with the ecstatic frenzy of heathen soothsayers, but implies perfect mental control as well as freedom. The inspired writers, therefore, were not the mere mechanical instruments of the Spirit; they arranged their thoughts, and even balanced their sentences, with care. To this extent there is a human element in Scripture. While the impulse to speak came directly from God, the writer conveyed the message in his own words. Great stress is laid by Origen upon the moral condition of the organs of revelation. So far does he make this a determinating factor in the case, that he bases upon it the claim that there are different degrees of inspiration, Christ ranking in this respect higher than Paul, and Paul than Luke or Timothy. Each vessel is filled according to its capacity, and the treasure is put into earthen vessels that the triumph of the truth may be due to no arts of human speech, but solely to the power of God.

Origen finds evidence of its inspiration in the general recognition accorded to the teaching of Scripture as compared with the reception given to any of the doctrinal systems elaborated by men. For the truths of revelation, irrespective of nationality and in face of persecution, many have abandoned their ancestral worship; whereas, notwithstanding all their parade of logic, none of the philosophers have succeeded in making disciples of any considerable fraction of even a single nation. The same conclusion is borne out by the fulfilment of prophecy. The Saviour's birth and dominion, the sins of the Jews and the election of the Gentiles, were all foretold. It had been clearly predicted that from the time of Christ onwards there would be no king in Judah, and that with His appearance the whole sacrificial service would be abolished. But the argument from prophecy, which proves the deity of Christ, proves also the divine inspiration of the writings which prophesied of Him. The divine origin of scriptural doctrine is further attested by the superhuman power that watched over, and was reflected in, the doings of the apostles. Finally, the very perusal of the sacred writings begets in the reader's own inner consciousness the feeling that they are inspired.

In every part of Scripture Origen traces the breath of the same Spirit, and views both Testaments as containing between them one complete covenant record. He strongly asserted, in opposition to the Gnostics, the unity of the sacred writings. His unswerving attitude on this point did more than any other influence to confirm the Church in the belief of the indissoluble connection between the Old and New Testaments. He loses no oppportunity of pointing out that in "the volume of the book" the doctrine of Christ has been gathered into one, and maintains that, like that of the Paschal Lamb, the body of Scripture is indivisible. He claims that the perfect harmony of law, prophecy, and gospel is shown by, among other evidences, the appearance of Moses and Elijah at the Transfiguration. While, however, essentially the same as regards their contents, the Old and New Testaments stand related to each other as shadow and substance.[1] Both contain the truth; but in the one it is hidden, whereas in the other it comes clearly to light. This is the result of the advent of Christ, which fulfils and explains every part of Holy Writ. The divinity of the prophetic declarations, as well as the spiritual nature of the truth embodied in the Mosaic law, is thus clearly disclosed, and the veil removed by which the light had been previously concealed. Origen's too exclusive treatment of the law as the shadow of gospel conditions prevented him, however, from doing justice to its ethical side.

According to Origen, the Spirit's chief object in Scripture is to communicate ineffable mysteries regarding the affairs of men, *i.e.* souls inhabiting bodies.[2] But, passing forthwith into the region of the transcendent, he remarks that among those matters which relate to souls we must rank as primary the doctrines

---

[1] His position with reference to this point is not quite consistent. For example, writing against the Gnostics, he even goes so far as to declare a preference for the Old Testament over the New; on the other hand, he asserts that for such as have true insight into the gospel the Old Testament has no further value.—*In Matt.* x. 412.

[2] *De Princ.* iv. 14.

bearing upon God and His only-begotten Son, namely, "of what nature He is, and in what manner He is the Son of God, and what are the causes of His descending even to the assumption of human flesh, and of complete humanity; and what also is the operation of this Son, and upon whom and when exercised." In the divine teaching a place had also necessarily to be given, he says, to the subjects of rational creatures, diversities of souls, the nature of the world, and the origin and habitat of sin. In short, the Scriptures are treated by Origen as a mine of speculative truths. Facts are of importance mainly as the vehicles of ideas; and the ethical is subordinated to the metaphysical, in keeping with the spirit of the age. But he never departs from the position that the Bible is the sole guide to those higher truths which, however they may vary as regards the form of their presentation, remain always the same in substance, and which, while to some extent we apprehend them here, can be fully grasped only hereafter. Hence he is careful to inculcate the practical duty of reading the Scriptures. They are the true nutriment of the spiritual nature, and it is by partaking daily of this food that we arrive at true fulness and richness of life, and are enabled ever more completely to consecrate it to God.

But according to Origen the Spirit had a second object in Scripture, namely, the concealment of spiritual truths under cover of some narrative of visible things or human deeds, or of the written legislation. Although thus in one sense mere wrappage, the letter of Scripture is capable of edifying "the multitude," who cannot investigate the mysteries. Seeing, however, there is much in Scripture besides the obvious, "the word of God has arranged that certain stumbling-blocks, as it were, and offences, and impossibilities, should be introduced into the law and the history," lest we should be beguiled from the true doctrines by the mere charm of the language, or rest satisfied with the letter. The ordinary narrative could sometimes convey the mystical sense, but where it was not suited for this, "the Scripture interwove in the history the account of some event that did not take place, sometimes what could not have happened; sometimes what could, but did not." Instances are given where the physical or moral impossibility of the case should stimulate inquiry after the inner meaning. Who, it is asked, can believe there was morning and evening before the sun was created, or an actual earthly paradise with a visible tree of life, or a mountain lofty enough for Jesus to view from its top all the kingdoms of the world? Some of the Mosaic precepts Origen declares to be on a literal interpretation irrational, as, *e.g.*, that against eating vultures, which famine itself would induce none to eat; and others impossible, such as that which requires sitting at home throughout the Sabbath. He speaks in a similar way of some of the Saviour's injunctions to the apostles, maintaining, for instance, that only "simple persons" would believe that he ordered them to "salute no man by the way." According to this view the literal sense of such passages as those recording the episode of Lot's daughters, the barbarities of the wars against the Canaanites, and imprecations upon enemies, is also discarded by the enlightened conscience. It seems strange that Origen, who was so careful to make out to the last detail the infallibility of Holy Scripture,

ORIGEN'S VIEW OF HOLY SCRIPTURE

should have also denied the historical credibility of such incidents as the sacrifice of Isaac, the cleansing of the temple, the feet-washing, etc. Perhaps the explanation is to be found partly in the inordinate idealism of his age, which led him to doubt the authenticity of whatever appeared to be contrary to reason or unworthy of God, no matter what ecclesiastical standards might teach. His doubts were certainly not due to a sceptical tendency, for he cordially accepts all the essential doctrines of the faith; rather may we with Redepenning regard them as the consequences of an excessive inclination to believe.

The great instrument for discovering and interpreting the deeper mysteries underlying the letter of Scripture is the allegorical method. Origen uses this in a twofold manner,—positively, so as by means of it to teach and elucidate the doctrines of the faith; and negatively, in order to defend it against the assaults of its adversaries. Allegorism in the interpretation of Scripture was in vogue before Origen's time, but he was the first who attempted to give it a scientific basis. Not satisfied, like Clement, to accept it as a traditional fact that the sacred books have an allegorical meaning, he sought an abstract ground of justification for this theory, as well as a more definite method of applying it, so as to ascertain, if possible by rule, the sense of particular passages. He starts from the position that earthly things in general, and sacred history and law in particular, are the shadows of things heavenly and invisible. If God made man in His own image, He may have made other creatures after the image of other heavenly things. Thus by means of the world that is seen the soul is led upwards

74 ORIGEN AND GREEK THEOLOGY

to the unseen and eternal. Upon the terrestrial the seeing eye can discern the stamp of the celestial. In connection with this "law of correspondence" Origen makes the pregnant remark: "He who believes the Scriptures to have proceeded from Him who is the author of nature may well expect to find the same sort of difficulties in it as are found in the constitution of nature."[1] This was the seed-corn from which sprang, fifteen centuries later, Butler's famous *Analogy*, and the words are fittingly appended by Southey to his inscription upon the bishop's monument in Bristol Cathedral.

Origen finds his ruling principle of interpretation in Prov. xxii. 20 (LXX),[2] and in an analogy between the Platonic doctrine of the constitution of man and Scripture, which has been given for man's salvation. As man is of a tripartite nature, consisting of body, soul, and spirit, so also does Scripture possess a threefold sense—the literal, the moral, and the spiritual. This triple sense he supports by an ingenious use of a passage from *The Shepherd of Hermas*, where Grapte, Clement, and Hermas are made to typify the three classes of readers to whom Scripture appeals.[3] Grapte

---

[1] *Philocal.* p. 23.

[2] The word translated (in A.V. and R.V.) "excellent things" literally means "thrice" or "in triple form," and is so rendered by the LXX (τρισσῶς) and Vulg. (*tripliciter*), perhaps with the idea of repetition to emphasise the truth. Origen uses the passage, so understood, as an argument for his view of a threefold sense of Holy Scripture. Perowne (*Cambridge Bible*, etc., *ad loc.*) says: "The word has been thought to denote the chief of the three persons who formed the complement of an ancient war-chariot, and so to mean principal or excellent." According to R.V. marg. "the word is doubtful. Another reading is *heretofore*."

[3] He also finds an allusion to the threefold sense in the waterpots "containing two or three firkins apiece" (John ii. 6). See *De Princ.* iv. 11, 12.

ORIGEN'S VIEW OF HOLY SCRIPTURE

represents the orphans who are unable to call God their Father, and who are fit to apprehend only the "body" or letter of Scripture; Clement, the more advanced, who are edified by its "soul"; and Hermas, the wise and grey-headed presbyters of the Church, the perfect (1 Cor. ii. 6, 7), who are capable of apprehending the spiritual law itself. This does not imply that from every passage a threefold meaning is to be extracted. Sometimes, where the literal sense is either sufficiently worthy of God or sufficiently surprising, Origen is content not to allegorise; it is only the commonplace that he considers it essential to explain. Some texts contain only the "soul" and "spirit" of Scripture, *i.e.* have no "bodily" or literal sense at all; others, as the Ten Commandments and all precepts of universal obligation, have an ethical import which is of itself sufficient.

It has frequently been held that Origen further divided the spiritual sense into an allegorical and an anagogical,[1] but this claim can scarcely be made good. Indeed it is not always easy or possible to differentiate between the moral and spiritual senses, which shade off into each other like dissolving views. In numerous instances, however, the threefold meaning is stated clearly enough. The grain of mustard seed, for example, is to be understood literally of the actual seed; morally, it denotes faith; spiritually, it represents the kingdom of heaven. The moral signification of the text seems to cover those uses of it which bear upon the practical life of the soul in its relation to God and duty; the spiritual extends to all "mysteries"

---

[1] In the Latin Church this found current expression in the couplet—
"Litera gesta docet, quid credis allegoria,
Moralis quid agas, quo tendis anagogia."

connected with the Church and its history, both temporal and eternal. But in many passages Origen satisfies himself with the broad twofold distinction between letter and spirit. Viewed purely as the rudimentary stage of Christian culture, the merely literal interpretation is at once useful and harmless, but unless men outgrow this it becomes injurious. Christ's woe pronounced upon the scribes and Pharisees he applies to such as concern themselves only with the literal meaning. To cling to the letter after the veil has been taken from the law is the root of much evil. For the Jew it means unbelief; for the Christian, a yoke of bondage; for the Church, a fruitful source of heresy; and for all, a misunderstanding of God.

It is, then, according to Origen, the function of allegorism to discover, exhibit, and expound the deeper sense of Scripture. Only through the Holy Ghost, however, can one acquire this noblest of all arts. The spiritual penetration necessary in order to the discovery of "mysteries" is essentially bound up with the possession of faith and love to Jesus Christ. While no one has absolutely lost the faculty of apprehending the divine, men differ vastly in respect of knowledge and receptivity. Some have not grasped the most elementary principles of morality and religion; others confound their systems of philosophy with the highest truth. Among Christians who really possess this, some cling to the letter alone; while others again, who have a deeper apprehension of truth, differ in proportion to their zeal. There thus opens up before the truly consecrated soul an ever-widening and illimitable prospect of larger knowledge.

ORIGEN'S VIEW OF HOLY SCRIPTURE

What led Origen thus to repudiate the literal sense of so many passages of Scripture? In general, it may be said that his Platonic spiritualism, his attachment to the Alexandrian idea of *gnosis*, and his extravagant conception of inspiration already predisposed him in favour of a mystical exegesis. More particularly it would appear that he was impelled in this direction by the immediate necessities of the polemic against Jews and heretics, and also perhaps by the homiletic requirements of the age. To a certain extent Origen is justified in claiming the Apostle Paul (*i.e. qua* author of the Epistle to the Hebrews) as a predecessor in the field of allegorical interpretation. Yet there is a world of difference between the allegorising of the New Testament Epistle and that of Origen, in which, while they cannot extinguish his brilliant merit as a biblical scholar, the most fanciful extravagances —etymological, cosmological, and even arithmetical— abound. His method is really a "play of the imagination, an excellent means of appearing to find what one already possesses, but not of discovering what one does not possess."[1] It is at once illusive and fruitless. Although involving much laborious exercise of the mind and the imagination, it is labour in vain; it furnishes him with nothing new, and is after all only the reflection of his own thoughts. He finds in it a convenient way of compelling Scripture to yield an answer to the many speculative questions that agitate his own restless brain. But it is no proper or satisfying answer that he thus obtains. Scripture is merely turned into a cipher, of which he has not the

[1] Denis, *De la Philosophie d'Origène*, p. 33. Cf. *in Exod.*, Hom. xiii. 2.

key. As a Jew, even Philo had to pay some regard to the literal and historical sense of the Old Testament; but the reins of Origen's imagination knew no such restraining influence. For him allegorical exegesis meant licence to father his own speculations upon a sacred text which was venerated as the depository of all truth.

In opposition to the Jews and Judaising Christians, who denied that their legal sacrifices and ritual were denuded of their value and importance by the coming of Christ, Origen maintained that to observe the law outwardly in the letter now that its spiritual sense has been revealed, is no longer religion, but superstition, and a hindrance rather than a help to piety. "Compared with the gospel, the law is like those earthen vessels which the artist forms before casting the statue in bronze; they are necessary until the work itself is finished, but their utility ceases with the completion of the statue."[1]

With Origen the aggressiveness of the Gnostics weighed even more powerfully than the conservatism of the Jews. Learned, versatile, speculative, this class of opponents devoted their oratorical and literary powers to wrecking the faith of the simple. Undoubtedly the strong point of Christian preaching was an unbroken tradition reaching from the Creation to the times of Christ. The Gnostics sought to undermine this position by violently separating the New Testament stem from the Old Testament root. They ridiculed the story of Noah's ark, and the God who had to send His angels to ascertain what was happening in Sodom. They criticised mercilessly whatever

[1] *In Levit.*, Hom. x. 1.

ORIGEN'S VIEW OF HOLY SCRIPTURE

in the Old Testament offended their moral sense, *e.g.* the atrocities of the Jewish wars, with the view of representing them as sanctioned by a cruel God utterly unlike the good God of the gospel. Cultured Greeks, although otherwise drawn to the sacred writings, were shocked at such tokens of barbarity, and hesitated to declare themselves Christians. Under these circumstances Origen does not, like Clement, content himself with pleading that in God justice and goodness are harmoniously combined. He boldly cuts the knot by maintaining that the narratives and commands to which his opponents took exception are not literally true; that the kings slain by the Israelites are only figurative names for vices that have dominion over men; and that the nations which they are said to have exterminated are not to be regarded as composed of men, but of the enemies that assail men's souls. What the Spirit has in view in such passages is not the narration of historical events, but the communication of mysteries, under the veil of facts, for the soul's edification. They thus serve a pædagogic purpose, and are vehicles of the highest truth. The forbidding aspect of the upper garment cannot alter the fact that "the king's daughter is all glorious within," and while it may repel the ignorant, it only acts as a spur to redoubled effort on the part of the spiritually enlightened. In the hands of Origen, therefore, allegorism in its negative aspect becomes an apologetic weapon, by means of which he defends Christianity against the hide-bound externalism of the Jews and the blasphemous criticism of the Gnostics; but as the result of his fantastic interpretations, the history itself, of course, disappears. Lest, however, his view should be

80 ORIGEN AND GREEK THEOLOGY

regarded as invalidating entirely both the historical and legislative portions of Scripture, Origen is careful to state that the passages having a purely spiritual meaning are few in comparison to those that are true historically, and that in regard to the Decalogue and such New Testament precepts as "Swear not at all," etc., there is no doubt that they are to be observed according to the letter, although in such cases a deeper meaning also may disclose itself to the advanced Christian.

It has been suggested that, even irrespective of any controversy with Jews or heretics, Origen would still have been driven to these extremities by the mere conditions of preaching in his time. The preacher's custom was one day to read and expound a page of Scripture, the next day to read and expound the page following. In the case of historical books, which were not written exactly for edification, one can understand what embarrassment he would often experience. Only by effacing their historical character could he draw edifying lessons from texts but little edifying in themselves.[1] Origen's *Homilies* certainly show how ready he was to sacrifice the literal sense, and at all hazards to discover a meaning suitable to the moral and spiritual needs of his hearers. Any other course would in his opinion have been wrong. "Those do injustice to Moses, who, when the Book of *Leviticus* or some portion of *Numbers* is read in the church, do not set forth spiritually what is written in the law. For necessarily those present on hearing recited in the church either the rites of sacrifice or the observances of the Sabbath and other similar things,

[1] Denis, p. 45.

ORIGEN'S VIEW OF HOLY SCRIPTURE

are displeased, and say, How is it necessary to read that here? Of what use to us are Jewish precepts and the observances of a despised people? That concerns the Jews; let them attend to it if they please."[1]

Bound up with the positive aspect of allegorism as the instrument for the discovery of mysteries was the doctrine of reserve, or economy, as it was called. This was based upon such passages as Prov. v. 16; Tob. xii. 7; Matt. vii. 6; Mark iv. 34; and while applied partly to the hostile heathen, was used by Clement and Origen chiefly as a justification for withholding from Christians of the less educated order whatever might tend to unsettle their simple faith. For such the only safe path was held to be that of implicit obedience to the divine law; in no case were they to ask the reason. "The holy apostles," says Origen, "in preaching the faith of Christ, declared with the utmost clearness whatever they thought necessary to salvation, even to those who are slothful in the investigation of divine science, leaving the reason of their assertions to be sought out by those who should deserve the excellent gifts of the Spirit, and especially the graces of utterance, wisdom, and knowledge. But as to other things, they affirmed indeed that they are, but why or whence they did not explain."[2] There is a sense in which the doctrine of reserve may be properly used by every teacher who would guard against confusing his pupils by a too early introduction to what is difficult and profound. But the Alexandrian Fathers carried it far beyond the limits of a prudential silence of this sort. They saw no harm in winking at superstitious beliefs which they

[1] *In Num.*, Hom. vii. 2.   [2] Preface to *De Princ.*

considered to be either harmless or positively helpful in the right direction. Such a standpoint reflects the influence of the Greek philosophy, which did not reckon Truth among the four cardinal virtues. It makes the doctrine of economy "the screen of an esoteric belief," and the domain of intellectual freedom the close preserve of the enlightened Christian. Additional interest is lent to this doctrine from the fact that, in conjunction with "tradition," it was made the basis of the Tractarian Movement in England in the nineteenth century.

Perhaps the most serious fault in Origen's position with reference to this whole subject is his failure to take account of the law of historical development in divine revelation. In his view Moses and the prophets had as deep an insight into the relations of the Persons of the Godhead as the apostles, and he could probably have found proofs of the resurrection as easily in the Book of Genesis as in the Pauline Epistles. From this standpoint there was, of course, nothing to prevent the gospel records from being supplemented by the prophecies; and in fact Origen treats the Psalms as sources for the life of Christ. He regards the whole truth as having been revealed by the Spirit under the Old Testament economy as well as under the New, the only difference being that in the former case comparatively few understood the spiritual significance of the law, whereas it is now understood by multitudes. It is true that in a certain degree the Old Testament prefigured the New; but meither was all symbolic, nor did what symbols there were amount to actual proofs of Christian doctrine. Even the shadows of good things to come were only shadows, but Origen confounded them with those good things themselves. Nothing has operated more prejudicially against a true understanding of the Bible than this absurd method of treatment. Its mischievous results have been reflected in all subsequent doctrinal development. For long the glamour of Origen's genius led to widespread acquiescence in his wildest extravagances. But with the dawn of grammatico-historical exegesis and the founding of the new science of biblical theology, this antiquated method of handling Scripture has for ever become impossible. At the same time "exact grammatical exegesis is by no means alien to his homilies and commentaries, and many of his strangest uses of Scripture may be viewed as practical applications rather than scholarly expositions."[1] Other extenuating facts are his prayerful spirit, his toilsome effort, and his recognition that Scripture is its own interpreter. When all is said, however, there remains the irrepressible regret that "the eagle eye of Origen" should have been so enchanted by a veritable Will-o'-the-wisp, and that his colossal abilities should have been so largely devoted to the building up of a false system of interpretation.

[1] Salmond, art. "Hermeneutics" in *Ency. Brit.*

CHAPTER IV

Religious Philosophy of Origen

THE view taken by Origen of the relation of Christian doctrine to Greek philosophy is substantially that of Clement, although he rates philosophers somewhat lower than does that writer. Truth he regards as a constant quantity, which from the beginning has been imparted to man only in scattered rays. Of these human wisdom, as embodied in the circle of the sciences, and in the secret doctrines of Chaldæans and Egyptians, Jews and Greeks, has supplied its quota. Divine wisdom, however, as revealed in Christianity, immeasurably transcends the philosophical knowledge of men. The Christian doctrine embraces whatever elements of truth are contained in the Greek philosophy, of which indeed it is the completion. While philosophy is a divinely ordained means of arriving at the truth, and is closely related to Christianity in respect of the fundamental ideas of God and moral justice which have been written indelibly by the Creator upon the human heart, it is far from being of uniform value. In the form of Epicureanism, for example, it is even hostile to the truth; in that of Platonism, it partly coincides with it. Where its development has been pernicious, this result is due to its corruption by demoniac transmitters and human teachers. On the other hand, besides the affinity necessarily existing between philosophy and Christianity as being both of divine origin, there is also the measure of resemblance caused by the borrowing of philosophical doctrines from the Old Testament.

The religious philosophy of Origen is thus marked by a finely tolerant spirit. Although viewing the Scriptures as the sole guaranteed source of truth, he shared Clement's opinion that human systems of thought also might be at least relatively true. Wherever a spark of good appeared, these Alexandrian teachers gave it acknowledgment. As the principle of perfection, their Christian gnosis taught them "to honour the whole creation of God Almighty," and to view everything from the relative standpoint. They were students of Greek culture, and had a high idea of what was becoming in a philosopher. "Origen could already estimate the relative progress made by mankind within the Church as compared with those outside her pale, saw no gulf between the growing and the perfect, and traced the whole advance to Christ." [1]

If, however, he recognised philosophy as furnishing a series of steps in the right direction, Origen was also strongly convinced of its inadequacy. While it formed an introduction to the higher wisdom, it was at best an uncertain guide. Philosophers did not succeed in conveying the truth to the popular mind; they were like physicians who attend only to the health of a select few and neglect the multitude. After uttering in the schools the grandest arguments about God, they

[1] Harnack, *Hist. of Dogma*, ii. p. 338.

86 ORIGEN AND GREEK THEOLOGY

straightway fell into idolatry and sanctioned polytheism. This was in sharp contrast to the practice of the very lowest Jew. The secret of the success of the unlettered disciples of Jesus in impressing men of various nationalities, as compared with the failure of the Greek philosophers to win adherents, lay in the fact that in the one case the speakers possessed a certain God-given power which was lacking in the other. This was none other than the power of the Logos, which everywhere manifested itself in the Church by abolishing polytheism, and bringing about the moral betterment of gospel hearers in proportion to their capacity and willingness to receive that which is good. In earlier times also through Moses the power of divine revelation had been shown on a national scale—" Would that the Jews had not transgressed the law, and slain the prophets, and conspired against Jesus: we should then have had a model of that heavenly commonwealth which Plato has sought to describe; although I doubt whether he could have accomplished as much as was done by Moses and those who followed him."[1]

The true goal of the Greek philosophy, as well as of the revealed wisdom proclaimed by the prophets, was the incarnation of Jesus, which focussed all previous self-communications of the Eternal Reason. A knowledge essentially devoid of error is thus guaranteed to us. Men could not reach this anterior to Christ's coming, because it was unattainable apart from the expiation of the world's sin. Without Him perfect knowledge is an impossibility. Clement held that a man's life is likely to be virtuous in proportion to his

[1] *Contra Celsum*, v. 43.

knowledge of the truth. Origen makes an advance upon this position by identifying human enlightenment with redemption. Men walk in light and practise virtue through Him who is the truth, and who has fulfilled all righteousness. By the union of the divine and human natures in His own person, Christ has become the source of the new life of humanity.

The character of Origen's theological system as a philosophy of revelation accounts for the Gnostic and Neoplatonic features mixed up with it. His speculations often recall the theosophic dreams and fantastic cosmology of Valentinus, and his methods are those of that prominent heresiarch, and of the Neoplatonic schools. In his doctrine of the pre-existence of souls, in his theory of a threefold division of human nature, and in his highly symbolic interpretation of the story of Paradise, his Christian theology clearly shows affinity with those systems. The agreement, however, is not in principle, but is due to the adoption in common of particular Platonic tenets. He is even more of an idealistic philosopher than Plato himself. At the same time he holds the Scriptures of the Old and New Testaments to be the only absolutely reliable sources for acquiring a knowledge of the truth, and there is something to be said for the contention that in Origen much has been ascribed to the influence of Platonism that admits of a simpler and more natural explanation.[1] According to this view the doctrine of the pre-existence of the soul, for instance, was not peculiar to Pythagoras and Plato, but was also current in the East, and may quite well have been suggested to Origen by certain Jewish apocrypha in which there

[1] Denis, *De la Philosophie d'Origène*, p. 57.

88 ORIGEN AND GREEK THEOLOGY

was a large admixture of Oriental ideas. So also with regard to the ultimate triumph of the good, the conversion of the devil, etc. The exaggerated and axiomatic significance attached by Origen to certain New Testament texts is further pointed to as the real basis of many of his semi-Christian, semi-Oriental theories. He finds, *e.g.*, the distinction of the upper, intermediary, and infernal worlds in the saying of St. Paul, "that in the name of Jesus every knee should bow, of things in heaven, and things on earth, and things under the earth" (Phil. ii. 10); and the pre-existence of the soul in the statements: "When Elizabeth heard the salutation of Mary, the babe leaped in her womb" (Luke i. 41), and "There was a man sent from God whose name was John" (John i. 6). Endowed with a very bold and lively imagination, and breathing so constantly the atmosphere of the supernatural, there was really no limit to the chimerical notions which he was able to read into and extract from the texts of Scripture. But his doctrines occupy another level, and, from whatever sources they are drawn, all bear the stamp of his own individuality. While refusing to believe that in any of its main essentials Origen derived his doctrinal system either from Plato or the Stoics, Denis willingly concedes that its linguistic framework, as well as many "hypotheses which are like the stage-dressing of his ideas," are borrowed from the Greek philosophers. He maintains, however, that the doctrines themselves, as distinct from their philosophical dress, were derived from other sources. Although the great Alexandrian owes his idealism to Plato, whether directly or through the medium of the Gnostics, it is not according to this view permissible to go into detailed analysis so as to say of particular doctrines, "This Origen borrowed from the Stoics, that from Plato." For the rest, they are severally stated with much logical acumen, and even where not originally evolved by his own mind, present combinations so novel, adjustments so exact, and transformations so profound, as to make them rank with the most noteworthy contributions to theological thought ever given to the world.

While, however, in loyalty to the Church's rule of faith he accepts the gospel as in itself "the power of God unto salvation to every one that believeth," Origen also attaches the greatest value to a scientific conception of Christianity. Hence the union in him of the Platonic philosopher with the orthodox traditionalist. Deeming it to be the object of Christianity that men should become wise, he not only asserts the rights of science in the Church, but distinctly subordinates faith to knowledge, and regards the former as a stage in the Christian life relatively inferior to the latter. For this position he finds ample warrant in Scripture, which contains many enigmatical and dark sayings expressly designed to exercise the understanding of its readers. The content of the Church's faith thus demands to be idealised, and the most suitable appliances for this purpose are the methods of the Greek philosophers. As the revelation of the highest reason, Christianity must lend itself to elucidation by the science of reasoning, and, in fact, it admits of being stated in clear dogmatic propositions. To attain to such a systematic grasp of ideas and doctrines is to reach the highest stage of the Christian life. This, however, Origen no longer designates *gnosis*, but *wisdom*. The spread of

Gnostic heresy had apparently rendered it desirable to employ a term not so liable to be misconstrued as that which had been used by Clement. In his public teaching that writer had also withheld more of this higher knowledge than did Origen, who considered it the only vital Christianity, and therefore showed more eagerness to impart it to all.

A theory of Christianity which emphasised the distinction between *pistis* and *gnosis* required twofold expression. Its teachers used one language for the people and another for the initiated. The idea of an exoteric and an esoteric Christianity will always be repulsive to some as savouring of dishonesty; yet there is another side to the matter. Even the modern Christian teacher must suit his language to his audience. A professor of divinity does not discourse to his students as he would to a home mission gathering, or even to an ordinary congregation. Different stages of attainment in Christian knowledge call for different modes of treatment on the part of Christian teachers. And if Origen drew a clear distinction between the simple and the perfect, he at all events did not separate the two classes by an impassable gulf. On the contrary, he sought to bridge over the distance between them by proclaiming the entire compatibility of the profoundest scientific culture with a sincere acceptance of the gospel. And it was just because of this that he was so successful as a Christian missionary to the Greeks. It would be wrong to say that he proclaimed two Christianities; what he really asserted was that one Christian saw much more in Christianity than another.

No doubt Origen's conception of Christianity had its

drawbacks. For one thing it amounted to the virtual obliteration of the historical element in Holy Scripture. Not that he denies in the majority of instances the actual occurrence of facts, but by the application of his hermeneutical methods he robs them of their significance. Thus even the Incarnation is emptied of its peculiar value. To the perfect, Christ is nothing more than the manifestation of the Logos who has been from eternity with the Father, and whose activity has also been eternal. It is not as the Crucified One, but merely as a divine teacher that He is of consequence to the wise. "He was sent indeed as a physician to sinners, but as a teacher of divine mysteries to those who are already pure, and who sin no more."[1] The gospel records are accordingly subjected to the allegorising process, with the result that their true and simple story disappears. Indeed the gospel itself is represented as merely "the shadow of the mysteries of Christ"; as such it occupies a middle position between the law and "the eternal gospel" (Rev. xiv. 6), which, as the full revelation of those mysteries, is the possession only of the spiritual Church. "In the final utterances of religious metaphysics ecclesiastical Christianity, with the exception of a few compromises, is thrown off as a husk. The objects of religious knowledge have no history, or rather—and this is a genuinely Gnostic and Neoplatonic idea—they have only a supramundane one."[2]

As a substitute for the outward revelation and ordinances which form the distinguishing characteristics of positive religion, Origen makes use of the results of the speculative cosmology of the Greeks. He is familiar

[1] *Contra Celsum*, iii. 62.   [2] Harnack, *History of Dogma*, ii. p. 343.

with the various mythological and philosophical theories as to the origin of the universe and the nature of matter. That we must largely trace to this source the inspiration of the marvellous and strangely complicated picture of the world [1] which finds a place within his broad and idealistic theology, is plain to every reader of the *Contra Celsum*. It was already recognised by Porphyry, whom Eusebius quotes as saying of Origen: "His outward life was that of a Christian and opposed to the law, but in regard to his views of things and of the Deity, he thought like the Greeks, inasmuch as he introduced their ideas into the myths of other peoples." His cosmology, in fact, is an essential part of his theology. To have a clear idea of God it is not enough to think of Him abstractly and apart from His relation to the world. It is precisely in connection with the latter point that these impressions are produced which determine the real standpoint of a theologian, and show whether he is pantheistic, dualistic, or Christian. That Origen belongs to the latter category is proved by his contention that there is only one eternal substance, by his conception of God as the direct Creator of the world, and by his view of Christ as the God-Man in whom and by whom all things consist.

The moral and religious ideal set forth in the system of Origen is one which has its roots partly in Neoplatonic mysticism and partly in Holy Scripture. It had long been a favourite theory with idealistic philosophers that the most perfect life open to man is that which consists solely in meditative introspection and contemplation of the eternal. According to this view actions have the effect of entangling us in all manner of worldly

[1] "L'espèce de poème cosmogonique conçu par Origène" (Denis, p. 163).

concerns, and therefore it is better for us not to act, but just to remain absorbed in the absolute and the unseen, and in the possession of a calm tranquillity which more than anything else tends to make us godlike. To have need of nothing is to be in closest contact with the Deity; to overcome the sensuous, and to live in the habitual contemplation of the invisible, is to attain at length the final aim of existence in ecstatic union with God. This is the view of life that prompted the ancient hermits to withdraw from the world and take to their cells, and it is this that has laid the foundation of the monastic system wherever it has been practised. Whether, however, this abandonment of the active for the contemplative life is in harmony with the true genius of Christianity may well be doubted; its note is not that of an isolated self-sufficiency, but that of a yearning aspiration after righteousness. In the Alexandrian Fathers we see the union of both tendencies. While with Origen the mystic element is not predominant, it is certainly present, and there can be no mistake as to his "hunger and thirst after righteousness." For him the ideal to be sought by the human spirit is "the state without sorrow, the state of insensibility to all evils, of order and peace—but peace in God." The way to attain this is through self-knowledge, repression of the sensuous, and due cultivation of "the meditative hour"; but in all this he sees nothing inconsistent with the most active endeavours to promote the kingdom of God. Christian productivity is a necessary consequence of Christian receptivity. There will always be visible fruits of the power of Christ working in the soul in the shape of freewill efforts after serving

94 ORIGEN AND GREEK THEOLOGY

God and doing good to the brethren. Through such service, through faith in and fellowship with the Logos, through loyal submission to Providence, and through the desire of heaven, the spirit of man becomes godlike and eternally blessed. Viewing the soul as the mirror of Deity, and believing that through the contemplation of herself the secret of deification is to be found, Origen uses the ethical systems of Greek philosophy as stepping-stones towards the ultimate attainment of this high destiny.

Worthy of note also in this connection is Origen's theory of knowledge and its relation to faith. In his view knowledge is essentially recollection. It is the result of recalling fundamental truths imprinted on the human soul by the Creator, and even in its growth through the continued energy of men's minds the divine element, *i.e.* the beneficent influence of the Logos, is at work. In this way knowledge may be gleaned from the field of philosophy as well as from that of revelation. It was this conviction that led Origen to incorporate so many philosophical doctrines with those of Scripture, and to weave them into one heterodox system, the essential harmony of which in all its parts was, however, probably clear enough to his own mind. And if he did admit elements alien to the genius of Christianity, he must at least be acquitted of having either accepted anything directly antagonistic to it or sacrificed any of its fundamental docrines.

Faith Origen views as a whole-hearted belief manifesting itself in a ready obedience. While accepting the doctrine of justification by faith alone, he holds that the faith which does not influence conduct is dead. A living faith cannot consist with continuance in sin, but changes the whole walk and conversation. If we really believe in Christ as our peace, we shall not stir up strife; if we believe that of God He is made unto us wisdom, we shall not turn again to folly; if we believe that He is the power of God, we shall not remain unfruitful disciples. Real faith, however, may be perfect or imperfect. Of the former description was that counted to Abraham for righteousness, seeing it had already accredited itself through obedience; of the latter is that of all who have still the spirit of fear and have not received the spirit of sonship. But even in its most imperfect measure real faith is always implanted in the soul by divine power, and when the true light thus comes to a man he will not fail to advance by the aid of human learning as well as through the enlightenment of the Holy Ghost to an ever clearer insight into the meaning of Scripture, and to an ever fuller apprehension of the divine glory of the Redeemer. Faith thus gradually develops into knowledge, and the life of faith advances with every increase in the number of doctrinal propositions the truth of which is recognised. While in its essential content Faith need not embrace more than the main articles of the Christian creed, its objects are alike numerous and manifold, and as a divinely given and gracious power within us it enables the true Christian firmly to grasp the truth in all its bearings. When Faith and Reason thus combine their forces, the resultant product is Christian science. In this higher knowledge there are two main stages — gnosis or understanding, and wisdom or the direct spiritual vision of truth.

In the investigation of truth there is, however,

no finality. Even to zeal reinforced by grace God's judgments are unsearchable, and His ways past finding out. Human knowledge at its highest reach is but patchwork; we see in riddles, we know in part. The figures we deal in only take us midway between the shadows of the law and the truth itself. As sinful mortals we have necessarily here a limited horizon, but through the gateway of death the perfected Christian shall pass to a state of larger knowledge in which he shall see no longer through a glass obscurely, but face to face. The treasures of wisdom and knowledge formerly hidden from his view shall then be thrown open to him; as a veritable son of the Highest he shall fully understand the Scriptures and feed upon the very food of Christ.

The main idea underlying the religious philosophy of Origen is that of the indestructible unity of God and all spiritual essence. If, therefore, the created spirit in the exercise of its own free will shall fall away from God, it must still return to being in Him. The ultimate deification of humanity is a leading idea in the Greek theology. At the same time there is no confounding of Creator and created; Origen distinctly contrasts the one transcendent Essence with the visible creation. He does not, with many pagan philosophers, conceive God as existing at an infinite remove and in absolute isolation from the world. On the contrary, he maintains that, as revealed in Christ, He is immanent in the whole creation. We live and move and have our being in God just because by His power and reason He fills and holds together all the diversity of the world. The task to which Origen addresses himself thus resembles in certain respects that attempted by the Neoplatonists; for him as for them the problem is how to establish the organic unity of God and the world, and counteract the dualism of Oriental theosophies. In general, the system of Origen has much affinity with that of Valentinus, but is distinguished from the latter by the prominence given to the idea of the freedom of the individual will, and by the rigid exclusion of a fall as applied to any part of the divine pleroma itself. The effort to maintain along with His absolute goodness the absolute causality of God, and to retain the transcendental nature of the human spirit while rejecting Stoic pantheism, has driven every form of mysticism to a twofold conception of the spiritual, and from this ambiguity the system of Origen is not free. As the unfolding of the divine essence, the spiritual belongs to God; as that which is created, it stands in contrast to Him.

Origen displays much ingenuity in bringing his essentially heterodox system into line with the rule of faith as already elaborated by Irenæus, who conceives revelation as the history of salvation, and seeks to find in the literal sense of Scripture and Church tradition the divine "categorical imperative" for men. It is usual to regard Origen's philosophy as embodying (1) the doctrine of God and the unfoldings of His essence, (2) the doctrine of the Fall and its consequences, (3) the doctrine of redemption and restoration.[1] Denis' division into (1) Theology, (2) Cosmology, (3) Anthropology, (4) Teleology, while it covers the ground, is somewhat too suggestive of the clear-cut categories of modern systematic theology.

[1] So, *e.g.*, Redepenning and Harnack.

CHAPTER V

THE WRITINGS OF ORIGEN

ORIGEN wielded the pen of a ready writer. He was probably a more voluminous author than even moderns like Calvin or Richard Baxter. It is, of course, impossible to accept the traditional figure of six thousand as any indication of the real number of his works; but Jerome's question, "Which of us can read all that he has written?" is a sufficient testimony to the magnitude of his literary labours. As a result, perhaps, of the growing suspicion attaching to his name in the Church, the greater part of his writings has perished; and much of what we do possess is in the form of a by no means accurate translation by Rufinus. The writings of Origen are not limited to any one department of theological investigation; they range over the entire field. Much, however, has been erroneously ascribed to him, as, *e.g.*, the *Philosophumena* or *Refutation of all Heresies*, which in tone and language appears to be a Latin product rather than a Greek, and the *Dialogues* of one Adamantius *De recta in Deum fide*. That he should have been the reputed author of the latter work within a century after his death is scarcely surprising in view of the fact that even during his lifetime he had to complain of undue

THE WRITINGS OF ORIGEN 99

liberties being taken alike with his works and with his name.

i. *Origen's Contributions to Textual Criticism*

Jewish opinion with reference to the Septuagint had been gradually changing. For long this translation enjoyed great popularity among the Hellenists, and seems to have been read even in some Palestinian synagogues. Josephus makes extensive use of it. But when by its help it was sought to establish the truth of Christianity as against Judaism, the Jews began to repudiate it as a mutilated rendering of the Hebrew Scriptures, and gave preference to other translations, especially to that of Aquila, which was more literal and Hebraistic. Traces of disputes between Jews and Christians regarding the LXX occur as early as Justin's time;[1] and a century later, when Origen was at the height of his activity, the advocates of Christianity had constantly flung in their teeth the taunt that the proof texts they adduced either did not exist, or were not recognisable in the Hebrew original. Through frequent collisions with Jewish opponents who entrenched themselves behind this position, Origen must soon have become cognisant of the corrupt state of the LXX text in the MSS. then current. Its wide circulation, the frequency and haste with which copies were made, and the tendency of transcribers arbitrarily to add or omit, to alter or improve, produced a tantalising crop of "various readings," and even in Origen's time must have rendered the recovery of the original text a virtual impossibility. Yet, so far as it was practicable,

[1] *Dialogue with Trypho*, chaps. 71-73.

the Herculean task of a critical restoration was undertaken by this dauntless teacher of Alexandria. As an example of sheer pluck and monumental industry there is perhaps nothing in the annals of scholarship to compare with this first achievement in the field of biblical criticism. In entering upon this work, at which he toiled for eight and twenty years, Origen's aim was partly critical and partly polemical. On the one hand, he aimed at the improvement of the text of the LXX by providing a recension more reliable than the text of any single manuscript then existing; on the other hand, he sought to exhibit the real state of the case as between the LXX and the Hebrew text, so that Christians might no longer be at a disadvantage in their disputations with the Jews. The critical task was the necessary preliminary to the securing of the controversial vantage-ground desired.

Financed and encouraged by Ambrosius, Origen began to collect MSS. of the Septuagint. His collation of these revealed an amount of wanton divergence that rendered it hopeless to arrive at the true text by mere comparison of MSS. Nor, believing as he did that the Hebrew text had been tampered with by the later Jews, could he hope by its means to reconstruct the Greek text in its original form, although in passages where there could be no reason to suspect intentional falsification, the Hebrew text might prove a valuable aid. There remained, however, one other important factor in the case. This was the existence of several Greek translations of the Old Testament other than the Alexandrian. Reference has already been made to that of Aquila, a Jewish proselyte of Sinope, which appeared during the reign of Hadrian, and was afterwards issued

THE WRITINGS OF ORIGEN

in a second edition even more Hebraistic than the first. Half a century later, Theodotion, an Ebionite of Ephesus, published what is practically a revised edition of the LXX with a new translation of the Book of Daniel, which entirely superseded the older Alexandrian version, and is still printed in copies of the LXX. Shortly afterwards a third Greek translation was executed by Symmachus, also an Ebionite, and of Samaritan extraction. His translation is freer than Aquila's, and is also characterised by greater elegance and purer Greek. In addition to these Origen made use of other three anonymous versions, known, in accordance with the position assigned to them in his great work, as the Fifth, Sixth, and Seventh. Of the latter, however, he only makes partial use; possibly they were incomplete, or the copies which he possessed may have been so. One of them was found by him at Jericho; another he discovered at Nicopolis, while journeying to Greece; when and where he secured the third is unknown. All of them were probably older, as they were also more of the nature of free paraphrases, than the translations of Theodotion and Symmachus. While unable to adjudge any one of these versions to be in itself superior to the LXX, Origen saw how the latter might be corrected and supplemented by comparison with them as well as with the Hebrew. They were more or less based upon (presumably different texts of) the LXX, and had not as yet suffered from arbitrary perversions. Having collected the available MSS., Origen set to work upon his great edition of the Old Testament. It is usually called the *Hexapla*, from the circumstance that each page consisted of six parallel columns, showing at a glance the whole of the material for arriving at the most reliable text of the Septuagint, and for ascertaining how far that text really coincides with, or deviates from, the original Hebrew. The first column to the right contained the Hebrew text, the second the same text transliterated into Greek, the third the translation of Aquila, the fourth that of Symmachus, the fifth the Septuagint, and the sixth the version of Theodotion. While the entire Old Testament was thus dealt with, certain of the books composing it were set down in two, and in some instances three, additional columns containing the so-called Fifth, Sixth, and Seventh versions.[1]

In forming his Hexaplar text Origen proceeded on the principle of retaining the original LXX, and making use of critical signs to indicate how and where it differed from the Hebrew. What was lacking in the LXX, but occurred in the Hebrew and in one or more of the other translators, was marked with an asterisk (*) and the name of the source;[2] what stood in the LXX, but had no equivalent in the Hebrew, he marked with an obelus (÷).[3] Where different MSS. of the LXX deviated from one another, he gave preference

[1] See specimen page in De Wette's *Introduction to the Old Testament*, or in Smith's *Dictionary of Greek and Roman Biography and Mythology*.

[2] These *lacunæ* were supplied mostly from Theodotion, but not seldom from Aquila, and sometimes from Symmachus.

[3] "In later copies these marks were unfortunately often omitted. The Hexaplar text became mixed up with the true LXX, and the modern critic is sometimes tempted to forget how much the Eastern Church owed to this first attempt to go back to the Hebrew Old Testament, in his impatience at the obliteration by the adoption of Hexaplar corrections of important divergences of the LXX from the Massoretic text" (W. Robertson Smith, art. "Bible" in *Ency. Brit.*).

THE WRITINGS OF ORIGEN

to the reading which had the support of the other translators.

Origen also prepared another edition of the Old Testament containing only the text of the Septuagint, and the versions of Aquila, Theodotion, and Symmachus. This was arranged on the same plan as the larger work, and was known as the *Tetrapla*. As to its precise relation to the *Hexapla*, however, scholars are not agreed. Some regard it as the earlier work upon which the *Hexapla* was based, and as having contained the LXX in the usual text merely; according to others, it was issued later than, and as a minor edition of, the *Hexapla*, with the improved text of the LXX reproduced from the latter, but without the critical signs and the suggested additions and omissions. To both works Origen supplied short marginal notes, a large proportion of which consisted of mystical explanations of Hebrew proper names, while some appear to have contained a Greek version of readings found in the Samaritan and Syriac texts.

Little now remains of these great early monuments of Christian erudition. They were too huge for transcription, and seem to have perished in the destruction of Cæsarea by the Arabians in 653. About the beginning of the third century they were brought to that city and placed in the library of Pamphilus, who in collaboration with Eusebius extracted the Hexaplar text of the LXX, along with its diacritical signs, etc., and circulated it broadcast among the churches of Palestine. Jerome, who speaks of these MSS. as *Palæstinensos codices*,[1] also made extensive use of it. As separate copies of the later translations were also

[1] *Præf. in Paralip.*

multiplied, many Church Fathers, even without access to the Hexapla itself, were able to avail themselves of its contents; and since Petrus Morinus (in the sixteenth century) led the way, several attempts have been made to restore as far as possible the lost work by collecting the extant fragments from the patristic writings.[1] In the seventh century a slavishly literal Syriac translation was made from the Hexaplar text of the LXX, retaining the Origenic signs, but without specifying the sources from which additions have been adopted. Arabic versions have also been prepared from the Greek Hexaplar text.

The important critical work done by Origen for the text of the Septuagint, his strong declaration as to the want of uniformity in the text of the Gospels,[2] and a misunderstanding of Jerome's references to "the MSS. of Adamantius,"[3] led to the erroneous belief that he also prepared a recension of the New Testament text. As an exegete, of course, he sought the correct readings, and the great amount of textual variation in the Greek MSS. of the New Testament caused him carefully to revise and correct obvious errors of transcription in his own manuscript or manuscripts.[4] His reverence for the letter of Scripture prevented him, however, from admitting any merely conjectural emendations into his text, although he adopted several

---

[1] Cf. especially Field, *Origenis Hexaplorum quæ supersunt*, 2 vols., Oxon. 1867–1874.

[2] *In Matt.* xix. 19.

[3] *I.e.* the MSS. used by Origen, and not a recension of his own.

[4] He used more than one, and did not confine himself to one "family," the text of Mark used by him for *in Matt.* being (according to Griesbach) *Western*, while that cited in the *in Joann.* is *Alexandrian*.

THE WRITINGS OF ORIGEN 105

in his commentaries.[1] It is further probable that Origen's purified text was, along with the major part of his works, copied by Pamphilus, that it was followed by Eusebius, whose quotations so remarkably coincide with those of Origen, and that it obtained wide currency in the fifty copies ordered through Eusebius by the emperor Constantine. Its influence is even clearly traceable in the *textus receptus* of the present day. Still, Origen made no such recension of the New Testament as he did of the text of the LXX in the *Hexapla*, upon which his fame as a critic mainly rests. Biblical scholarship owes to him a lasting debt of gratitude as the brilliant pioneer of that critical treatment of the sacred writings which has yielded such valuable results in our time.

ii. *Apologetic Work of Origen*

Towards the close of the reign of Marcus Aurelius (*c*. 176) a strong attack upon Christianity was made in a work entitled Ἀληθὴς λόγος, or the *True Discourse*. This was written by Celsus, doubtfully identified by some with Celsus the friend of Lucian, who wrote a work on magic, and was an Epicurean. The standpoint of the author of the *True Discourse* is substantially Platonic. Origen, who does not profess to know the facts, suggests that he either concealed his Epicurean views, and had become a convert to a better system, or was merely a namesake of Celsus the Epicurean

[1] In Matt. viii. 28 and parallel passages he supports the reading Γεργεσηνῶν, although he found it in no MS., and in John i. 28, misled by a popular legend, he preferred to read "Bethabara" for "Bethany"; but although both of these readings gained currency through his influence, it does not appear that he actually inserted them in his text.

(iv. 54); and while he himself on the whole inclines to the former of these alternatives, the real state of the case favours the latter.

Great interest and importance attach to this work as the first onslaught upon Christianity by one possessing a fairly competent knowledge of its real character and claims. Celsus perceived that it was a power which had to be reckoned with, and in his acute and able treatise, which anticipates many of the scientific arguments used against Christianity in modern times, he virtually urged all that could be said against the religion of Christ from the standpoint of cultured paganism. Celsus was not ill-fitted for his task. He was familiar not only with Greek thought and literature, but also with the Christian literature of the period (iv. 52, viii. 15); he had some acquaintance with the Old Testament; he knew the Four Gospels, especially that of Matthew; he had an idea of the main trend of the Pauline theology; he had obviously made diligent inquiries among the Jews, and had apparently read some Jewish and apocryphal works; he had travelled much, and had frequently conversed with Christians. Not only, however, is he well informed; it is scarcely an exaggeration to say that no more plausible dissertation against the Christian faith has ever been penned. As an illustration of the art of putting an opponent's case in the worst light it is singularly clever. Yet it "lost its whole point" owing to a serious misconception on the part of Celsus. Although aware of the distinction between "the great Church" and the heretical sects (v. 59), he nevertheless treats as Christian doctrine whatever any sectary calling himself by the Christian name chose to teach, and is thus guilty, as Origen complains, of the grossest misrepresentation (iii. 13, vi. 24).

Another interesting feature of the *True Discourse* is that it shows Celsus and Origen to have been not so far apart in their fundamental postulates. Philosophically and theologically, they were more closely allied than Origen suspected, and he is sometimes able to meet his antagonist only by speculatively reconstructing the Church doctrine in dispute. Both were Platonists, but with a difference. As an eclectic philosopher Celsus strove to bring his Platonic principles into harmony with the doctrines of Heraclitus, Pythagoras, and others; Origen rejected the dualism which lay at the root of these systems. Celsus held that matter is uncreated and coeternal with God; Origen taught that God is the Creator of all things. Even where their presuppositions do coalesce there are divergences; yet with all these there is affinity. Celsus conceived God as pure Intelligence, revealing Himself in the totality of ideas, of which the world of sense is the reflection. Sun, moon, and stars are revelations of God, who exercises a general providence through the laws of nature, and a special care for His creatures through the mediation of the " demons " or lower deities. These are the gods of the old national religions, Greek and barbarian alike. They are superintending spirits who guard the various quarters of the earth (v. 25), and this is the element of truth underlying the ancient mythologies. Some of them are scarcely higher than man, others are almost purely divine. As the gods of those who can rise to virtue but not to knowledge, their relation to the life of the soul is Gnostic rather than Christian; yet on the whole they form, in the system of Celsus, a sort of counterpart to the Christian doctrine of angels.

If, however, Celsus and Origen may be said to have started from principles common to both, they nevertheless arrived at diametrically opposite results. Origen was all for Christ; Celsus had not a good word either for Christ or for Christians. Even for the impressive sufferings of the former, and the silent martyrdom of the latter, he had only insulting epithets of mockery and scorn. In the bitterness of his attack upon Christianity he at once outdistanced all its opponents —many of whom, *e.g.* Plotinus and Porphyry, acknowledge the piety of Jesus while they freely lash His followers—and abandoned the ground so firmly taken up by Origen, who evidently grudged him the name of Platonist, and would fain have classed him with the less honoured Epicureans. As a fierce antagonist and merciless critic of the Christian [religion, Celsus was "the Voltaire of the second century."

Owing to the extensive verbatim extracts preserved in Origen's reply, and the consecutive method therein adopted, we can form a tolerably accurate notion of Celsus's treatise as a whole. In his Introduction he charges Christians with maintaining secret associations in violation of the law, and then proceeds with an air of impartiality to refer to their doctrinal and ethical systems. The one is of barbarian origin, and the other contains nothing new. The attitude of Christians towards idolatry is correct, but was adopted by Heraclitus long before them. Christ was a sorcerer, and His followers practise incantations. One might as well worship the phantoms of Hecate as exercise the blind faith of Christians, who say, "Do not

THE WRITINGS OF ORIGEN 109

examine, but believe." In order further to asperse the origin of Christianity, he excludes the Jews from the category of ancient and learned nations holding in common certain rational principles by means of which they all laid some stone on the cairn of truth, and asserts that Moses borrowed his doctrines and laws from Egyptian and other sources. In the main body of his *Discourse* Celsus, availing himself of the *a fortiori* argument, attempts to show (1) that Christianity is untenable from the standpoint of Judaism, as Jesus does not fit the character of the Jewish Messiah; and (2) that as the Messianic idea of the Jews is in itself preposterous, Christianity is thus deprived of the last vestige of support. While this expresses accurately the general trend of his work, he does not strictly follow any clear-cut plan. He cared little for artistic effect so long as he could deal a deadly blow at Christianity. To strike at it through Judaism showed consummate skill in tactics, although in view of the renewed attack from his own philosophical standpoint it involved a certain amount of repetition and confusion.[1]

The main part of his work, in which he seeks to destroy the fundamental doctrine of Christianity, Celsus supplements by a critical review of particular dogmas. Among the doctrines thus dealt with are those concerning humility and the kingdom of heaven, a supercelestial God, Satan, the Son of God, the creation of the world, and the sending of God's Son to a corrupt race like the Jews. What is true in Christianity is represented as an inferior version of the teaching of the Greek philosophy, or as a feeble

[1] For a careful summary of the *True Discourse* the student is referred to Patrick's *The Apology of Origen*.

echo of other religious systems. All the religious conceptions of Christians, even that of eternal life, are characterised as grossly material, and many of them as inconceivably absurd. The *True Discourse* closes with a spirited defence of pagan worship, and a somewhat pathetic appeal to Christians to co-operate with the king as loyal citizens. This is creditable both to the sagacity and to the temper of its author. But " when the persecutor thus found his weapons break in his grasp, and stooped to appeal to the generosity of his victim, it is evident that the battle was already lost."[1]

During the reigns of Gordian and Philip the Arabian, the Church was happily free from persecution. The effect of this was to accelerate its growth to an extent which could hardly fail to arouse the opposition of the heathen. In view of the weight attached in pagan circles to the work of Celsus, and in view also of their own incapacity, many Christians avowedly desiderated a thoroughgoing defence of their faith, to which they could confidently refer every gainsayer. Accordingly, more than half a century after its publication, the work of Celsus was sent by Ambrosius to Origen with a request that he would refute it. Although singularly well equipped for the task, Origen undertook it with reluctance, believing Christianity to be its own best apology. Yet he threw himself into the controversy with characteristic energy, and in his reply kept in view not only the demolition of the arguments of Celsus, but also the positive presentation of Christian truth. Needless to say, the eight books which compose the treatise against Celsus, and which are extant in the original Greek, are of great value as a source for

[1] Bigg, *Christian Platonists*, etc., p. 267.

the history and condition of the Church in the first half of the third century. They are marked by keen spiritual insight, vast erudition, masterly ability, and mature thought. They form the Apology *par excellence* of Christian antiquity, and have been the armoury from which weapons have all along been drawn for the defence of the Christian faith. According to Eusebius of Cæsarea, Origen's reply, as a refutation of all objections, actual or possible, past or future, left nothing to be desired; while centuries later it was still spoken of as "a golden work which can never be sufficiently praised."[1] Still, the *Contra Celsum* is not without its defects. The brightness of Origen's own faith in the ultimate triumph of Christianity leads him to underrate his antagonist, of whose work, in spite of its learning and ability, he constantly speaks in very disparaging terms. The method adopted is also confusing and tiresome for the reader. Departing from the systematic treatment at first contemplated by him, he takes up the objections of Celsus *seriatim*, and replies with great vehemence to each. This change of plan may have saved time to Origen, but has had the opposite effect for his readers, involving, as it does, needless repetition, besides marring the unity of the work. "As the book stands, we have all the materials for an apology, but they lie without order or proportion; it is 'a quarry of weighty dogmatic disquisitions,' but not a symmetrical building; and it is only by bringing together isolated and scattered thoughts that we can ascertain what Origen taught on the great problems of Christian Apologetics."[2] It must further

[1] Voss, quoted by Fabricius, *Delectus Argumentorum*, p. 63.
[2] Patrick, *The Apology of Origen*, p. 119.

be admitted that in details Origen's reasoning occasionally descends to the level of casuistry. Celsus brings forward objections which he either ignores or—considering that he is dealing with one who does not share the Christian presuppositions—fails fairly to meet. Yet, when all is said, the fact remains that many of the best things Origen ever wrote are contained in this apologetic work. It is, moreover, pervaded by a fine Christian spirit. In spite of the provokingly biting sarcasm of his opponent, he never indulges in anything like abusive language; "this low jester Celsus" (iii. 22) is perhaps the worst epithet he applies to him. With the most persevering patience he traverses nearly every specific objection raised by that writer against Christianity, and he candidly admits that on some points he is correct in his view (iii. 16). Every justice is done to the culture of the ancients. In the entire work there is nothing out of keeping with the ideal of Christian meekness so impressively drawn in its opening sentence: "When false witnesses testified against our Lord and Saviour Jesus Christ, He remained silent; and when unfounded charges were brought against Him, He returned no answer, believing that His whole life and conduct among the Jews were a better refutation than any answer to the false testimony, or than any formal defence against the accusations."

The nature of Celsus's attack necessarily determined the general scope of Origen's reply. It was not within his purview to combat the essential errors of paganism; his task was the narrower one of answering the specific objections urged against Christianity. Meanly enough, Celsus had prefaced these with the declaration that its

THE WRITINGS OF ORIGEN 113

votaries were disloyal rebels who adhered to an illegal secret system, well knowing that to bring such a charge was a virtual sentence of death. Origen replies that, so far from being unpatriotic, Christians are pre-eminently benefactors of their country. If they do not fight for kings with the sword, they render them still more effective help by their prayers; if they decline public offices, it is that they may perform a diviner service in the Church of God (viii. 73–75). Their "secret associations" amount to nothing more than a league against the tyranny of the devil (i. 1); their doctrine is better known to the world than the tenets of philosophers (i. 7). What likelihood is there of those rebelling against the State whose Master forbids slaughter, violence, and revenge (iii. 7, 8), and whose religious principles require a willing subjection to civil rulers? Philosophers are not censured for abandoning their country's customs; why then should Christians be? A distinction must be made between the written law of cities and the law of nature, *i.e.* the law of God; and where these clash, Christians are only reasonable in seeking to regulate their lives by the prescriptions of the latter, which is "king of all things" (v. 35–40).

As a philosopher, Celsus is biassed against Christianity on several grounds. For one thing, he views it as fit only for unlettered rustics. The style of the sacred writings he despises as rude and simple, and their contents, where true, as a coarse *rechauffé* of what has been more elegantly expressed before. He cites the Christian precept, "Whosoever shall smite thee on thy right cheek, turn to him the other also," and represents it as a vulgar reproduction of the

Platonic version of the same truth: "We must never do injury to any; we must not even, as most people think, take revenge for evil done" (vii. 58). To this Origen wisely replies that the style of address adopted in Scripture and by our Lord Himself was one suited to a gospel intended for the multitude, and that while comparatively few have profited by the beautiful and polished style of Plato, books written in simpler style have been of service to many. This Origen says without disparaging Plato, "for the great world of men has usefully produced him also."

Another thing laid by Celsus to the charge of Christianity is that it exalts faith at the expense of reason, and so puts a premium upon foolishness. It was the habit of Christians, he says, to represent that there was no need for investigation, and to keep repeating, "Your faith will save you." Origen answers that this is not a true statement of the case; that in the Christian system there is ample scope for investigation; and that in laying stress upon faith Christians are only giving effect to a principle underlying all things human. The sailor exercises faith when he puts out to sea; so does the farmer when he casts seed into the ground. Even into the choice of a particular school of philosophy faith must enter; and if we must repose faith in the founder of such a school, is it not more reasonable to trust in God Himself, and in Him whose words exert such a marvellous power in the lives of the believing? However desirable it might be for all to study philosophy, only a few have leisure and talent for this. Is it not therefore well that so many should have been redeemed from the practice of wickedness through faith alone, and apart from philosophical reasons?

The rooted antipathy of Celsus to Christianity was further due to its attitude towards the sinful and the worthless. In this aspect it ran counter to his philosophical beliefs, "for to change nature thoroughly is exceedingly difficult," as well as to his sense of propriety, for he fully endorsed the Pharisaic complaint, "This man receiveth sinners." Origen replies that there is no absolute preference shown for the sinner as such; it is only where the element of penitence comes in that he is ranked higher than one who is reckoned a lesser sinner, but who is devoid of the consciousness of sin, and proud of his good qualities. Moreover, although the gates of the Church are open to the most sinful, it is from the ranks of the virtuous that her adherents are mostly drawn (iii. 65).

Celsus does not content himself with giving expression to such prejudices against Christianity; he deliberately seeks to undermine the foundation on which it rests. To begin with, he denies the need for a revelation. Origen shows that, apart from such a source, no adequate knowledge of God can be acquired by men, and quotes from Plato's *Timæus* to prove that this is acknowledged by philosophers themselves. Celsus goes on to affirm that, even assuming a revelation to be necessary, the Scriptures do not possess that superiority, that originality, or that worthy conception of Deity which would alone entitle them to such a character. While granting that philosophy and Christianity have some truths in common, Origen asserts that on a comparison the superiority of the latter is disclosed; that in no case has a Christian dogma been borrowed from Greek philosophy; and that it is absurd to suppose that uneducated men like Peter and John should have based their teaching about God on a misrepresentation of passages in the epistles of Plato. The originality of the Christian doctrines is attested by their moral force. Philosophers will gravely discourse about the soul, and then straightway sacrifice a cock to Esculapius; whereas the power of those Scriptures which Celsus calls "vulgar" is such as to convert multitudes from vice to virtue, and inspire cowards with a moral courage that despises death (iii. 6). The scriptural conception of God is not, as Celsus maintains, debasing and purely material; its anthropomorphisms are simply an adaptation to our weak capacity, and are to be understood figuratively. Origen agrees so far with Celsus that man's knowledge of God is limited, but affirms that we know some of His attributes. Although being incorporeal He cannot be seen, the vision of Him is yet possible to a pure heart. It is the inner man that is created after the image of God.

Celsus's criticism of the Scriptures is positive, however, as well as negative. The Mosaic cosmogony and Old Testament records in general he views as replete with silly absurdities, and the distinctive rites of Judaism as borrowed from other nations. He denies that a race like the Jews could have been "beloved of God," and represents Christianity as at once based upon and in sharp conflict with Judaism. Origen defends the inspiration of the Mosaic writings, and points to the monotheism as well as to the lofty standard of morality that obtained among the Jews in proof of their divine calling. They were forsaken by God only when they sinned, and were never utterly abandoned until they slew Jesus. Circumcision and

THE WRITINGS OF ORIGEN

abstinence from swine's flesh may have been practised by others than Jews, but with a different motive. The divine authority of Scripture is attested by the fulfilment of prophecy. Christians accept the inspiration of the Hebrew Scriptures, but differ from the Jews as to their interpretation. It is not with the letter, but the spiritual truth of Judaism that the Christian has to do; for this is not a national, but a cosmopolitan religion. "We have to say, moreover, that the gospel has a demonstration of its own, more divine than any established by Grecian dialectics. And this diviner method is called by the apostle the 'demonstration of the Spirit and of power': of 'the Spirit' on account of the prophecies, which are sufficient to produce faith in any one who reads them, especially in those things which relate to Christ; and of 'power,' because of the signs and wonders which we must believe to have been performed, both on many other grounds and on this, that traces of them are still preserved among those who regulate their lives by the precepts of the gospel" (i. 2).

But it was the doctrine of the Incarnation that constituted the main point in the controversy between Celsus and Origen. In attacking this Celsus had tried to storm the citadel of the Christian faith. With great vigour Origen repels the assault, and shows that Celsus proceeds upon a misapprehension as to the nature of God, the value of man, and the moral results of Christianity. No Christian, he says, maintains the descent of God into humanity in the sense that He thereby vacated His throne in heaven. It was man's work, not God's, that needed repair. The advent of Christ was not the outcome of a sudden impulse, but the final stage in a long development. That He who was previously in the form of God should lay aside His glory so as to be accessible to men involves no such change as that alleged by Celsus;—not from good to evil, for He did no sin; nor from honour to shame, for He knew no sin; nor from happiness to misery, for He humbled Himself, and was none the less blessed. Who would suggest such a process of degeneration in connection with the work of a physician, whose benevolence leads him to view and handle repulsive objects in order that sufferers may be cured?

If Celsus thought that the Incarnation degraded God, he also considered that it unduly exalted man. In his pantheistic materialism he virtually puts man on a level with the brute creation. Origen, on the other hand, affirms man's position in creation to be unique. To liken to a worm of the earth him who was made in the image of God is to calumniate human nature. While Celsus cannot conceive of God as coming into contact with matter, Origen knows no pollution save that of moral evil. The consecrated body is the temple of God. It is for man chiefly, though not exclusively, that all things have been framed by the Creator. The dogs eat of the crumbs which fall from the master's table. The comparison which Celsus makes between the actions of men and those of ants and bees affords no proof of their equality. God is not angry with apes or flies, but He punishes men who transgress His law. While according to Celsus there is in this perfect universe no moral disorder, no sin, and therefore no need of redemption, Origen maintains that in the exercise of his freedom the rational creature has brought moral confusion into

THE WRITINGS OF ORIGEN 119

the cosmos, and that in order to repair this disaster God has revealed Himself through conscience, prophecy, and the Incarnation.

Celsus was further led by his doctrine of evil to maintain that the end of the Incarnation is unattainable. Redemption is impossible; moral evil cannot be cured; everything revolves in a circuit; history literally repeats itself. "If this be true," Origen replies, "our free will is annihilated; Christians will be redeemed and unredeemed by turns, and Celsus will periodically write over again this treatise of his!" Necessitarianism like this is, of course, fatal to Christianity, which makes its appeal to the moral nature of man as a free agent. There is a flavour of piety about the saying of Celsus, that apparent evil may promote the good of the whole; but evil is none the less evil because it is overruled for good. The position taken up by Celsus amounts to the negation of moral evil. "This is the opiate administered by pantheism in all ages to soothe conscience, deaden human sensibilities, and enable men to contemplate with philosophic indifference the moral condition of the world, as at once irremediable and not needing remedy."[1] While Origen recognises the value of the evidence of prophecy and miracle, he bases his apology chiefly on moral grounds. To him *the* proof of the truth of Christianity is the power which it exerts over the hearts and lives of men. In answer to the contention of Celsus that Christians were the adherents of One who had failed, Origen triumphantly appeals to the circumstance that Christian Churches were everywhere rising up like stars in the surrounding darkness, and that although

[1] Bruce, *Apologetics*, p. 14.

120 ORIGEN AND GREEK THEOLOGY

it was most influentially opposed, the progress of the gospel was in inverse ratio to the hostility directed against it. All the assertions and arguments of its opponents were invalidated by the incontrovertible logic of visible fact.

iii. *Exegetical Writings of Origen*

In this department Origen's labours are prodigious, and range over nearly the entire field of Scripture. They comprise (1) *Scholia*, brief notes, mostly grammatical, and not necessarily always original, upon obscure and difficult passages ; (2) *Commentaries*, which, in spite of the allegoric and dogmatic elements with which they are cumbered, in many respects still serve as models for commentators; (3) *Homilies*, or expository lectures which aimed at edification. Of these works not much has been preserved in the Greek original, but considerable portions are extant in Latin translations by Rufinus and Jerome.

Properly speaking, Origen was the first exegete. Everything done in this direction previously (*e.g.* by Theophilus of Antioch, Melito of Sardis, and even Pantænus and Clement) had been merely preparatory to a scientific interpretation of Scripture which views each separate passage in relation to the whole. While, of course, no fair comparison can be made between him and modern commentators, it is no exaggeration to say that the best of them are debtors to Origen. One of his great merits is that he never shirks a difficulty ; indeed, from pure love of discussion he frequently suggests doubts to the reader. Nothing could exceed his passion for verbal and grammatical accuracy, or

THE WRITINGS OF ORIGEN

his linguistic and critical insight, while his knowledge of the ancient theology is unique. And despite recent attempts to belittle his scientific attainments,[1] there can be no doubt that, relatively to his own age, these were of the highest order. If in handling the Septuagint he was hampered by his imperfect acquaintance with Hebrew, he was under no such disability with reference to the New Testament. The Greek grammar and language he knew as thoroughly as any Greek scholar of his time. His commentaries, however, are not without faults. They are marred by their excessive length and discursiveness; they often lack clearness; they are overloaded with irrelevancies and wearisome repetitions. His view of inspiration compelled him also to adopt the allegorical method, according to which the sacred books are treated ostensibly as an encyclopædia of philosophical and dogmatic wisdom, but in reality as a peg on which to hang the commentator's own ideas. The plan he follows is that of giving consecutively verse by verse the literal, moral, and spiritual sense. By means of his allegoric spiritualism he can thus gain from any word an outlook into the universal.[2] "The text is but the

---

[1] See Denis, *Introduction*, p. 12 ff.

[2] The strange blending of grammatical and speculative exposition so distinctive of Origen is well illustrated in what he gets out of the Inscriptions of the Psalms. The word usually rendered "For the chief musician" he renders "To the end." This leads to an enumeration of the notions of different philosophers upon the subject of the end, and is followed by a discussion about the essence and name of God. "Upon Gittith" he interprets to mean "concerning the wine-press," and finds in this the idea of the Church, where the devotion offered to God represents the combined outpouring of many hearts, just as in the wine-press the contents of many grape-clusters go to form the wine.

threshing-floor on which he pours out all the harvest of his knowledge, his meditations, his hopes."[1]

Origen's principal New Testament commentaries are those on St. Matthew, St. John, and Romans. Chronologically, the commentary on St. John was his first great exegetical work. It was composed of more than thirty-two books, of which, apart from fragments, we possess only nine. Like our modern commentaries, it is prefaced by a general Introduction, dealing with the peculiar characteristics of the Fourth Gospel, and according to it the highest place on account of the stress it lays on the divinity of our Lord. The exposition itself is marked by that breadth of treatment which is a feature of all Origen's writings. The style is on the whole clear, but sometimes involved and usually diffuse. "In the beginning was the Word"— this forms the subject-matter of the whole of the first book. At the outset he gives all possible senses of this statement, with special consideration of the meanings put upon it by heretics. This is followed by a discussion of "the Word," and this again by a disquisition upon the doctrine of creation out of nothing. The second book continues the exposition only as far as chap. i. 7.

The commentary on Romans was written after his sixtieth year. It was translated, edited, and abbreviated by Rufinus, and it is not always possible to distinguish between what is his and what is Origen's own. But from Greek fragments still extant, and from other translations, as well as from what we otherwise know of Origen's views, it is clear that Rufinus allowed himself a good deal of latitude in excising whole pas-

[1] Bigg, *Christian Platonists*, p. 131 f.

THE WRITINGS OF ORIGEN

sages and in correcting what be deemed heterodox. This is very noticeable as regards, for example, the doctrine of the Trinity.

A still later date must be assigned to the commentary on St. Matthew, the nine opening books of which have almost entirely perished. The remainder of the work still exists in a somewhat uncouth, but apparently faithful, Latin translation. As might have been expected, these later products of Origen's pen exhibit a soberness of spirit, a maturity of judgment, and a freedom from exaggeration in strong contrast to the vehement impetuosity of his earlier days. In them he expresses himself with the calmness of one who has had experience of human life and the feelings incidental to it. Nor does he hesitate in his commentary on Matthew to retract the view of chap. xix. 12 which led to his own youthful indiscretion. But with all this there is no deviation from the essential principles of biblical interpretation and exegesis held and practised by him all his life through, and certainly there is no reason to suppose with Ernesti that allegory was merely a weakness of his old age.

Speaking with tongues was distinctly a gift of a transient kind (1 Cor. xiii. 8). In Origen's time a growingly rigorous Church discipline had virtually banished the practice from Christian gatherings; only among the Montanists did it to some extent linger on. A substitute for it was found in the Discourse or Homily. This was the name given to the popular expository address which was now regularly delivered in the Churches. Divine service was conducted twice daily, but except on Sundays and feast-days was only very sparsely attended. The audiences were not always

124 ORIGEN AND GREEK THEOLOGY

devout, and it was particularly difficult to secure silence on the part of garrulous and gossiping women. The Scriptures were read consecutively, and the preacher expounded a portion of what was read, either choosing his text himself or having it given to him by the presiding bishop or by the presbyters. All were welcomed at the daily services, but the unbaptized were not admitted to the Lord's Supper. In respect of intelligence and moral fibre the audiences were of a decidedly mixed character. Some took a very materialistic view of gospel promises; some conceived God as ruling with despotic cruelty; others were lax enough to frequent the racecourse as well as the church.

To Origen belongs the distinction of being the first great preacher. In his Homilies he aims chiefly at the edification of his hearers, and concerns himself more with allegorical interpretation than with the literal sense of the passages expounded. There is, however, little of the sentimental or pietistic vein about his discourses. The products of a robust mind, they appeal in the main to the intellect rather than to the emotions, and are based on the principle, "Come now, and let us reason together." They are marked by lofty dignity, transparent sincerity, deep moral earnestness, and width of outlook. Their author's cultivated scriptural intelligence is reflected in the numerous biblical quotations with which his discourses are interspersed. The hortatory element is not conspicuous, but in the closing sentences his hearers are usually urged to the performance of some Christian duty. Frequently[1] he concludes with a summons to rise and pray. Of the Homilies still extant the most important

---

[1] *E.g. in Luc.* 36, 39.

THE WRITINGS OF ORIGEN 125

are those on the Pentateuch, Jeremiah, and St. Luke. A large proportion of the whole were delivered at Cæsarea after Origen was sixty years of age. They were taken down by shorthand writers, and owe their inornate and diffuse style to their extemporaneous delivery. They have, however, a charm of their own. "Origen is emphatically 'a man of God,' strong and subtle, yet infinitely humble and gentle, a true *Ductor dubitantium*, because he knew there was much that he did not know, and yet was not afraid."[1]

iv. *Origen's Dogmatic Works*

Of Origen's dogmatic works there is only one complete specimen extant, namely, the ΠΕΡΙ ΑΡΧΩΝ (*De Princpiis, On the Fundamental Doctrines*). It is, however, a work of first-rate importance, being indeed the most notable production of the ante-Nicene age. For the most part, unfortunately, we possess it only in the Latin translation of Rufinus. Believing that Origen's works had been malevolently corrupted by heretics, this writer undertook the translation on the express understanding that he should follow the method adopted by Jerome in his translation of the *Homilies*, that, namely, of excising or amending heterodox statements. His motive was, he says, to prevent Origen from being slandered; and so far as he may have been able to free the text from real corruption his work was no doubt praiseworthy; yet on many accounts it is permissible to wish that his editorial supervision had been spared. As it is, one can never be certain as to what is Origen's and what is due to Rufinus, except

[1] Bigg, *Christian Platonists*, p. 130.

126 ORIGEN AND GREEK THEOLOGY

indeed where the original Greek has been preserved.[1] Happily, however, it is frequently possible to ascertain the real views of Origen from the *Philocalia*,—a selection of "choice thoughts" from his works jointly compiled by Basil the Great and Gregory of Nazianzen. There are also preserved in Photius and in the defence of Origen by Pamphilus certain fragments which are useful for purposes of comparison.

Written prior to A.D. 228,[2] the *De Principiis* falls within the earlier period of Origen's literary activity. It reflects, however, with substantial accuracy the views of his later years. Intended for readers familiar with the philosophical teaching of the times, it aims at giving objective reality to the metaphysical abstractions in which men busied themselves, and is notable as the first attempt at a scientific Christian dogmatic. By such a presentation of the leading doctrines of the one positive religion Origen sought to supersede the gnosis which meant speculation about all forms of religion; and although frequently the fundamental truths themselves are overshadowed by the general philosophical speculations of the age, the work displays throughout a spirit of unswerving loyalty to Scripture and to the creed of the Church. The former supplies the material, the latter regulates the use to which it is put in the building up "by all the resources of the intellect and of speculation" of the first system of Christian dogma. As individual opinions are freely expressed in connec-

---

[1] This applies to considerable sections of Books III. and IV.

[2] So Harnack. Schnitzer, apparently upon insufficient grounds, would date it as early as 213; while Redepenning, erring probably in the opposite direction, thinks it must have been composed after Origen's fiftieth year (235).

tion with the elucidation of the several doctrines, the book is really a philosophy of Christianity—though not, as some have thought, a Christian philosophy of the origin of being[1]—and in its measure a solution of a problem unattempted by Clement. Judged by modern standards, it may lie open to criticism on the ground of occasional vagueness, strained interpretations, digressions, repetitions, etc. It may also appear as if the peculiar "truths of salvation" are kept too much in the background owing to Christian doctrine being treated as a matter of knowledge. To the former criticism it is sufficient to reply that Origen's was the first attempt "to form a connected series and body of truths"; to the second, it may be answered that for Origen Christianity was essentially a doctrine of salvation. In his view, however, men need not only to be saved from sin, but also, and very specially, from error in science and religion. This explains why to him and to his age doctrine formed the essential content of Christianity.

Origen's starting-point is the Christian tradition. The facts and customs thus transmitted are to be implicitly accepted as the basis of all further investigation. But the apostles did not clear up everything. Frequently they contented themselves with a brief statement of doctrines, leaving the scientific proof of them to be established by the exercise of Christian talent. In some instances they left the disciple to rely upon science even for the precise definition of dogmas, as well as for the elucidation of their mutual relations and the deducing of the consequences. The

[1] This has been conclusively shown by Schnitzer (p. 22 ff.) in his excellent remarks upon the meaning of the title Περὶ ἀρχῶν.

faith has been once for all delivered to the saints, but it is the function of the enlightened Christian reason to formulate and develop it, and to apply it to the practical wants of men. In short, there is perfect liberty of thought and opinion on every point not included in the apostolic tradition or rule of faith, of which, according to Origen, this is the sum—(1) there is one God who created all things out of nothing, who is just and good, the Father of our Lord Jesus Christ, and the God of the Old and New Testaments; (2) Jesus Christ was begotten of the Father before all creatures, was the servant of the Father in the work of creation, and became man without ceasing to be God; He was born of a virgin and of the Holy Spirit; He did truly suffer, rise again, and ascend into heaven; (3) the Holy Spirit is associated in honour and dignity with the Father and the Son, and inspired all the saints both under the old and under the new economy; (4) there will be a resurrection of the dead, when the body which is sown in corruption will rise in incorruption, and hereafter the soul will inherit eternal life or endure eternal punishment according to its deeds; (5) every rational soul is a free agent, lured to sin by evil spirits, and helped by good angels to salvation, yet not forced to act rightly or wrongly; (6) the Scriptures were written by the Spirit of God, and have not only an obvious meaning, but also a hidden sense perceived by those only on whom is conferred the grace of the Holy Spirit in the word of wisdom and knowledge.[1]

Although the work is not strictly methodical, it is broadly accurate to say that the first book treats of God and the spirits; the second, of the world and

[1] *Preface*, p. 4 ff.

man; and the third, of sin and redemption. In each of these three books the entire Christian conception of the world is set forth from a different standpoint. The fourth book deals with Holy Scripture.

In the first book Origen discusses the nature of God and the special relations of the Three Persons of the Godhead to men, who "derive their existence from God the Father, their rational nature from the Word, and their holiness from the Holy Spirit." The true goal of humanity is union with God; but this can be reached only by a gradual process of enlightenment and purification. "By the renewal of the ceaseless working of Father, Son, and Holy Spirit in us, in its various stages of progress, shall we be able at some future time perhaps, although with difficulty, to behold the holy and the blessed life, in which (as it is only after many struggles that we are able to reach it) we ought so to continue that no satiety of that blessedness should ever seize us; but the more we perceive its blessedness, the more should be increased and intensified within us the longing for the same, while we ever more eagerly and freely receive and hold fast the Father, the Son, and the Holy Spirit" (i. 3. 8). Negligence may, however, induce general declension; man may sink lower as well as rise higher. And, in fact, the present position occupied by each rational being has been determined by his previous use of his opportunities and gifts; it is not due to some having been created essentially holy, others essentially wicked, and others still capable both of virtue and vice. It is because of merit, and not from constitutional necessity, that some rank higher than, and exercise power over others; just as it is owing to their own actions that some have degenerated into malignant demons. In Origen's view the human race was formed of those occupying an intermediate position, *i.e.* of those removed from their primal state of blessedness, but not irrecoverably so. He clung to "the larger hope," believing that while at the end of the world God will bestow on each what he deserves, the divine goodness in Christ may bring all His creatures together into a great unity. "Meanwhile," he says, "both in the ages which are seen and temporal, and in those which are not seen and eternal, all rational beings who have fallen are dealt with according to the order, the character, the measure of their deserts. Some in the first, others in the second, some, again, even in the last times, through greater and heavier sufferings, borne through many ages, reformed by sharper discipline, and restored at first by the instruction of the angels, and subsequently by the powers of a higher grade, and thus advancing stage by stage to a better condition, reach that which is invisible and eternal." But though the rational soul may thus pass from one order to another, it can never sink into the condition of irrational animals (i. 8. 4).

Under the head of incorporeal and corporeal beings Origen raises a curious and, as he says, "bold" question as to the position of the heavenly bodies—the sun, moon, and stars. On what he regards as adequate scriptural grounds, he maintains that they are living and rational beings; that their spirit was implanted in them from without, and did not come into existence along with their bodies; and that at the end of the world they shall be released from their bodies, and from the bondage of giving light to the human race, and shall form part of the kingdom which

Christ shall deliver up to God the Father that He may be all in all.

The second book is mainly devoted to a consideration of the present condition of the world and man,—the renewing influence of the incarnation of Christ, and the doctrine of the last things. According to Origen, the great diversity of condition among rational beings is due to the varying degrees of their declension from goodness. But in his ineffable wisdom and power God "grasps and holds together all the diversity of the world," and adapts the vast medley of motives and movements to one harmonious whole. Bodily nature he regards as the result of the infusion of certain qualities into created matter, and as destined to dissolution when all have been subjected to Christ. Another fall of rational creatures, however, would necessitate its coming again into existence, though the new world thus called into being would not be a duplicate of the old.[1] After showing that there is no demiurge, but that the God of the Old Testament is identical with the Father of our Lord Jesus Christ, and unites in Himself the attributes of justice and goodness, our author proceeds to deal with the incarnation of Christ. On this important subject he advances beyond the position of Clement, who had spoken of the union of the Logos with a human body but not with a human soul, and goes on to develop the doctrine of the Saviour's perfect humanity as accepted by the Church

[1] Origen suggests two other possible views with reference to the end of all things and the supreme blessedness,—the one that the bodily substance will be changed into an eternal condition corresponding to the merits of those who assume it, and the other that beyond the planetary spheres there is a good land, the abode of the meek, and forming part of that "heaven" which is the home of the perfected.

ever since. He then reverts to the subject of the Holy Spirit and the manifold nature of His working. This is followed by a section upon the soul, which he derives from the understanding (*Nous*), and to which he assigns an intermediate position between the weak flesh and the willing spirit. Of rational creatures there is a definite number, sufficient for the adorning of the world. They have the power of voluntary action, and may develop in a good direction or a bad; hence the great diversity of circumstances among them. Diversity was not the original condition of the creature, but is the result of each one's lot being equitably ordered according to the deserts of his previous life. The book closes with a discussion of the doctrines of the resurrection, future punishment, and the life everlasting.

The third book treats of free will, the conflict with the evil powers as well as with error and temptations of purely human origin, and the ultimate realisation by man of the divine likeness in the consummation and restoration of all things. Nothing is more distinctive of Origen's system than the doctrine of free will. This constitutes its ethical basis. Just because man is at all times free to choose between good and evil, it is on the one hand made possible for him to attain to perfection, and on the other impossible for him to divest himself of responsibility for failure. While the decision in each case rests with ourselves, it is none the less true that all that happens to us is sent of God. Origen does not strictly regard sin as inherited, but assumes that guilt has been contracted by the individual in a pre-mundane existence, and that his present material and spiritual endowment has been determined accordingly. In spite of the struggle involved in the existence of

THE WRITINGS OF ORIGEN

hostile powers and inner temptations, all (including Satan himself) may advance towards the dignity of the divine likeness. The final re-establishment, however, of a state of unity in which God shall be all in all must be slow and gradual, "seeing that the process of amendment and correction will take place imperceptibly in the individual instances during the lapse of countless and unmeasured ages, some outstripping others, and tending by a swifter course towards perfection, while others again follow close at hand, and some again a long way behind (iii. 6)."

The substance of the fourth book, containing Origen's views on Scripture and its interpretation, has been already dealt with. A brief résumé of the principal topics discussed in it brings the work to a close.

v. *Origen's Letters and Treatises on Practical Religion*

Of Origen's letters only two have been preserved, the one addressed to Julius Africanus, and the other to Gregory Thaumaturgus. The circumstances of their composition, and the nature of their contents, have been already referred to.[1] His extant works on practical religion are also two in number, and treat of *Prayer* and *Martyrdom*. Between them they cover practically the whole subject of the appropriation of salvation.

Origen's treatise on *Prayer* was addressed to Ambrosius and Tatiana,[2] with the view of clearing up certain difficulties felt by them upon this subject. The exact year of its composition cannot be determined. Pam-

---
[1] See p. 58 f.   [2] Perhaps the sister of Ambrosius.

philus groups it along with the works on *Martyrdom* and the *Resurrection* as being written more directly from the heart than any others of Origen's numerous writings. Besides being comparatively free from his characteristic faults, it contains many spiritually suggestive, tender, and inspiring thoughts. Of this nature are, for example, his remarks on the utility of so composing the mind for prayer as to realise the immediate presence of God; on the peculiar love and sympathy shown by the holy dead for those who are still fighting life's battle; on the saintly life as one great ceaseless prayer; and on the devotional spirit as implying the laying aside of all anxieties and grudges, and the lifting up to God of the soul before the hands, of the mind before the eyes.

Origen starts from the position that the highest truth is incomprehensible to our fallen nature, and can only be grasped by us through the rich and immeasurable grace of God, ministered to us through Christ and the Holy Spirit. There is nothing good in the creature save what has been bestowed by the Creator. Hence the necessity of prayer. But of ourselves " we know not what we should pray for as we ought"; we need the Spirit of the Lord to direct us. After tracing the scriptural meaning and usage of the word prayer, Origen proceeds to deal with two arguments against the efficacy of prayer which had caused perplexity to his correspondents. These were that prayer is vain (1) if God foresees the future as it will actually unfold itself; (2) if all things happen according to His will, and His decrees are fixed, and nothing of what He desires can be changed. Origen's reply is that, although His foreknowledge is of the character represented, God answers prayer nevertheless; for while He foresees, He does not control, the nature of our choice, our actions, and our desires. Divine prescience neither interferes with the exercise of our free will, nor divests us of responsibility for our actions. By way of enforcing the duty of prayer, the writer points to the example of Christ and the saints. The Son of God is the high priest of our oblations, and our advocate with the Father; He prays for those who pray. So do the angels who are sent to minister to us, and the souls of the saints who have already fallen asleep. If Jesus prays, nor prays in vain, but through prayer obtains His requests, and presumably would not obtain them without prayer, which of us can neglect to pray? He who always prays will always be heard. In the Babylonian den the lions' mouths were closed by the prayer of Daniel; Jonah was heard from the whale's belly. These are emblems of spiritual experiences, of deliverances from more hurtful beasts, and from the billows of keener trial. Besides being in itself a valuable moral tonic, prayer brings down the fertilising rain of spiritual blessing which has been retarded by sin, dissolves the poison instilled into the prayer-neglecting soul by the powers of evil, and quenches the fires of temptation. It is more properly concerned with those spiritual and heavenly things of which things earthly are but the shadow. Prayer should penetrate the whole life, yet not so as to sink the special exercise in the general devotional attitude of the soul. Thrice daily at least, as well as once during the night, ought one to pray. Many words, or polished sentences, are not necessary, but the prayer must be without wrath or excitement. Founding upon

1 Tim. ii. 1, Origen distinguishes four varieties of prayer, and illustrates these by examples from Scripture. His conclusion is that while intercession and thanksgiving may fitly be offered to men, and all three lower forms of petition to the saints, "prayer" strictly so called must be addressed to God only. It is not proper to pray to the Son as apart from the Father, nor to the Son conjointly with the Father; our prayers must be directed to God alone, the supreme Father of all, to whom the Saviour Himself also prayed. But they must be offered through the only-begotten Son as the high priest whom the Father Himself has appointed; and without Him no prayer can be offered to the Father. Origen bases his view on the Saviour's words, "Whatsoever ye shall ask the Father, He will give it you in My name." By putting the question, "Are we not divided if we pray some to the Father, some to the Son?" he seems to indicate that at the time he wrote there was a lack of uniformity in the practice of the Church upon this point, and that he was urging a return to earlier usage. Prayer to Christ as God is nowhere disallowed by him; on the contrary, he justifies it by a reference to the prayers of the thief on the cross and of the martyr Stephen. And in several passages of his writings he practises it himself.[1]

Was Origen consistent in this? At some points, perhaps, his doctrine requires correction. He writes, of of course, throughout as a subordinationist and an advocate of the view that Christ's humanity ceases with His exaltation. It is certain, however, that his position upon this subject was not dictated by any want of devotion to Jesus, or by any doubt as to His

---

[1] *Hom. in Jer.* 4 ; *in Ezech.* 12 ; *in Luc.* 15, etc.

THE WRITINGS OF ORIGEN 137

divinity. Rather may it have been due to a fear lest in the mind of the Church the Father should be overshadowed by the Son. In the Western Church more particularly there was a tendency to confuse the First and Second Persons of the Trinity and to practise the absolute adoration of the Son in a manner derogatory to the sovereignty of God. It was a further and later consequence of the same tendency that the glory of the Son was hidden behind the halo that surrounded the Virgin and the saints. Certainly Origen did great service in emphasising the need for a more exact conception of what prayer is,—even although his exposition of 1 Tim. ii. 1, and his use of other parts of Scripture in which the same words occur, be somewhat arbitrary,— and in clearing up the Son's relation to the Father and to the fellowship of Christians. His view practically amounts to this, that there is an invocation of the Son which is permissible and proper, but which is different in degree from the adoration of the Father. We may directly supplicate the Son for blessings which it is his prerogative to confer, but in the highest act of worship the soul must reach forth to Him whose Being is absolute and underived.

A considerable section of Origen's work on *Prayer* (chaps. 18–30) is devoted to an exposition of St. Matthew's version of the Lord's Prayer, with reference also to the similar prayer recorded by St. Luke. In the closing chapters (31–33) Origen enters into particulars regarding the proper spirit of prayer, the fit place and posture for the exercise, the direction in which the suppliant is to turn, and the component parts of which his prayer should consist. He who would pray aright must approach God with reverent

138 ORIGEN AND GREEK THEOLOGY

composure, and talk with Him as to an actual onlooker and listener. It is also fitting that he stand upright, with hands outstretched and eyes uplifted. Except in sickness, no one should pray sitting or reclining. The penitent should pray on bended knee. It is advisable to have a set apartment for prayer, and that one which is never desecrated. Of all places the most suitable to pray in is the church, where the faithful are gathered in the immediate presence of the angels, of the power of our Lord and Saviour, and of the spirits of the departed. Origen thinks it natural that in prayer we should turn to the East as symbolising the outlook of the soul upon the dawn of the true light. The parts of prayer are these:—the ascription of glory to God through Christ in the Holy Spirit; thanksgiving, general and special; confession of sin; petition for great and heavenly things both for one's self and for all, particularly for acquaintances and friends. As prayer begins, so should it end with praising and glorifying the Father of all through Jesus Christ in the Holy Spirit, to whom be glory for ever and ever.

The treatise on *Martyrdom* was addressed to Ambrosius and Theoktetus (a presbyter of Cæsarea), who were cast into prison during the persecution under Maximinus Thrax. It has been justly styled "a golden work." Even the essay on *Prayer*, in which Job is held up as "the athlete of virtue," contains a rich vein of comfort for the afflicted; but in the *Exhortation to Martyrdom* we have a solid reef of this spiritual gold. The subject is one upon which Origen was preeminently qualified to speak, and in his little book " we catch the prolonged echo of the manly words which in

THE WRITINGS OF ORIGEN

childhood he sent to his captive father: "Flinch not for us."[1]

He begins by reminding his friends that in accordance with the principle laid down in Isa. xxix. 9-11 (LXX) they must, as no longer babes in Christ, expect trial upon trial, but that he who has borne tribulation like a strenuous athlete receives also hope upon hope. On this he founds the exhortation to steadfast endurance of temporary suffering. Perfect love to God implies not only a willingness to put off the earthly tabernacle, but the withdrawal of the soul from everything corporeal. Origen does not, however, with certain of the Gnostics, excuse denial of Christ upon the plea that it is only the inner faith of the heart that is important. Those who believe on Him with the heart must confess Him with the mouth. Nor is it, as some pretend, a matter of indifference whether we worship God as Jehovah or Jupiter or Apollo; we must call upon Him by proper and scriptural names. A great reward in heaven awaits those persecuted for righteousness' sake, while he who denies Christ is divided from Him as it were by a sharp sword. The faithful martyr's endurance of pain and utter self-denial will be recompensed by the direct vision of God. Origen exhorts his readers to act in terms of their baptismal vows, and to recollect that their struggle to maintain the Christian religion is witnessed by all the angelic and infernal powers. Their victory would give delight in heaven; their fall would be hailed by the demons with glee. He points them likewise to the examples of Eleazar and the seven brethren, to show how piety and the love of God can triumph over

[1] Pressensé, *Early Years of Christianity*, ii. p. 320.

the most cruel tortures. Martyrdom is further set forth as the ideal expression of gratitude to God for His benefits. It is "the cup of salvation." Although we cannot again be baptized with water and the Spirit for the remission of sins, there is given us the baptism of martyrdom, which carries with it the expiation of post-baptismal sins. The souls of those who have been slain for the testimony of Jesus surround the heavenly altar and minister forgiveness of sins to those who pray. In offering up himself the martyr is an immaculate priest who offers an immaculate sacrifice, and in this respect resembles the great high priest Jesus Christ. For him the winter storms are followed by the flowers of spring. So much may be gathered from the Saviour's warning forecast to the apostles regarding the treatment they should receive from the world, and from His declaration that those who confess Him before men will be confessed by Him in heaven, while those who have denied Him He will in turn deny. No one therefore need be ashamed to carry the cross of Jesus. "Be slow to love the things which pass away, but do the will of God, that you may be worthy to be made one with the Son and the Father and the Holy Spirit according to the prayer of the Saviour: that they also may be one in us."[1] Created in His image, the human soul yearns for this union with God; yet man loves life. Why should we hesitate to accept freedom from the burden of the flesh, that with Christ we may enjoy the rest of the blessed? Let us show that the good seed has found in our souls receptive soil, and that we have built our house upon the rock; let us, as those who despise the trials and cares, the

[1] *Orat.* 39.

THE WRITINGS OF ORIGEN

wealth and pleasures of this world, in the spirit of wisdom and freedom from anxiety hasten towards the riches that do not deceive, and towards the joys of paradise. The martyr's blood cries to heaven like the blood of Abel. Perhaps, too, as we were purchased by the precious blood of Jesus, so also may some be purchased by the precious blood of martyrs, since these occupy a rank superior to that of the merely righteous. By their death they exalt themselves and glorify God. Origen concludes by expressing the hope that what he has written may for the present be useful to his friends, and that through the words and wisdom of God, which far excel anything human, they may gain a still clearer insight into the divine mysteries and be made perfect.

CHAPTER VI

ORIGEN'S THEOLOGY: GOD AND HIS SELF-
MANIFESTATIONS

i. *The Nature of God*

IN his teaching with reference to the divine nature, Origen puts in the forefront the absolute immateriality of God. He is pure Spirit, and devoid of every element of corporeity; pure intelligence, and not to be conceived in a physical sense either because compared in Scripture with fire and light, or because many saints participate in the Holy Spirit. "It must not be supposed, then, that God is either a body or in a body; He is a simple intellectual nature, admitting of no addition at all. There is in Him no greater or less, no higher or lower, for He is the monad, unit, mind, the fountain of all mind."[1] Strictly speaking, perhaps, God is not substance, being *beyond* it; but if the corporeal element be excluded, this term may be applicable. Either way, however, it is inaccurate to say that God partakes of substance, for He does not partake of, but is partaken of by, whatever has being. He is "of nothing," the One in contrast to the many, the absolute Existence as contrasted with conditioned

[1] *De Princ.* i. 1. 6.

ORIGEN'S THEOLOGY

existences, and revealed by the dependence, the order, and the yearning of the manifold as the Source of all good.

Since in its operations mind is independent of time, space, and bodily magnitude, God as entirely spiritual is also eternal and unchangeable. His work in the field of the temporal may produce the impression that He is Himself subject to change. In reality He is above it, exalted above time in an everlasting *now*, and dwelling in space only as the architect may be said to inhabit his work. Not that He is to be considered the soul of the world in the Stoical sense; His all-comprehending presence takes the purely spiritual form of an almighty superintending providence. He is potentially everywhere, and His presence in one place does not imply His absence from another. His throne was not left vacant when, rich in mercy, He came down in the person of Jesus to share and to elevate the life of humanity.

Subject to no change, God is also devoid of passion. Only in condescension to our weakness does Scripture ascribe to Him vengeance, anger, regret, and the like. As He is altogether impassible, these are feelings quite foreign to His nature, and such passages as ascribe them to Him are not to be interpreted literally; we are to "seek in them a spiritual meaning, that we may think of God as He deserves to be thought of." If, for example, He is called a consuming fire, it is only in the sense of destroying the evil that finds its way into our minds, and so into our actions. To speak of the wrath of God will yet become an impossibility through the final restoration of all things. No man is hated by God, who loves His whole creation.

144 ORIGEN AND GREEK THEOLOGY

Punishment is not His work, but the inevitable wages of sin.

Abstract as are many of his notions with respect to the Deity, Origen holds firmly to the absolute causality of God as a self-conscious Being who gives expression to His will in that which He creates. His conception of God is therefore more personal than that of the Neoplatonists, who view Him as first developing the consciousness of Himself through the Logos. Accordingly, while conceiving God as entirely free from the emotional disturbance of passion, and as framing His decrees in the calmness of wisdom, Origen by no means regards Him as devoid of attributes. "The Father Himself and God of all," he says, "is long-suffering, merciful, and pitiful. Has He not then in a sense passions? The Father Himself is not impassible. He has the passion of love."[1] This may seem scarcely consistent with his general position as indicated above, and indeed occasionally Origen is tempted to go so far in this direction that he virtually withdraws his own statements.[2] It is perhaps a fair thing to say that he "had experienced that state of consciousness exemplified for us by all exalted Christian spirits, in which joy and sorrow cease to be passions and are no longer contraries. He did not clearly see that what is true of goodness and justice is true of love and sympathy. They differ not in themselves but in their objects."[3]

In opposition to the Gnostics, who sought to distinguish between the just God of the Old Testament and the merciful Father of the Lord Jesus Christ,

[1] *In Ezech.*, Hom. vi. 6.
[2] *E.g. in Num.*, Hom. xxiii. 2.
[3] Bigg, *Christian Platonists*, p. 158, note 1.

ORIGEN'S THEOLOGY

Origen stoutly maintains their identity. Not only so; he maintains the identity of the attributes of goodness and justice themselves. In this he diverges from the view of Irenæus and Tertullian that these are opposite attributes, yet necessarily coexisting in God. According to Origen, the indiscriminate bestowal of benefits upon all, irrespective of conduct, argues a perverted notion of goodness, whereas punishment inflicted as a deterrent from evil implies real goodness. God recompenses in justice and punishes in kindness; with Him justice is a manifestation of goodness.

Although a relative knowledge of Him is derivable from the Manifold, God is in fact incomprehensible. Clouds and darkness are round about Him; His ways are past finding out. It is possible through strenuous effort and by the aid of enlightening grace to go a certain length in this direction, but behind what we may thus discover there stretches so to speak a boundless region of unexplorable territory. He dwells far above the reach of our feeble perception. As the sunbeams that stream through a chink in the wall to the sun itself, so is the knowledge of God derived from the beauty of His works. These are merely "rays as it were of the nature of God in comparison with His real substance and being." Brighter is the revelation which we have in Christ, "the image of the invisible God." He that has seen Him has seen the Father, yet only in the measure made possible to him by divine grace. That God is meanwhile incomprehensible to us is not due to anything in the divine nature or in our own. God is light, and in proportion as we get nearer to Him will the shadows flee away. One day He shall impart to us His Spirit without measure, and we shall know Him as He is known by the only-begotten Son, and see Him face to face.

Inasmuch as he never conceives of God apart from revelation, which is necessarily partial, Origen does not hesitate to bring in his relative view of things even with respect to the Deity. God is not without limitation either as to His knowledge or His power. He foresees, indeed, all that comes to pass; but this is due to the fact that in the beginning He created, according to a definite standard of number and measure, as many rational beings and material bodies as He knew would admit of being governed by Him and be sufficient for the adorning of the world, as well as to the further circumstance that the duration of the world is limited. In respect of omnipotence also God is not unconditioned. From the very nature of the case His power is limited. Were it not so, it would be incomprehensible even to Himself. But in fact He can do only what He wills.[1] He is thus limited not by the resistance of created matter, but through His own nature, in virtue of His own reason and His own goodness. It is, moreover, morally certain that God cannot do what is evil, and logically certain that He can do nothing contrary to nature, although some of His miracles may *appear* to be incredible. Finally, there are evils inseparable from the carrying out even of the wisest plans of the Creator: "Evils in the strict sense are not created by God; yet some, though but few in comparison with the great,

[1] *Contra Celsum*, v. 23. Origen was afterwards accused by his enemies of teaching that God cannot do anything that He has not done. This was perhaps in reality only an inference from his teaching—not quite unwarrantable, it must be said; but this view was in later times expressly taught by Abelard, who further maintained that God cannot leave undone anything that is good.

ORIGEN'S THEOLOGY

well-ordered whole of the world, have of necessity adhered to the objects realised, as the carpenter who executes the plan of a building does not manage without chips and similar rubbish, or as architects cannot be made responsible for the dirty heaps of broken stones and filth one sees at the sites of buildings."[1] The truth is, Origen has none of the modern reverence for the word *infinite*. To him as a Christian Platonist it is nearly equivalent to *evil*, and the very perfection of the divine attributes lies in their mutually limiting character.

It is upon this consideration that Origen bases his view of the created universe as at once limited in extent and timeless in the sense that there was no time when it was not. If æons did elapse before it existed, then in those æons God cannot have been what He is as Lord of all. But to grant this would be to deny His unchangeableness, and to suppose Him capable of a transition from lower to higher, from the potential to the actual—an impossible position, which amounts to a denial of His perfection. The idea of a Creator necessarily involves that of a creation; it is in virtue of creating that God becomes Creator. As, however, time did not exist before the world, and has an end, God as First Cause of the world is above time, and must be conceived as existing prior to matter. Matter is therefore not coeternal with Him whose being is everlasting and timeless, with whom it is always *to-day*. If it be suggested that in this case God must have been idle before the world began, Origen replies that God's work did not begin with the making of this world, which was preceded, as it will be followed, by countless others.

[1] *Contra Celsum*, vi. 55.

ii. *The Doctrine of the Trinity*

The doctrine of the Trinity had been clearly defined in the baptismal formula, and had been mentioned by Justin and others as a necessary part of the Church's creed. Towards the close of the second century we find it definitely named, and its significance grasped as affirming both unity in trinity and trinity in unity. From this time it became *the* problem of Christianity. The conception of one God in three Persons had been distinctly reached, but as to the nature and relations of these Persons somewhat vague notions still prevailed. Writers like Athenagoras and Tertullian show, however, the general trend of ecclesiastical tradition with reference to these questions. This was a lead which Clement and Origen felt constrained to follow. If they were bold speculative thinkers, they were also loyal sons of the Church, and their attachment to the latter proved the dominating influence. What renders this all the more remarkable is that Greek Christianity undoubtedly drew much of its inspiration from Jewish theosophy. For the thought of Clement and Origen the Apologists of the second century are of little account, it is Philo who is their "guide, philosopher, and friend." Yet, although it is in the writings of this brilliant Alexandrian that the first traces of Trinitarian doctrine occur, their Trinity is not Philo's, but a fuller development of the New Testament doctrine on the lines already marked out by the tradition of the Church. While it is true that "Clement neglects almost as much as Philo the third hypostasis of the Trinity," he at any rate avoids the inconsistency which leads that writer to suggest several different trinities. And if Clement says nothing explicit as to the nature of the third Person, His relation to the other two Persons, and His special function, the writings of Origen exhibit a most palpable advance in this respect. To some extent this is true even as regards his treatment of the first two hypostases of the Trinity, but is most notable in his discussion of questions pertaining to the Holy Spirit.

Already in Origen's time, particularly at Rome, the air vibrated with strife as to the sense in which God is One, and at the same time Three. The latter aspect of the problem formed the more immediate subject of controversy. It was not so much the truth of the divine unity that exercised the minds of disputants as the precise significance to be attached to certain real distinctions in the divine Essence, the existence of which is a matter of revelation. Of most crucial importance was the question as to the distinct personality of the Son. What Origen and the theologians of his age were chiefly concerned to show was, that while Jesus is God He is nevertheless not the Father. But, broadly speaking, the task they set themselves was the elaboration of the doctrine of three Persons or Subsistences in the Godhead.[1]

The Father.—Although maintaining that God is incomprehensible, Origen yet regards Him as to some extent knowable, for apart from a certain knowledge of Him we could not even know that He is incomprehensible, and in what respects He is so. On the question as to how we attain to a knowledge of God, Origen

[1] *Substantia* and *persona* are used by Latin writers as the equivalents of the Greek *hypostasis* and *ousia*. It was peculiarly unfortunate, and the prolific source of much misunderstanding, that the Greek word for *person* should have been thus interchanged with the Latin word for substance.

holds as against Celsus that the notion of God cannot be arrived at by analysis and synthesis, but only through "a certain grace inborn in the soul, not without God, but with a certain enthusiasm." It is a special gift of intuition. This position is equally subversive of the method of abstraction employed by Clement, who attempts through a process of exhaustion—namely, by eliminating in succession the conditions of creaturely existence—definitely to determine the idea of God. It was a fundamental axiom in the thought of Origen, as subsequently in that of Leibnitz, that God is not to be discovered by any scientific demonstration, but is near us in our hearts.

In the idea of God thus intuitively implanted within us there is a positive element which the method of negation only serves to bring into sharper relief. According to Origen, this is the idea of goodness;[1] and however incomprehensible God may be in the depths of His being, yet because of the intimate relation in which the idea of the good stands to reason, He becomes intelligible to His rational creatures. Goodness is in Him an essential attribute of His nature; with Him to be is to be good. To Him alone belongs the fulness of being and of goodness. Partaking of nothing, whilst He is Himself partaken of by all, He is the principle alike of existence and of Deity. He is God in Himself, the true God, the God of gods. It is only, however, through the study of the relation of the First Person of the Trinity to the Second and the Third that Origen's theory of the Father can be exempted from the category of obscure generalities.

[1] This is simply Plato's idea of the good, but in a somewhat more personal form.

ORIGEN'S THEOLOGY

The Son.—It belongs to the idea of God as the absolutely good to reveal or communicate Himself. The life which has its source in Him must necessarily flow forth to other beings. And as God is unchangeable, this process never had a beginning; it is eternal. But it is only through the Logos that God acts upon the world. He must lay aside His absolute apathy as pure Intelligence, and assume this form in order to come into close touch with the Manifold. While Origen's doctrine of the Logos bears a general resemblance to that of Philo, and is not free from the contradictory elements contained in the latter, it is characterised by more crispness of definition, and by a clearer affirmation of the distinct personality of the Logos, whom he identifies with Christ. According to Origen, the Logos who appeared in Christ is the Word or Son of God, His Wisdom hypostatically existing, eternally begotten, and of like essence with the Father. He is the truth and life of all things which exist. He is not an emanation from God, who is indivisible, but the complete self-revelation of the Father, "the brightness of His glory, and the express image of His person." As Creator of the world He is immeasurably exalted above it; yet as Himself derived, He is subordinate to the Father, who is the alone Absolute. He is truly God, but "second God." Origen contends equally for the independent personality, and for the true divinity, of the Son, although he is led by the exigencies of debate sometimes to emphasise His subordination to, and at other times to claim for Him virtual equality with, the Father. His aim, of course, is to represent the Father as the one foundation of Godhead, while at the same time conserving true Deity for the Son. The main positions here demand, perhaps, somewhat fuller state-ment.

The Son is coeternal with the Father: "there never was a time when He was not." God and His Wisdom are as inseparable in thought as are light and splendour. Something like an act of the will, which proceeds from the understanding without being divided from it, is the begetting of the Son by the Father. He proceeds from the Father's essence as the Son of His will. It is not, however, an act that has taken place at some definite moment, for it had no beginning, and is a continual and eternal process. Neither by thought nor figure can this begetting be adequately explained to the human mind; but the resultant Logos is a living being,[1] a second person, with an independent existence. This thought of the eternal generation of the Son, which the Christian Church has accepted as "the truest human expression of one side of the mystery of the essential Trinity," was first worked out by Origen.

As incorporeal and invisible, as the perfect image of God's person and the unspotted mirror of His power, as being, so to speak, the very soul of God, the only-begotten Son is truly God, sharing in His essence, possessing all His attributes, and therefore also coequal with Him—"the same in substance with the Father." That the omnipotence of Father and Son is one and the same is, he says, shown by the words of St. John in the Apocalypse: "Thus saith the Lord God, which is, and which was, and which is to come, the Almighty." "For who else was 'He which is to come' than Christ?" As the purest efflux of the glory of the Almighty, Wisdom,

---

[1] "Animal vivens." Origen quotes the expression from the *Acts of Paul*, a spurious ecclesiastical treatise mentioned by Eusebius.

ORIGEN'S THEOLOGY

which is Christ, can say, "All Mine are Thine, and Thine are Mine"; and also, as the stainless mirror of the working of God, "What things soever the Father doeth, these also doeth the Son likewise." From this point of view Origen concludes that there is "no dissimilarity whatever between the Son and the Father."

When, however, he asserts that this is true only in relation to the world, the statement loses much of its force. Although from our standpoint He is the manifest essential God, yet "as soon as the category of causality is applied, and the particular contemplation of the Son in relation to the Father gives way to the general contemplation of His task and destination, the Son is not only called creature and demiurge, but all the utterances about the quality of His essence receive a limitation."[1] His coequality with the Father is conditioned by the fact that the Son's existence is something derived. Although not created, He is begotten. As distinct from God the Father, who is the First Cause, the Son is "that which is caused." Thus the Father is greater than the Son. What He is the Son derives from the Father, so that even those properties which belong to His Deity do not exist in Him in the same absolute sense as in the Father. As the first stage in the transition from the uncreated One to the created Many, His unchangeableness is only relative. His goodness is not absolute, but the perfect image of the absolute goodness of the Father, who is exalted above the Son as far as the Son Himself is exalted above all thrones, principalities, and powers. The all-embracing Kingdom of the Father is more extensive than that of the Son, which is confined to rational

[1] Harnack, *History of Dogma*, ii. p. 357.

154 ORIGEN AND GREEK THEOLOGY

beings, and which in turn is greater than that of the Holy Spirit, which extends only to the saints. Christ's Kingdom comes to an end; after all has been subjected to Him, He shall be subjected to the Father, and God shall be all in all. There is nowhere any attempt to detract from the divinity of the Son; on the contrary, prayer may be made to Him. But along with this there is everywhere the reminder that God is the Father of all that is. Strictly speaking, however, the subordination here taught by Origen is not a subordination of essence, but one of function in relation to the manifestation of the Persons of the Godhead to creatures; that is to say, the Son as Son is inferior to the Father as Father. Its basis, moreover, is scriptural rather than metaphysical. It was dictated by no spirit of presumption, but by a loyal and courageous acceptance of Christ's own testimony when He says, "None is good save One," and "My Father is greater than I."

The Son's relations to the world are set forth in Scripture under a variety of titles. While in this respect the Father as the highest absolute unity can only be One, the Son is Manifold. As the perfect image of the mind of God He is first of all Wisdom; then as the medium of revelation He is the Word; further, as the source and sustainer of rational beings and inanimate nature, He is the Truth and the Life. But these qualities, which belong to Christ immutably as the only-begotten Son of God, Origen distinguishes from those human and accidental properties which He assumed for the purpose of redemption. To this latter class are reckoned His functions as the God-Man, Physician, Shepherd, Lamb of God, etc. The two categories Origen likens to the higher and lower steps

ORIGEN'S THEOLOGY

of the ascent to the Holy of holies. With all this he disclaims any intention of introducing a distinction into the essence of the Son. It is not implied that Christ will ever divest Himself of His glorified body, or that we shall ever be able to do without Him as the Life and the Truth. If one day we shall see the Father even as the Son sees Him, and the work of redemption and mediation thus take end, this will only be because we shall be "of one spirit with the Lord."

In Origen's doctrine of the Logos, however, far more stress is laid upon His significance as Creator and Teacher than upon His work as Redeemer. Indeed it is the mark of the true Christian that he has outgrown the need of redemption viewed as forgiveness, and no longer requires the Physician's healing or the Shepherd's care. Thus, in order to the fulfilment of the purpose of redemption, we must ultimately pass beyond the crucified Jesus to the Word. As this is, according to Origen, the path to the higher life, it is small wonder that, often as the name recurs in his writings, the Person of Christ is of no real importance to his conception of the Logos. The weakness of Origen's position lies indeed just here; he confounds the two conceptions Logos and Son, and fails firmly to grasp that of the premundane personality of the Logos.

The Spirit.—Origen remarks that while the Greek philosophers have by the light of nature and of the human mind been able to recognise God as the Father of the universe, and in some cases also have even attained to an idea of the existence of the Son as the word or reason of God, the belief in the Holy Spirit is confined entirely to Christianity. This effectually disposes of the contention of those who would ascribe his heterodox views upon the Trinity to his fondness for Plato. No speculative necessity led him to place the Spirit alongside of the Father and the Son; he did so entirely out of deference to the rule of faith, according to which the Holy Spirit is "associated in honour and dignity with the Father and the Son." In affirming the three Persons, he, of course, implies the distinct personality of the Spirit, and He expressly speaks of His divinity,[1] although he nowhere definitely calls Him God. The thought, however, is unquestionably present to his mind; it lay wrapped up, indeed, in the baptismal formula. Prayer may be directed to Him as to the Son. His essential Godhead, moreover, involves His eternity; it is He who in the beginning moved upon the face of the waters. He is the inspirer of both prophets and apostles, and is designated in Old and New Testament alike Spirit or Holy Spirit. It is through the Spirit that men are enabled to receive Christ as Justice and Wisdom; it is through the Spirit that they are sanctified and perfected.

Although Origen represents the Spirit as sharing in the work of creation,[2] he states that the Church in his time had reached no settled view as to whether He Himself is created or uncreated. This is a point, he says, demanding "careful investigation," but he fails to formulate any clear and consistent doctrine regarding it. In general, he avoids language which would suggest that the Spirit is a creature; but while sometimes he asserts that He is not to be reckoned among the "all things" made by the Son, at other times he takes the very opposite view.[3] In spite of this vacilla-

[1] *De Princ.* ii. 7. 3. [2] *De Princ.* iv. 30.
[3] Both views are expressed even in comments upon the same passage (*John* ii. 6).

tion, he appears to arrive at the conclusion that the Spirit "is become" through the Son. In other words, the Spirit is created, but in a peculiar sense; He is the first creation of the Father through the Son, and therefore subordinate to the Son, as the Son is to the Father. In connection with His acceptance and treatment of the mysterious dogma of the Trinity, it is very apparent on the one hand that Origen does all he can to eliminate every idea that savours of the created, and on the other that in passing from the consideration of the concept God to that of the two other divine Persons, he experiences extreme difficulty in avoiding the use of language which tends to reduce the Son and the Holy Spirit to the rank of creatures. Although his doctrine of the Holy Spirit is worked out with an explicitness unknown to any of his predecessors, he was certainly far from happy in his mode of conceiving the Spirit's personality.

While all things derive their existence from God the Father, and are subject to His power, and while the Son as the principle of reason imparts reason to all rational beings, the Spirit's sphere of action is limited to the saints. Hence the special ministry of the Spirit, although the most important, is also the most circumscribed. That of the Father and of the Son extends without distinction to every creature, but only the sanctified have a share in the Holy Spirit. The difference in the circumference of these concentric circles into which existence is thus divided is, however, only of temporary duration, for in the end the whole rational creation will be raised to the level of the holy. This result is attained through the grace of the Holy Spirit. Not that His dignity is greater than that of the Father and the Son; on the contrary, the Father's power is greater than that of the Son, and that of the Son greater than that of the Holy Spirit. But from the point of view of Origen's system, this formula really lacks the precision which it seems to possess. For as only the rational creation is abiding, all else being doomed to vanish away, and as all rational beings are destined to holiness, the action of the three Persons of the Trinity in relation to creatures does not ultimately vary in extension. The terms Father, Son, and Holy Spirit merely mark, as regards its three principal movements, the one though diverse activity of God.

Father, Son, and Spirit form a Trinity in which there is no difference, and in which accordingly nothing can be called greater or less. The three Persons are of the same nature and essence, equal in dignity and honour. Their consubstantiality is such that the Spirit of the Father is the same as the Spirit of the Son, the same as the Holy Spirit. Hence the Trisagion of Isa. vi. 3; the cherubim are not content with crying "Holy" once or twice, but their threefold ascription corresponds to the triple sanctity of God as represented by the Father, the Son, and the Holy Spirit. In spite of this apparently explicit statement as to the equality of the Persons, which is possibly due to the correcting hand of Rufinus, Origen's Trinity is a graduated one, based upon the absolute Godhead of the Father, from whom the two other Persons proceed. Clement and Origen had completely established the coeternity and consubstantiality of the three Persons, but it was reserved for the Fathers of the fourth century to put the finishing touch to the labours of the great Alexandrian teachers, by divesting themselves entirely of the

ORIGEN'S THEOLOGY

swaddling-clothes of Jewish-Christian tradition, and unequivocally asserting their equality as well. As God cannot be thought of apart from revelation, this Trinity, which in Origen's view constitutes the deepest mystery of the faith, remains a Trinity of revelation. "The gift of the Spirit is made known through the Son, and operated by God the Father."

Not only the Son and the Holy Spirit, but all other rational beings as well, proceed by a sort of timeless emanation from the primal Deity, and in some way share in the divine life and the divine nature, without however having identity of essence as parts of the Godhead. According to Origen, the rational element is one and the same throughout the entire domain of the spiritual. Indeed this is the pivot upon which his whole doctrinal system turns. The restoration of the oneness of the spiritual through the removal of the disturbance caused by the development of the worldly in antagonism to the divine—in other words, the deification of humanity—is the goal, as it is also the starting-point, of the Greek theology.

Although not so immediately concerned with the question of the unity in trinity as with that of the trinity in unity, Origen and his school were already being challenged by Celsus and other opponents to explain their position with reference to the former problem. Their doctrine of the threefold Personality, it was contended, could not consist with belief in the divine unity. An endeavour was made to impale them upon the horns of a dilemma. Either Christianity was monotheism as conceived by Celsus, in which case it was merely on a level with the religion of the ancient

Persians; or it was monotheism as conceived by Noetus,[1] in which case the work of Jesus was purely visionary. In spite of the humble diffidence with which he expresses himself regarding these profoundly mysterious themes, Origen tenaciously adheres to the view that God is at once Three and One. While affirming the distinction of Persons, he denies that there is therefore actual division; "for to ascribe division to an incorporeal being is not only the height of impiety, but a mark of the greatest folly."[2] He holds that between Father and Son there is complete mutual circumincession or interpenetration, unity of substance, and identity of will; and the same thing holds good with regard to the entire Trinity.

[1] Noetus was a presbyter of Smyrna, who held by "modalistic monarchianism," *i.e.* the opinion that Jesus was a mere man, and constituted the Son of God only because of the unique degree in which He was filled with divine power and wisdom.

[2] *De Princ.* i. 2. 6.

CHAPTER VII

Origen's Theology: Creation and the Fall

i. *The World of created Spirits and the Conception of formal Freedom*

The ultimate reason of the creation of rational beings, which are of different ranks, and include human souls, is the divine goodness; God desired those on whom He might lavish His benefits. Although to us they are innumerable, the number of these intelligences is not infinite. Called into existence through the Son, they are in reality the unfolding of the fulness that dwells in Him. But inasmuch as the idea of createdness was already more firmly coupled with the Holy Ghost than with the Son, the former rather than the latter marks the transition to the inferior spirits. While, however, in the graduated series of spirits which represent created reason these occupy the stage next to Him, there is nevertheless between them and the Holy Spirit a wide gulf of cleavage. For although He is the first of the creatures, who are all of the same substance, it is the essential property of His nature to be good. The inferior spirits, on the other hand, while destined for the highest good, must yet reach it through their own free choice.

That free will is the prerogative of all moral creatures

is a doctrine of cardinal importance in the system of Origen. "Every rational creature is capable of earning praise or blame—praise, if, in conformity to that reason which it possesses, it advance to better things; blame, if it fall away from the right course."[1] It is as much the characteristic mark of the created spirit to be free, as it is that of the Deity to be unchangeable. Not that the Son and the Holy Spirit have not freedom, but in their case, as in that of the Father, freedom and necessity are one. It belongs essentially to their nature constantly to embrace and hold fast the good, whereas the lower spirits, having only a capacity for the highest good, may and do abandon it, and must regain it through renewed effort.

In opposition to the Gnostics, who held by the doctrine of absolute predestination, Origen vigorously defends his theory that free will is bound up with reason, and is the possession of every created spirit. While inanimate things such as wood and stone are moved from without, animals and plants have their motive power within themselves. But in the case of rational beings there is, further, the faculty of reason, which enables them to choose good or evil. Such freedom implies responsibility. Those who possess it are not the helpless prey of external influences. One man, for example, will fall before some particular temptation; another will resist it. Some rise from vice to virtue, others fall from virtue to vice. But in either case, whether there be a transformation for the better, or a process of degeneration and declension, we are to trace the change not to external causes, but to the decision of the will.

[1] *De Princ.* i. 5. 2.

ORIGEN'S THEOLOGY

In support of this contention Origen adduces passages of Scripture which presuppose the freedom of the human will, and place clearly before men for their deliberate choice the alternative paths of life and death.[1] Special stress is laid upon the words of Jesus,[2] and of the Apostle Paul.[3] At the same time he discusses with great minuteness other passages which seem to preclude the idea of free will, and which were therefore the favourite weapons of the Gnostics. The mere fact that God "hardened Pharaoh's heart" disproves the assertion that his was a ruined nature incapable of salvation. Turning for an illustration to the Epistle to the Hebrews, Origen insists that just as the same rain makes cultivated ground fruitful and leaves neglected soil barren, so "by one operation God has mercy upon one man while He hardens another, although not intending to harden." The hardening of some is due to their inherent wickedness. The same sunshine melts wax and hardens clay; and the same divine influence that hardened Pharaoh prevailed with some of the Egyptians who cast in their lot with the Hebrews. Many bad slaves are made worse through the kindness of their masters, and many sinners are hardened through their contemptuous disregard of the riches of God's goodness. It may also be said that God hardens those whom He abandons for their own advantage, reserving the cure of their sin for the other life, as a wise physician who knows all, and governs souls with reference to the future. Again, changing the figure, he remarks that the great Husbandman, who is acquainted with the seasons and the nature

---

[1] Mic. vi. 8 ; Deut. xxx. 15 f., etc.
[2] Matt. v. 39, vii. 26, etc.   [3] Rom. ii. 4–10.

of the soil, frequently refrains from casting the seed on rocky ground, where it would spring up too precipitately. When this does take place the object is by gratifying its desire to lead the soul subsequently to receive the slower husbandry which is more beneficial for it. It is not always for the advantage of the sick to be rapidly cured, and in bestowing benefits God occasionally procrastinates rather than communicate things which, when seen and heard, would only add to the sin of those whom even such peculiar privileges would fail to convince. When God engages to substitute for stony hearts the heart of flesh, the promise is not made without reference to the will of those concerned; on the contrary, they must lend their co-operation by voluntarily submitting themselves to His power, just as an ignorant person must yield himself up to his instructor to be taught, and as the sick were cured only by coming to the Saviour to be healed. When it is said that "it is not of him that runneth, but of God that showeth mercy," all that is meant to be conveyed is that God does far more for our salvation than we do ourselves. Although it is God that saves the ship from destruction, it is not brought safe to port without skilful navigation on the part of the crew. If the apostle speaks of God as "working in us both to will and to do," this is simply on a level with the general statement that our power of locomotion is from God. It merely asserts the divine origin of our power of volition and of action; we may use this power either in a good or an evil direction. In conclusion, Origen discusses the difficult passage Rom. ix. 18 ff. Unless we are to charge the apostle with self-contradiction, how are we to reconcile his censure of the wicked

(2 Cor. v.) and praise of the virtuous (2 Tim. i. 16 ff.) with the view that according to him it is the fault of the Creator that one vessel is in honour and another in dishonour? Besides, does not St. Paul himself say that "if a man purge himself ... he shall be a vessel unto honour, sanctified, and meet for the Master's use" (2 Tim. ii 21), thereby referring the whole back to ourselves? The two forms of statement are not really contradictory; they are the opposite poles of a higher truth which we must extract from both.

When hard pressed by his opponents, Origen had always a second line of defence to fall back upon. He fought them stoutly, and on the whole successfully, on the scriptural arena; but he could retreat, if necessary, into the stronghold afforded by a doctrine almost as dear to him as that of free will itself—the doctrine of the pre-existence of the soul. That one vessel has been created for honour and another for dishonour is due to causes antecedent to the present life.

Origen looks on everything from this standpoint of freedom; for him it is the key to the interpretation of the cosmos as it exists. We have already seen that in his system human souls form one of the orders composing the category of created spirits. In the interest of the divine omnipotence, moreover, it is necessary to assume that the whole of the spirits were created from all eternity, for "He must always have had those over whom He exercised power." Otherwise we are landed in the absurdity of reducing the Almighty to the level of a finite being who came into possession of them by a kind of progress. God created all the spirits equal and alike, because there was in Himself no reason for producing variety and diversity. Viewed with respect to their origin, they are of the same divine substance, share the same spiritual light, and are immortal in essence. That some have advanced through imitation of God, while others have failed through negligence, is due to the freedom of the individual will and to the different offices assigned to them. Although, strictly speaking, all rational natures are incorporeal, yet as liable to change, and as finite beings who have been created, they are weighted with a kind of materiality, and possess from the first a body or envelope suited to their environment. This is true alike of angels and of men. Absolute immateriality belongs to God alone. It is further noteworthy that, idealist as he is, Origen confines his attention to the actual constitution of the spirit world, and does not in the least concern himself with the question as to what would have been the proper development for all. He is content to view them in their existing relations and diverse conditions as regulated by their progress in, or departure from, goodness.

In the matter of overcoming evil the ability both to will and to do is the gift of God; only the actual choice is our own. As the will to embrace the good is thus due to the influence of the Holy Spirit, bestowed in proportion to our merit, there is in every good deed of ours a commingling of our own choice and the divine aid; but the latter plays infinitely the greater part. The freedom of the created spirits is therefore only relative, and amounts to no more than the power of controlling their own destiny for a time. It is on every hand conditioned, and exists only within very narrow limits. The rational creature has his environment given to him; it is beyond his power to command

ORIGEN'S THEOLOGY

the success of his own action; and even the decision to act is dependent upon earlier decisions. After these deductions are made, and in view of the fact that all rational existence must ultimately find its goal in God Himself, what is there left to the province of free determination? What appears as freedom is in reality nothing else than the necessary evolution of the created spirit. Origen refrains, however, from drawing this inference himself. For him freedom means unfettered liberty of choice, the unconditioned possibility of descending from the higher to the lower, and of again ascending to the good; and it means no more. His conception of freedom is limited to this its purely formal side, no account being taken of what lies beyond the mere act of choosing, namely, the attainment of the good, and the consummation of freedom in the onward progress of the being. What escapes him is that freedom is essentially free devotion to the good, which, originating in freedom of choice, afterwards becomes an inalienable spiritual possession. Origen indeed ascribes to God a higher freedom than mere liberty of choice; but the constant necessity of dealing with Gnostic and Neoplatonic denials of freedom apparently prevented him from perceiving that for the created spirit free will is only a stepping-stone towards that higher freedom which consists in voluntary adhesion to the divine law and the consequent normal development of the being. Owing to this inadequate conception of freedom, "religious history becomes, in the system of Origen, a drama without a conclusion, which is perpetually recommencing, and, as it were, repeating itself."[1] This defect is, however, in some

[1] Pressensé, *The Early Years of Christianity*, iii. p. 314.

degree atoned for by the lofty *morale* pervading the view of the world with which it is associated.

ii. *The Fall and the Creation of the material World*

In Origen's view the Fall was premundane; it took place before time began. The possession of free will made it possible for rational creatures either to advance to the point of attaining divine wisdom or to become involved in wickedness. When the good that was in them potentially becomes their own they reach perfection, and give place to a succession of worlds which serve as scenes of discipline for those who stand in need of it. For not all created spirits have chosen the path of virtue. In some cases " slothfulness and a dislike of labour in preserving what is good, and an aversion to, and a neglect of, better things, furnished the beginning of a departure from goodness," and the lack of goodness is positive wickedness. Their sin, which assumed a multiplicity of forms, in every case involved a diminution of true being, which is one with the good. Where the movements of souls are wrongly conducted, the power implanted in their substance by the goodness of their Maker disappears; it was not their own originally, and may be taken from them as it was given to them.

It was with a view to the purification of the fallen spirits that God created the visible world. What we are accustomed to regard as the creation of the world is thus, in Origen's conception, not the commencement, but an intermediate stage of spiritual history. It is the result of occurrences prior to the existence of the earth, which is both a place of punishment and a house of

ORIGEN'S THEOLOGY

correction. Life on earth is the continuation of an antecedent existence. Our present lot is the logical and moral consequence of our conduct in a prior state. The diversity that is in the world is due to the varying degrees in which rational beings have fallen from the primal unity in which they were at first created by God. Hence the different orders and ranks of angels; hence the inequalities among men. If one man is born to the life of an uncivilised savage, another to the enjoyments of learning and the fine arts, and another to the privileges of Christian fellowship, this must be regarded as the result of their own individual previous choice, and not, as the Gnostics maintained, of predestination. Every man's earthly circumstances are to be interpreted as a judgment passed upon his behaviour in a pre-existent state.

The most immediate consequence of the Fall was corporeal being. In order to give external shape to moral decisions, God created matter as a mobile substance capable of undergoing all manner of transformations, and thus of serving as a shroud to the soul, whatever may have been the extent of its rebellion. As the servant of angelic beings it shines in celestial splendour; when dragged down to furnish the habitat of beings of a lower order it assumes a grosser form. No longer harmoniously united in God, the spirits diverge from one another upon the assumption of their material garb, which, owing to its infinite adaptability as the outward expression of the manifold tendencies of the spiritual nature, becomes a veritable "coat of many colours." Those who steadfastly adhered to that which is good have obtained the rank of angels, and inhabit the ethereal bodies of the stars. Their exact place in the heavenly hierarchy of "gods," thrones, dominions, principalities, and powers, has been determined by their own quality and merit. Those who have utterly fallen away from God and goodness have become demons, with a passionate thirst for evil. These have had their glory turned into dust, and exist in hideously ugly, though invisible, dark bodies.[1] In addition to these good and evil powers the spirit world includes the intermediate and probationary class of human beings. Deeply as men have fallen from their primal state of blessedness, they have not sunk so low as the malignant demons; the love of God has not in man's case been wholly quenched. It has, however, become cold; to use Origen's own expression, the spirit has "cooled" into a soul. The moral character of "souls" varies according to the degree in which the lower or higher nature gains the upper hand; yet all souls are at least capable of being restored through chastisement to a condition of perfect spirituality.

Although they differ vastly from each other in their mental conformation and in their motives, God by His ineffable wisdom has contrived that the various purposes of the creatures shall be usefully adapted to the harmony of one world, and that their collective activity shall make for one end of perfection. That every spirit shall be free to take his own course, and that while some, for example, should need help, others should be in a position to give it, is the deliberate arrangement of God with a view to ensuring the salvation of all

[1] Cf. what Dante says of those toil-worn souls whose avarice has landed them in hell—
"That ignoble life
Which made them vile before, now makes them dark,
And to all knowledge indiscernible."—(*Inferno*, vii. 53-55.)

His creatures. In spite of its varied complexion, the condition of the world is not one of internal discord; rather is it like "some huge animal kept together by the power and reason of God as by one soul." On the other hand, however, this vast and orderly creation does participate in the misery attendant upon sin; "the whole creation groaneth and travaileth together in pain until now." The heavenly bodies and the angels of God must act perforce as ministering spirits to man, being thus made subject to vanity "not willingly, but by reason of Him who hath subjected the same in hope," namely, of "the manifestation of the sons of God." The far-reaching evil of sin is further evidenced by the fact that the glory of the Saviour Himself is not perfect without His people, for whom He waits in order to "drink wine" in the kingdom of God.

iii. *The Doctrine of Man*

Jerome wrongly charges Origen with holding the doctrine of the transmigration of the soul from one human body into another, or even into the body of a beast. But if at this point the Christian theologian of Alexandria severs himself from Platonism, he certainly puts himself in line with it on the question of the soul's pre-existence. This latter doctrine forms an integral part of his philosophical system. He does not, like many of the early Fathers, regard man as virtually the sole end of creation, but constantly assumes that he is merely one factor in the general world of spirits.[1] So essential is the belief in pre-existence to his whole theory of the universe that he is not even careful,

[1] This is quite consistent with his reply to Celsus.

either by means of Plato's expedient of partial recollection or otherwise, to offer an explanation of the lack of any connecting link in consciousness between the present and the former life. By the position he takes up with reference to the pre-existence of souls he of course ranks himself as an opponent of both the creationist and traducian theories as to the origin of the human soul.

In his psychology Origen adopts the Platonic and Pauline doctrine of trichotomy. The constitution of man is threefold, consisting of spirit, soul (ψυχή, *anima*), and body. Of these elements of human nature the highest is the spirit, which has descended from the upper world, and is joined to the body through the medium of the animal soul. The soul thus stands midway, so to speak, between the weak flesh and the willing spirit, and constitutes the peculiar individuality of the man. To Origen this triple division of man's constitution is necessary in order to account for our antagonism to God, which can be traced neither to a purely physical cause, nor to the rational spirit, which must remain intact. This is scarcely in keeping, however, with what Origen says about the spirit in man having been "chilled" or transformed into a soul. Such a process involves a certain measure of defection from God, and where this takes place the integrity of the rational spirit must necessarily be impaired. Nor is his fanciful derivation of the Greek name for soul from a verb signifying to wax cold, and his consequent description of the soul as divorced from the divine fire, easily reconcilable with his statements regarding the sinless soul of Jesus. In fact "the soul is treated just as inconsistently as the Logos; it is a spirit grown

ORIGEN'S THEOLOGY

cold, and yet no spirit."[1] It is, however, only fair to say that Origen particularly disclaims dogmatism with reference to the conversion of the understanding into a soul, and the different degrees in which in different instances the intelligence is thus sensualised. These and other kindred matters he brings forward, he says, "as topics of discussion for our readers."

The fallen human spirit still retains its freedom, and has not lost the power of restoring itself to its former condition. By our culpable descent to this world, however, we form part of a system of things which inevitably affects us for good or for evil. To this extent Origen felt with Tennyson that

"The individual withers, and the world is more and more."

The individual cannot entirely dissociate himself from humanity in the aggregate. Between parents and children there is a subtle spiritual affinity of such a kind that all who are born into the world are "not only the sons, but the disciples of sinners." Yet there remains in fallen man a spark of the divine, a germ of goodness through the development of which he may rise not only to the level of the angels, but even to complete likeness to God Himself. According to Origen, "the image of God" stamped upon man at his creation guarantees to him the possibility of attaining to perfection; but the perfect realisation of the divine "likeness" is reached only through the exercise of his own diligence in the imitation of God.

In his intermediate position between the angels and the demons man is constantly subjected to two cross-winds of inspiration and impulse. His present position

[1] Harnack, *Outlines of the History of Dogma*, p. 161.

is therefore one of severe mental and moral conflict. The hostile powers of evil, with Satan at their head, instigate him to sin. Saints have to "wrestle not against flesh and blood, but against principalities, against powers," etc. On the other hand, they are assisted by the angels of God, who are stationed over the way of light as are the angels of Satan over the way of darkness.[1] Everyone has his good angel who incites him to well-doing, and his evil angel who lures him on to wickedness.[2] We may resist the evil suggestion, and we may disobey the divine call to better things. Under every temptation we have the necessary power to enable us to overcome it. If we choose to exercise it diligently we shall conquer, but if we use it slothfully we are defeated. All depends upon the use we make of our faculty of free will. Victory consists in the due mastery of the passions, in keeping them, that is, within the natural bounds of moderation, and in free devotion to the good. It is achieved through prayer, which weakens the influence of the demons. God is "the just president" of the struggle, and nothing that befalls us happens without His permission, or even in the last resort apart from His providential guidance, though the latter is, of course, exercised subject to the liberty we possess.

Origen's conception of sin is dominated on the one hand by the doctrine of pre-existence, and on the other by that of free will. The first establishes the fact, the second the guilt, of sin. Already in its former state the human soul was stained with sin, so that it enters upon terrestrial life in a sinful condition. Sin is in-

[1] *Epistle of Barnabas*, chap. xviii.
[2] *Shepherd of Hermas*, Com. vi. 2.

ORIGEN'S THEOLOGY

separable from man's whole earthly environment; it is the inevitable shadow cast upon the spirit that has wandered from its source. Origen appears to have been satisfied with this view of the case until in Cæsarea he encountered the practice of infant baptism, with its manifest bearing upon the question of original sin. This led him further to conclude that there is a certain hereditary pollution attaching to all the children of Adam. "Spermatic germs" of good and evil are inherent from the first in every human being. The narrative of the Fall in Genesis he interprets allegorically as a delineation of the defection of the entire human race. Adam is the type of moral agents generally. But though Origen thus regards the sin of all men as inherited from their first father, he by no means accepts the doctrine of total depravity. Man is moved by noble impulses which are the fruit of long latent germs of good. He has an innate disposition not only towards the lower realm of things that appeal to the senses, but also towards the divine, eternal, and invisible. In other words, he has a conscience, which is virtually a reminiscence of a former and better existence. This is the peculiarly spiritual element in man, and is directly related to the Spirit of God. It is, in short, the law of God written upon the heart.

The guilt of sin is bound up with the idea of freedom. Even since the Fall man might have conquered evil, but he has chosen to listen to the solicitations of the demons until to his original sin there has been added much actual transgression. Not that the body, although the result of the Fall, is in its nature impure. The devil is not the cause of our natural appetites. For instance, concupiscence is not in itself sinful; guilt is contracted only when we yield to it. In view, however, of our fleshly constitution, which renders evil inevitable, and in view of the error inseparable from temporary wrong development, our freedom is to a large extent illusory. No man can be sinless. In Adam all sin, just as in Adam all die. Moral evil does not originate in God, although in His government of the world it is made subservient to the good; nor does it spring from matter, which is consequent upon sin; it has its source in the freedom of the created spirit, that is, not in freedom itself, but in the free act of declension from God. Origen conceives it, however, as something negative; in its essence it is neither real nor eternal. It is the opposite of true being, which is one with the good. With God's aid evil is not invincible. In point of fact Origen believes strongly in the ultimate complete triumph of the good. The rebellious spirits must therefore return to God, the devil himself not excepted. When this consummation is reached, the present material world will come to an end.

CHAPTER VIII

Origen's Theology: Redemption and Restoration

In the matter of salvation Origen insists upon the necessity of the utmost moral effort on the part of the individual spirit. But in view of the extent to which, through our own fault, the powers of evil have gradually tightened their grip upon us, he is equally explicit in affirming the necessity of divine help being extended to us on a grander scale even than that implied in the assistance of all the good powers, if we are to be delivered from Satan's thraldom and restored to a state of perfection. God Himself must come to our help. Thus no human effort can save apart from divine grace.

i. *The Four Revelations*

Ever since the Fall God has been rendering help through the medium of a manifold and progressive revelation. To begin with, He has placed us under the tuition of the natural law of conscience, which is binding upon all rational creatures, angels and sidereal spirits, equally with men, being subject to its sway. No man has perfectly kept this law; "there is none that doeth good; no, not one." Yet where, through the cultivation of the ray of light thus implanted in the human spirit, something has been accomplished in this direction, men shall not go altogether unrewarded. Philosophy, however, is no passport to the kingdom of heaven, from which the pagan is shut out because he does not believe in Christ, and is not born again of water and the Spirit.[1] Elsewhere, it must be said, Origen speaks with more hesitancy. What he clearly says is that the natural light of reason, implanted by the Word, is insufficient.

The next stage in the onward march of revelation for the relief of the fallen spirit is that reached in the law and the prophets. Through the precepts and sacrificial system of the Mosaic law the power of sin received a distinct check. Yet it was only a shadow of better things to come, the clay model as it were of the future bronze figure, the schoolmaster whose training smooths the way for the reception of more perfect principles. Even when supplemented by prophecy, it cannot conquer sin and error. The prophets were pure spirits whose bodily nature was not the result of their own declension from God. Although clothed in mortal flesh, they were sent by the Word to minister to men battling with temptation, and to shed upon their moral darkness some rays of celestial light. Their mission was confined to a selected nation, so that it might become the centre from which the salvation of God should go forth to the ends of the earth. But these measures still proved inadequate.

The light of conscience and the force of law having failed to bring back the fallen spirits to the divine life, the Word Himself had to appear in order that this end

[1] *In Rom.* ii. 7.

might be achieved. Hence the humiliation of the only-begotten Son. Although man could not rise, He could stoop. The Word and Wisdom of the Father assumed the form of a servant in order that by His obedience unto death He might teach the art of free obedience to those for whom there is no other road to blessedness. This is the fuller revelation of the gospel—a revelation adapted to the various needs of the different orders of rational creatures, from the highest angel down to the lowest demon. To all men burdened with this corporeal nature the Word has at length visibly appeared to bestow upon them redemption and eternal blessedness according to the measure of their receptivity. The two factors in our justification are our faith and Christ's blood; "of the two, however, it is much more the blood of Christ than our faith that justifies."[1]

Even this is not the final revelation of God to men. The gospel is related to the perfect truth as the Old Testament to the New, or as the legislation of Deuteronomy to the rest of the Pentateuch. It is only the shadow of the realities to be ushered in after our æon has run its course. Temporary and mutable, it awaits its full unveiling through the second advent of Christ. Then it will resolve itself into the *eternal gospel*, which as the complete revelation of the divine purposes has "no outer shell and no representation." This eternal gospel lies concealed in Scripture, although to some extent it is discernible to the reader who can understand the mystic sense. It is the help afforded to the perfect, and in heaven the saints shall live according to its laws.

[1] *In Rom.* v. 8 f.

ii. *The Incarnation*

To Origen's mind the wonder of wonders is that the very Word and Wisdom of God should have existed within the frame of that Man who appeared in Judæa, should have been born and uttered cries as an infant, should have sorrowed, died, and risen again. The combination in Him of qualities so human and so divine baffles the understanding. If we think of a God, we see a mortal; if of a man, we behold Him returning from the grave laden with the spoils of vanquished death. Indeed this is a mystery the explanation of which is perhaps hidden from even the celestial powers. In speaking of it therefore Origen is careful to state that he is not dogmatising, but only surmising.

A true-hearted Christian, Origen loyally accepts this fundamental doctrine of the gospel; he is deeply touched with the love of the Saviour who "abased Himself . . . in order to benefit our race." Viewed in itself, moreover, and apart from his system, his teaching upon the Incarnation takes rank with his best work. In this connection he may even be said to have rendered special service, for never until he did so, through an able analysis of its constituent parts, had the completeness of the *human* nature of the Redeemer been adequately set forth. But obviously the dogma of the Incarnation does not fit well into his speculative system, one of the root principles of which is the immutability of the divine life. Upon such a presupposition the Word could neither suffer nor die. Besides as pure spirit He could not unite Himself directly with sin - tainted corporeal nature. These apparent contradictions Origen tries to solve by means of his ingenious doctrine of the intermediary human soul of Jesus. It was with this soul, which was alike capable of assuming a body and of receiving God, that the Word united Himself: His union with the body existed only in so far as it was mediated through the soul. In thus indicating the metaphysical basis of this redemptive union with the Word, Origen makes it clear that the soul chosen for this honour was one that had never fallen away from God or ceased to live in closest fellowship with the Word. Not that the soul of Jesus was in any respect different from all other human souls; but in the exercise of its freedom it elected to love righteousness, and that with such ardour as to destroy all susceptibility for change. It was thus raised beyond the possibility of sin; from being a fact its sinlessness became a necessity. The Logos, however, did not so dwell in the soul and body of Christ as to preclude his operation on other receptive souls according to their merit; on the contrary, His action continued to be as widespread as before. But in no case was the union so close as in that of Jesus. The various functions and attributes of the Word made flesh are presented by Origen as a flight of steps, so to speak, which the Christian ascends as his knowledge increases. But here too the ideal ethical union is that between the Word and the human soul of Jesus. Through the immensity of its love the latter was so closely joined to God as to be of one spirit with Him. Using an illustration of epoch-making importance in the history of dogma, Origen compares the union of the two to a mass of redhot iron. The soul lies perpetually in the Word, the humanity in the divinity, as iron in the fire. As the metal is capable of cold and heat, so is the soul capable of deification; the soul of Christ is completely transfused with the divine fire; "in all that it does, feels, and understands," it is God, and that immutably. Accordingly, in Scripture the human nature is frequently spoken of in terms of the divine, and *vice versâ*. Real and intimate as this union is, however, it does not amount to actual intermingling of the soul and the Word; rather does the former cleave inseparably to the latter by a constant exercise of will.

Although the Alexandrian theologians rejected Docetism in its grosser forms, there is nevertheless a certain Docetic tinge about their views regarding the Lord's body. Clement especially comes very near to divesting it of all reality. According to him the body of Jesus, being sustained by a divine power, required no food. It was also impervious to pain. His doctrine of the human soul of Christ enabled Origen to ascribe to it the sensations incidental to bodily existence, and to maintain the impassibility of the Logos. Jesus really hungered and thirsted, was tired and slept, experienced sorrow and suffering; but these sensations were confined to the soul and the body, which were both truly human. Yet through its intimate union with the divine the body of Jesus had a special character of its own. Not only was it pure and undefiled, as the offspring of a virgin conceived by the Holy Ghost; through the will of the Logos acting upon matter, which is essentially mobile, it also possessed the property of assuming the particular form most calculated to impress the beholder. That Jesus appeared thus in different forms to different persons, according to the measure of their ability to receive Him, is shown by the exclusion from the Mount of Transfiguration of all His apostles except the three who were alone fit to behold His glorification. He had one aspect to the sick, another to the strong who followed Him up the mountain slope where He taught them the Beatitudes. To some He was without form or comeliness, but for others the divine beauty shone through the material frame. At Gethsemane it needed the traitor's kiss to disclose Him to the insusceptible crowd. It is thus evident that Origen's view of matter as a changing substance qualifies to some extent his admission of the reality of Christ's body. On this account it has even been said that "the incarnation, as he represents it, is more nearly allied to the religion of India than to that of the apostles."[1]

It was further held by Origen that during Christ's earthly life there took place a gradual glorification of the soul by the Logos, and of the body by the soul, so that from this standpoint also the body of Jesus had no stereotyped form even prior to the resurrection. After that event, which was a reality and no mere appearance, it was a uniformly glorified body, and became more and more glorified until it reached the point of complete volatilisation. This explains why he showed Himself alive after His passion only to the disciples; there was no longer about Him anything which the unenlightened could see.[2] Transformed at length into pure spirit, and received into the Godhead, He is no longer man, but is identical with the Word.

In building up his theory of the incarnation Origen

[1] Pressensé, *The Early Years of Christianity*, iii. p. 327.
[2] *Contra Celsum*, ii. 64.

makes use of material gathered from sundry sources. Indeed, with the single exception of "modalism," it is hardly too much to say that "all conceivable heresies are here touched upon, but guarded by cautions."[1] Apart from the Docetic element already alluded to, perhaps the most notable blemishes in Origen's theory are its vacillation between a personal and an impersonal Logos, its virtual subversion of the reality of the union of the Word with humanity (seeing that according to his own system the perfect soul of Jesus cannot be a human soul at all), its semi-dualistic conception of the Redeemer's person, and its suggestion that human nature is but a temporary garb, and not destined for eternal glorification. On the other hand, the great merit of Origen's conception is that within the framework of a scientific Christology an ample place is found for the humanity alongside of a full recognition of the divine nature and personality of the Word. Thus at length the human nature came to its rights, and the idea of the *incarnation* was really accepted.

Origen was the first to use the term God-Man. In striking out this bold expression he sought to indicate the value of Christ's person, not only as the revelation in bodily form of the fulness of the Godhead, but also as showing the possibility of the human spirit becoming wholly divine. In the incarnation of the Logos we see the restoration of the original unity between the divine and the human, and the earnest of the re-deification of the entire spiritual world. He did not, like the Latin theologians, propound a doctrine of two natures, but set himself to show that the man Christ Jesus became

[1] Harnack, *Outlines of the History of Dogma*, p. 184.

gradually one in will and in feeling with the Deity, and is in this respect a model for the perfect Christian to whom alone His person can be known. The tendency of his speculation, however, was to obscure the reality of the Redeemer's person. By representing Him as all that Christians can conceive Him to have been, Origen virtually reduces Christ to the symbol of a many-sided redemption. For the advanced Christian His humanity together with its history has no real significance. What the true Gnostic finds in Him is the revelation of the divine Reason. The only important consideration for him is that whereas, hitherto, the Logos had dwelt only very partially in mankind, his indwelling in Jesus inaugurates his more complete indwelling in men. He is not concerned with Christological problems. Questions regarding the divinity or humanity of Christ are only for imperfect Christians, who, however, are entitled to look to the perfect for their solution, and for the defending of the same against error, whether Docetic or Ebionitic.

iii. *The Sacrifice of Christ*

In Origen's view redemption is in no sense an exaltation of the created spirit to a higher position than that which it originally occupied; rather is it essentially a restoration to that position of perfect life in God which the spirits in the exercise of freedom deliberately abandoned. The redeemed are those who, purified from every stain of sin, find once more in God their all in all. It is through Christ that this consummation is reached. In Him the unity of God and the created spirits, which had been broken by the rebellion

186 ORIGEN AND GREEK THEOLOGY

of the latter, is again actually established; and He is thus the rallying point for the re-elevation of the entire spiritual world to the divine.

No one can read Origen without being struck with the vastness of the atmosphere. The wide sweep of his imagination, his speculative boldness, and his noble spirituality are in evidence almost on every page. It was a natural result of his view of the solidarity of all things that he should have regarded the death of Christ as a sacrifice for the whole world. Its beneficial effects are not limited to men; they extend to angels as well. After His ascension He became to the angels an angel, as He had become a man to men, and so is made all things to all. His blood, shed on Calvary for men, has been mystically sprinkled upon the heavenly altar for the redemption of celestial beings, if not for sin, yet in order to an increase of their blessedness. Christ was thus a double victim, by the blood of whose cross the Father has reconciled all things unto Himself, whether they be things in earth or things in heaven. The effect of the Saviour's offering of love extends to the utmost reach of the disturbance that has marred God's plan of creation. Even in Hades, whither His soul descended whilst His body lay in the tomb, His salvation was imparted to the spirits that were willing to receive Him. So true is it that "in the name of Jesus every knee shall bow, of things in heaven, and things in earth, and *things under the earth.*"

Origen was the first among the early Fathers to elaborate a theory of the Atonement. In doing so he made use not of the Scriptures only, but also of such current popular conceptions as appeared to him ethically

REDEMPTION AND RESTORATION 187

valuable. Among those, one of the most widespread was that which viewed the death of Christ as a ransom paid to the devil, who held us in bondage. Through sin we sold ourselves to him, the coin he paid for us being that of murder, adultery, and theft. Christ's death was necessary to redeem us from this slavery. With this view Origen linked on the Gnostic notion, (founded, doubtless, upon the ancient principle that sincerity towards an enemy is not obligatory), that the devil allowed himself to be duped. God offered to him the human soul of Christ in exchange for the souls of men. This the devil himself greatly desired, considering that with Jesus in his power he could make an easy prey of the whole human race. Through the Lord's betrayers and murderers he took possession of the soul of Jesus, as he had erstwhile done of Job's substance. But the torments caused him by that sinless soul were so intolerable to him that he could not retain his hold upon it. Jesus has thus vanquished death and him that had the power of it. Not only so; His victory is also the emancipation of all who believe on Him. The true King dethroned the usurper even where he had set up his dominion; He went down into the realm of death to set the prisoners free. Thus, then, is Christ our ransom. The God who became man, the divine high priest within the Redeemer, paid the price of our redemption from the sovereignty of Satan; and the offering which He laid upon the altar was that of His human soul. The body, as essentially unreal, could have no share in the atonement, and His spirit the Saviour had already committed to the Father.

Origen further regards the death of Christ as an expiation offered to God. Christ has reconciled us to the Father by suffering the punishment of death to which our guilt had rendered us liable. Although Origen did not develop the conception of the vicarious character of Christ's sacrifice, as was subsequently done by Anselm, he undoubtedly took this view of it. So much is implied even in his constant use of the epithet "our Saviour"; but we find this standpoint definitely adopted in his writings, which represent Christ as having put on, so to speak, our filthy garments, and drunk the cup of suffering that we might be spared its bitterness, while God has "willed the intervention of a propitiator, that those might be justified by faith in Him who could not be justified by their own works." It was divinely decreed that salvation should rest upon sacrifice, that the power of sin should yield only to the power of crucified love. In Origen's view punishment is never "identified with vengeance, but is always connected with the amendment of the sinner." There is no such thing as divine wrath. When through the dominion of sin chastisement no longer availed to make men better, then in His love the Father sent the Son, who, through His self-sacrificing death, destroyed the power of sin, and won for us remission from punishment. Christ's sacrifice is thus a satisfaction not to God's penal justice, but to His loving will.

By His death upon the cross and His glorious resurrection Christ has also, according to Origen, triumphed over the demons and freed us from their dominion. Their weakness stands out in sharp relief against the bright background of the holiness revealed in the Redeemer's sufferings. It is this holiness that gives to these sufferings their power. In virtue of it the demons are repulsed, and we are enabled to enter upon the new life of those "risen with Christ." If His death has overcome all hostile powers of evil, it is no less efficacious in subduing sin in believers themselves. But only those who in penitence and faith yield themselves wholly to Him can experience the sanctifying power which goes forth from Him, and which consumes sin in everyone who receives it, as fire consumes the flesh of the sacrificial victim. It is through His death, which was in every way indispensable to the world's redemption, that this divine power of salvation has come to full realisation. Freed thereby from every corporeal and local limitation, He places His divine love at the service of all, and by the breath of His mouth withers up evil. In the martyrdom of the saints there is a virtual continuation of the crucifixion. As a true priest offering the sacrifice of himself, the martyr too, in his own measure, conquers evil. All innocent blood diminishes the empire of evil, its efficacy in this direction depending upon the value of him who surrenders his life.

While Origen does not, like the Gnostics, deny the historical character of Christ's redemptive work, nor, like Clement, virtually ignore its objective character; while, on the contrary, he maintains that for less advanced Christians it is quite essential, he yet holds that this aspect of the truth is not the highest. Owing to the diversity of the spirits, particularly of men, the redeeming work of the Word is not confined to one stereotyped form. While its material aspect as a visible redemption from the powers of evil appeals most strongly to those of weaker capacity, there are others to whom the work of Jesus is primarily one of enlightenment. In communicating to them fulness of knowledge He also makes them sharers of His own life. Through the help of the Divine Teacher they are restored to fellowship with God and attain to deification. This is the goal for all, and the object of Christianity in all its stages; but the true Gnostic reaches it not through faith in the crucified, but through knowledge and love. In this way he rises above the historical Christ, and lays hold of the very essence of the Son revealed through His teaching in the eternal gospel. The Christ of the perfect is not the Christ of faith, but the Christ who dwells in us; not the Christ of history, but the Christ of experience. In thus maintaining the objective reality of Christ's sacrifice, while yet relegating it to a subordinate position, Origen has recourse to what Harnack calls his "masterly art of reconciling contradictions," in this case the respective views of the orthodox Christians and of the Gnostics. But the clear-cut manner in which he separates the divine and human elements in the person of Jesus, to the destruction of its unity, constitutes the chief blot upon his theory.

iv. *The Soul's Return to God*

If, by His conquest of sin and Satan, Christ has rendered our salvation possible, there must still be on our part an appropriation of it. The human will must co-operate with the divine grace. Christ's work leaves scope for our freedom and our faith. No doubt "in good things the human will is of itself weak to accomplish any good, for it is by divine help that it is brought to perfection in everything,"[1] yet it is equally

---
[1] *De Princ.* iii. 2. 2.

REDEMPTION AND RESTORATION 191

true that "God wishes us to be saved by means of ourselves." It is only when we have freely chosen the good part that grace comes to our aid. The measure of its bestowal is regulated by our spiritual progress. As the soul ascends by successive stages to the divine, it is gradually and proportionately endowed with grace.

In the soul's return to God the starting-point is repentance, which must be earnest, and repeated with every new transgression. Like John the Baptist, it is the Lord's forerunner, preparing His way in the soul. Even a good man will stumble, but he does not, like the wicked, abide in his sin; rising up again, he turns to the Lord with bitter tears and fasting, and so escapes like a bird from the snare of the fowler. In the absence of repentance Christ's redemptive work is rendered nugatory, but it will avail us even after grievous post-baptismal sin if we abandon it in true penitence. As punishment is proportioned to transgression, so is forgiveness to repentance; a partial repentance means only a partial salvation. True repentance finds vent in confession, not only to the Lord, but to such Christian brethren as are wise spiritual physicians, and especially to "a priest of the Lord," by whose instruction and warnings the sinner may be helped to overcome his sin. Christ has been expressly commissioned in order that the (evil) thoughts of many hearts may be revealed, and that through his atoning death they may be destroyed. If we thus acknowledge our sin now, the Lord will heal us; but if we fail in this way to anticipate our accuser, we must, in that day when all secrets shall be disclosed, share his fate in hell. The genuine penitent is also careful to reform his life. Apart from such amendment, repentance is vain and conversion unreal.

No less necessary in order to our spiritual recovery is faith, or the reception into the heart of that which is believed. For faith is not mere assent, but a heart-fellowship with God which expresses itself in corresponding works of righteousness. It is our own act, although for all increase of faith we are dependent upon divine aid. Faith is the essential prerequisite of true knowledge; to know Christ we must believe on Him. In seeking Him we must aim at no partial appropriation of His grace and truth. It is towards the whole Christ " in His indivisible and higher nature " that our desire must be directed. Yet we may and do partake of Him in different degrees. The majority know Christ only according to the flesh, *i.e.* as crucified; and while even so they occupy a higher position than the idolater or star-worshipper, or heathen philosopher, they are yet but the slaves of the Lord, who must rise by successive stages to be disciples, little children, children, brothers of Jesus, and sons of God. Christ is thus formed in us only gradually, and dwells in every soul in proportion to its receptivity.[1] Our knowledge is a growing quantity. Beginning with the religious apprehension of things visible, it rises to that of things invisible. From the vision of the crucified, the mind passes to the contemplation of the glorified, Redeemer, and grasps, so far as in it lies, the divine essence itself.

---

[1] If Origen was a speculative latitudinarian, he was also a sincerely pious mystic—a forerunner of Bernard of Clairvaux and the unknown author of the *De imitatione Christi*, of Tauler and Behmen, of Fénélon and Madame de Guyon.

REDEMPTION AND RESTORATION 193

This result, however, is not reached through knowledge alone, apart from love. The true knowledge is not of a cold and purely intellectual nature; it is essentially love, and its fruit is holiness. Man's God is what he superlatively loves. The cooling of the spirits in their devotion to God was their fall, for it meant that they turned with zest to the inferior. Man is so constituted that he must love, whether the object of his affection be the truly or only apparently good; and where he chooses wrongly, and becomes addicted to any form of idolatry, God recalls him through loving chastisement to the right path. The lever that raises us is the divine power in Christ; and when we have by this means ascended from the depths of sin and worldliness to the heights of holiness, we once more love God in Christ with all our heart and soul. This love also manifests itself as obedience; it inspires us to leave all and follow Him. In doing so we become spiritually regenerate. The work of Christ throws open to us the path of regeneration; but, as conceived by Origen, this is not a definite renewal of the inward nature. It is merely a process, which is lifelong; and, owing to our constant liability to deteriorate, it may be tortuous. Of regeneration in the sense of a new birth or radical change of heart, accompanied by Christ's royal rescript sealing our pardon and opening for us the heavenly sanctuary, Origen's theological system knows nothing. This means that no one can make sure of heaven. But thus to take away the element of assurance is to emasculate religion by depriving men of the peculiar rest and enjoyment which the doctrine of forgiveness is fitted to afford. While, however, in this way the

very marrow of evangelical doctrine may be said to
be alien to Origen's system of thought, he is not
careful always to wear the strait waistcoat. Not
only does he style baptism the bath of regeneration:
again and again, in setting forth the love of God the
Father, and the blessings of adoption and sonship
"first given in the new covenant," his words reflect
in no inadequate degree the true message and spirit of
the gospel.

In its progress Godward, then, the soul rises step
by step, and advances from one stage of recovery to
another. Beginning with faith in the crucified Redeemer and the acceptance of Holy Scripture in its
literal sense, our knowledge of the truth is deepened
and widened through the enlightening influence of the
Spirit, until its sanctifying power cleanses us from sin
and elevates us once more to the level of the heavenly.
Faith becomes a higher knowledge which reaches its
consummation in the direct spiritual vision of truth.
Enlightenment by the Spirit is bestowed concurrently
with, and in proportion to, the sanctification of the
heart, and as the result of this twofold spiritual process the redemption brought by Christ is realised in
us. In other words, this is the path along which
humanity can reach its destined goal of deification.

Although he confidently contrasts the Christian with
the heathen, Origen admits that owing to the inborn
tendency to sin as well as the constraint of evil habits,
there is in every case much required in order to complete sanctification. But the Spirit of God can effect
this in the face of all obstacles. Where there is the
willing heart, and no lack of spiritual exercise, there
will be progress in holiness. What is evil in us will

be cast out; what is hostile to our spiritual life will be overcome. The Saviour waits to wash hands, and feet, and head, until we be entirely purged from sin. Perfect sinlessness, however, is not always effected wherever Christianity is embraced; indeed, this result is attained by but few professing Christians, and apart from the acceptance of Christian doctrine it cannot be attained at all.

In Origen's system Christian ethics is based on Christ as "the substance of the virtues." The moral quality of an action is determined by its ultimate relation to Him. Those who profess to be His disciples, and yet let the cares of this life or the deceitfulness of riches crush him out of their minds, are wreathing his brow afresh with the crown of thorns. It is not slavish obedience to the outward letter of the law, but the free obedience of the spirit proceeding from love, that constitutes true holiness. It is in the heart that good and evil are really accomplished, and to the pure in conscience all things are pure. Under the Christian dispensation the only fasting of real value is fasting from sin, and the only consecrated altar is that of the believing heart. Neither is there any such distinction of days as in Judaism, for all days alike are days of the Lord. Lofty as is the spiritual character of this teaching, Origen takes a somewhat narrow view of certain points connected with individual and social ethics. This was no doubt due to the fact that in his time the State was based not upon Christian but upon pagan ideas. He was thus constrained to teach that Christians may serve kings by praying for them, but must not bear arms or "slay men." They must even decline public office in the interests of a diviner service

ORIGEN AND GREEK THEOLOGY

in the Church of God.[1] "Things strangled" are not fit food for a Christian; an oath of any sort is not for him. To contract a second marriage is highly censurable; to attend a theatre or a circus is to commit sin. Most astonishing of all is it to find Origen following Plato in maintaining the necessity of "the medicinal lie" because of its corrective effect upon the patient. In spite of these blemishes, however, his ethical standpoint must be pronounced singularly exalted and pure.

In his idea of the Church Origen dissociates himself from the view accepted in the West since Cyprian's time, that it consists of all who are baptized. He lays stress upon the distinction between the Church visible and invisible, and in this particular he represents a distinct advance upon the view of his predecessor Clement also. For Origen the Church is the community of the hóly, the one family of the saints in heaven and upon earth, the great company whose ruling impulse is the will of God. It is the Lord's bride, His house, His temple, His body, and is without spot or wrinkle. Its members are confined to those who truly believe, and outside of it there is no salvation. In the visible Church, despite the utmost effort to secure purity, there will always be some tares among the wheat. Open sinners are to be cast out of the congregation, as are also even lesser offenders whom repeated warnings fail to affect. As Origen, however, had reason to know, there may be such a thing as unjust excommunication on the part of "envious and self-seeking bishops," but in this case there is no exclusion from the kingdom of heaven, just

[1] *Contra Celsum*, viii. 73-75.

REDEMPTION AND RESTORATION

as, on the contrary, such exclusion does take place in the case of the sinner against whom no ecclesiastical sentence has been pronounced. Those who are wrongly cast out of the Church must bow to the unjust decree, and await the unerring judgment of the future.

The unity of the Church is spiritual, and exists under a variety of outward organisation. Many churches go to form the Church visible, which in Origen's view, as in Clement's, is the reflex of the heavenly Zion. Noteworthy and interesting in this connection is his attitude towards the Roman See. While not animated by the hierarchical spirit of the West, and while maintaining that every Christian who adopts Peter's confession shares in the privilege conveyed in the Saviour's words, " Whatsoever thou shalt bind on earth, shall be bound in heaven; and whatsoever thou shalt loose on earth, shall be loosed in heaven," he nevertheless felt a genuine veneration for the antiquity of the Church of Rome, and was ready in a limited sense to admit its primacy. If the Lord did not found the Church upon Peter to the exclusion of the rest of the apostles, He nevertheless by His words distinguished him above them all. Origen did not regard this distinction as the hereditary possession of Peter's successors at Rome, but at the same time he looked upon "the eternal city" as the most ancient and honourable seat of the Christian faith. With great zest he made a pilgrimage to it in order that he might witness and hear for himself the worship and doctrine of what had already become the leading Church in Christendom, and perhaps his keenest pang in connection with his condemnation by Demetrius was caused by the knowledge that it was acquiesced in by the Italian See.[1]

According to Origen every Christian is a priest in virtue of the spiritual sacrifice which he offers. Through almsgiving, charity, self-mortification, martyrdom, we share in the sacrifice of Christ, and so in His priesthood. But it is only in this moral and figurative sense that any layman can be called a priest. Origen did not allow the treatment meted out to himself to lead him to belittle the office of the ministry. He magnifies it more than Clement does, and shows a distinct leaning towards a restricted use of the priestly name. Those who bear it, however, must have a character in keeping with it. In short, "his doctrine of clerical authority is not unlike that of Wiclif. The power to bind and loose depends upon the spiritual worthiness of him who wields it."[2] No fixed conclusion had been arrived at regarding the extent of this power. A distinction was generally made between mortal and venial sins, but it remained a question whether mortal sins such as murder or idolatry, committed after baptism, could be forgiven on earth. In some cases a single absolution was allowed, but already in Origen's day the Church of Rome regarded no sin as unpardonable if duly repented of. His own view on the subject appears to have undergone a change. In his earlier writings he uncompromisingly affirms that no death-sin can be forgiven by the Church. Not that in such a case the sinner is hopelessly lost; God may forgive him in some

---

[1] At all events, if we may trust Eusebius, he wrote to Pope Fabian in vindication of his orthodoxy, and requesting to be readmitted to fellowship. See above, p. 53.

[2] Bigg, *Christian Platonists*, p. 215.

future æon. Latterly, however, he represents the most heinous sins as the subjects of priestly absolution, and reserves the excommunication of the Church for the obdurately impenitent.

Origen was no sacramentarian. He attached but little importance to the visible. In his view the sacraments have only a symbolic value, and belong to the category of veiled forms and images by which the truth can be communicated to the "common man." For the latter, indeed, they are essential, while even to the advanced Christian they are of some consequence.

Baptism with water is merely the symbol of the soul's purification. It does not effect this; it only represents it. The purification itself is antecedent to baptism; we must be dead to sin before we can through baptism be buried with Christ. A certain impurity, moral as well as physical, attaches to birth, but in baptism we have the visible counterpart to this. It is thus a second birth, by means of which the stains of the first are erased. Not that this result is due to the water, for baptism is essentially a birth from above through the Holy Ghost. Where it is not such, it has no purifying power. Those who seek baptism without laying aside their sins do not thereby obtain pardon. While the Saviour baptizes the holy with the Spirit, He relegates the sinful to the fire. The same outward ceremony may thus be fraught with salvation or with condemnation. To receive baptism unto salvation is far from easy. There is no magical or necessary connection between baptism with water and the reception of the Holy Spirit. But where it is properly received, and the Spirit communicated, the symbolic character of baptism is transcended, so to speak, and it becomes, through the power of the invocation of the Trinity, "the beginning and source of divine gifts of grace," operating the forgiveness of all former sins, and filling the heart with the Holy Spirit. The pardon of post-baptismal sins must be procured by ourselves through repentance, charity, constant striving after what is good, and should it so please God, through the bloody baptism of a martyr's death. In accordance with apostolic tradition, the Church administers baptism even to infants in recognition of the fact that in every human being are real stains of sin which require to be washed away by water and the Spirit.

Quite in keeping with this view of baptism is Origen's doctrine of the Lord's Supper. In no case does he attach value to the external and the material, and accordingly it is not the sign but the thing signified that has importance for him. Not that the water in baptism or the bread and wine in the Supper are worthless; they do confer something, but only in the same way as the external in the life of Christ whose miracles were fraught with temporal advantage to those on whom they were wrought, while yet as helps to faith their true significance was a spiritual one. With the sacrifice of the Lamb of God for the sin of the world, other sacrifices have ceased. In the Eucharist, therefore, there is no material sacrifice, no bloodless repetition of the sin-offering on the Cross, the only sacrifice associated with it being that of the Christian himself; and no material presence of Christ, who is, however, really and spiritually, and really just because spiritually, present. When the Saviour speaks of His body and blood, He does so in a spiritual sense. These terms refer to His teaching. When we receive them we are said to eat His flesh and drink His blood. "For it was not that visible bread which He held in His hands that God the Word called His body, but the word as a symbol whereof that bread was to be broken. Nor was it that visible cup that He called His blood, but the word as a symbol whereof that wine was to be poured out."[1] The body and blood of Christ can only be that word which nourishes and delights our souls. "Inasmuch as He is perfectly pure, His whole flesh is food; and because His every act is holy and His every word true, His whole blood is drink. For by the flesh and blood of His word, as if by pure food and drink, the whole human race is refreshed."[2] Of this true bread from heaven the desert-manna was the type, and the Lord's Supper is the appointed memorial. In this commemorative feast we are re-endowed with the grace of God, not, of course, through the mere external act of communicating, but through the spiritual enjoyment of the mystic bread. We renew the memory of Christ's body and blood by exercising trust in Him and by expressing our confidence in prayer. Although Romanists have claimed his support, there is no ground for the opinion that Origen held the doctrine of transubstantiation in any form. No change takes place in the elements used; they do not "become" the body and blood of Christ. He does, however, refer to the idea of a bodily presence in the Supper as distinctive of the elementary Christian who is in bondage to the letter, so that already in his time this strange superstition had apparently arisen. Origen calls attention to the fact that Christ did not say, "This is the bread of the New Testament," as He said of the cup, "This is

[1] *In Matt.*, Series 85.   [2] *In Lev.*, Hom. vii. 5.

My blood of the New Testament," because the bread is the word of righteousness or of the Old Testament, while the wine is the word of the knowledge of Christ. Old Testament righteousness cannot confer blessedness apart from faith in His passion. It is written, "Blessed is he that shall eat bread in the kingdom of God." There, however, there will be no eating and drinking of a corporeal nature, but a partaking of that angelic food of which our Lord speaks when He says, "My meat is to do the will of Him that sent Me." This is meat indeed and drink indeed. The elements used in the sacrament are merely symbols to assist our weakness. The bread in itself is and remains corruptible. It can do us no good apart from a living faith, a pure heart, and an upright conscience. It is not leaving off to eat of the consecrated bread that works us harm, but the wickedness that leads to such omission; nor does the observance of the sacrament do us good if we be lacking in regard to a virtuous life. In listening to Christ's words we drink His blood as truly as we do in the Supper; the only difference is the introduction in the latter case of the symbolical. What is of service to those who observe it not unworthily is not the material bread, but the prayer of faith which has been uttered over it; and what injures those who partake of it unworthily is not the bread itself, but the power of the truth in the words bound up with it.

v. *The Last Things*

Origen dissociates himself entirely from those who paint the future in colours of sensuous attractiveness, and look to it for a repetition on a luxurious scale of such bodily pleasures as may be tasted in this life. He rejects the notion that the earthly Jerusalem will be rebuilt, and that the favoured inhabitants will live on the wealth of other countries, whose sons shall minister to their enjoyment. To cherish such mistaken ideas is to interpret the Scriptures "in a sort of Jewish sense," and to show an incapacity to understand metaphor. It is absurd to suppose that, when the Saviour makes a promise to the disciples concerning the joy of drinking wine with them in His Father's kingdom, or asserts the blessedness of those who hunger and thirst, He intends His words to be applied in a grossly literal sense. This would be to extract from them a meaning unworthy of the divine promises. The food of the saints will be the bread of life, and their drink the cup of divine wisdom. So far from being of a sensuous character, the future glory of God's kingdom will be such as it hath not entered into the heart of man to conceive.

When a soul departs this life, the evil spirits endeavour to make a prey of it. In this they are successful, should it reflect their own avarice, envy, and other bad qualities; but those souls that have followed Christ are delivered from their power. Only a few, such as the saints and martyrs, are fit to enter at once on the direct vision of God; the vast majority require to undergo a process of purification before they can reach the highest blessedness. At death the good are borne by angels to a great lofty island situated somewhere upon this earth.[1] This earthly paradise is the first

[1] Cf. Dante—
>"Me God's angel took,
>Whilst he of hell exclaimed: O thou from heaven!
>Say wherefore hast thou robbed me?"
>
>   (*Purgatory*, v. 101-103.)

204 ORIGEN AND GREEK THEOLOGY

place of trial, and witnesses the initiatory stage of purification from those heaver offences which could not be visited with due chastisement in this life. Origen describes it as "a school of souls," in which they are taught by angels the meaning of what they saw on earth, and also receive some insight as to the course of future events. Here, too, they are instructed regarding the nature of soul and spirit, as well as the full significance of Holy Scripture. From this lower paradise souls ascend to a higher, in order to undergo still further purification. This ascent does not take place with uniform speed; some rise more slowly than others. But each as he mounts upwards through the spheres to the kingdom of heaven sees what is done in these regions of the air, and discovers why things are so done. At last, having passed through all gradations, and being purged from every defilement, the soul rises in the pure ether to God, and passes into the heavens as a follower of Him who has said, "I will that where I am there ye may be also." In this way many may reach the kingdom of God before the final consummation of the world.

The souls of the wicked are incapable of such an ascent, and remain behind in Hades, the place of punishment. Indeed, till Christ descended and released them, even the souls of the patriarchs and the prophets could not pass the fiery sword that barred the way to paradise. Those who died before His advent had to wait for Him in Hades.[1] Now, however, though all

[1] Cf. Dante's lines—

> "I was new to that estate,
> When I beheld a puissant one arrive
> Amongst us, with victorious trophy crown'd.
> He forth the shade of our first parent drew,

must still pass through the fire, the righteous can do so unscorched, because in them there is nothing on which it can seize.[1] But the godless are "tormented in this flame," which the Lord has kindled to consume evil; they are, that is to say, the prisoners of remorse. For the flames of Hades are not material; they are the tortures of an accusing conscience, a vivid recollection of sin, and the agony caused by the separation of soul and spirit. But for the guilty this is punishment enough. Indeed we can no more conceive the misery of the condemned than we can imagine what God has prepared for them that love Him. There is, however, a limit to their punishment; it is not really eternal, though so called. Still, it may last for ages, for the uttermost farthing must be paid. But sin that is unpardoned in this, may be pardoned in some future æon. Punishment, too, has always been a purifying power; its sole purpose is to purify; and the time must come when the worst may escape from the penal fire. Every soul must ultimately pass out of purgatory, and every world-epoch must end in the rescue and deification of all spirits in order to make way for a new one. "The end of the world, and the final con-

> Abel his child, and Noah righteous man,
> Of Moses lawgiver for faith approv'd,
> Of patriarch Abraham, and David king,
> Israel with his sire and with his sons,
> Nor without Rachel whom so hard he won,
> And others many more, whom he to bliss
> Exalted."—(*Inferno*, iv. 49-59.)

[1] So, too, Dante :—

> "I am so framed by God, thanks to His grace!
> That any sufferance of your misery
> Touches me not, nor flame of that fierce fire
> Assails me."—(*Inferno*, ii. 90-93.)

summation, will take place when every one shall be subjected to punishment for his sins; a time which God alone knows, when He will bestow on each what he deserves. We think, indeed, that the goodness of God, through His Christ, may recall all His creatures to one end, even His enemies being conquered and subdued." Thus did Origen cling to the larger hope, although He regarded this as an esoteric doctrine; "for the multitude it is sufficient to know that the sinner is punished."

Corresponding to this development of the destiny of the individual soul after death there is a general development of God's kingdom upon earth. The gospel gains increasing acceptance; the Jews are converted; and there is a reign of peace. So far, however, even under these circumstances, is sin from being destroyed, that there will be a final rally of all the powers of evil under Antichrist, in accordance with the prophecy of Daniel and the writings of St. Paul. After a period of war and famine, earthquakes and pestilence, during which some repent while others persist in wickedness, the end of the world shall come suddenly and unexpectedly, while men eat and drink, buy and sell, build and plant. The dissolution of the earth by fire, which only the more simple understand in the literal and material sense, is merely a metaphorical way of delineating those inward heart-throes by which evil is erased from the souls of the penitent. There will, however, be a new heaven and a new earth, in so far as "the fashion of this world passeth away." But this does not involve the destruction of the material substance of the universe; it implies only a change of quality.

At the close of the present æon Christ will return to judge the world in righteousness. This event is spoken of in Scripture after the analogy of a human tribunal in order to give it vividness, but in fact there will be no outwardly visible appearance of the Lord. His return is not material, but spiritual. The symbolic imagery used by the prophets in speaking of this subject is to be spiritually interpreted. Christ appears actually, in power and glory, revealing His true nature to all, to the wicked as well as to the righteous, yet not otherwise than He even now unfolds Himself to the eye of faith. Although this is the sense in which he understands the second coming, Origen is careful to explain that he does not reject "the second presence of the Son of God more simply understood." Not men alone, but all spirits must appear before Christ for judgment. To the demons are meted out the punishments reserved for them, and in the endurance of which their wickedness will be gradually purged. By this means the very devil himself will in the end be recovered to goodness. Even although, strictly speaking, he is not to be classed as a universalist, never certainly has universalism found more thoroughgoing expression than in the thought of Origen. In regard to the particular question of the salvation of Satan, it is curious and interesting to find an answering echo to the boldly optimistic creed of the great Alexandrian in the breast of our own Scottish poet Burns—

> "But, fare you weel, auld Nickie-ben!
> O wad ye tak a thought an' men'!
> Ye aiblins might—I dinna ken—
>   Still hae a stake:
> I'm wae to think upo' yon den
>   Ev'n for your sake!"[1]

---

[1] *Address to the Deil.*

The doctrine of the resurrection of the body Origen accepted as an integral part of the Church's creed, and even defended it in opposition to heretics. What made it possible for him to take up this position — that he had difficulties about the ecclesiastical doctrine is evident from *Contra Cels.* v. 14 ff.—was the language used by St. Paul regarding a spiritual body. This enabled him to get rid of his doubts, and to take refuge in certain characteristic refinements upon the apostle's words. In this way he was led to hold that at the resurrection we shall be clothed a second time with the body that we now inhabit. It will be the same, but with a difference. Owing to a change in its material substance, it will be spiritual, glorious, incorruptible. By the power and grace of the resurrection there will be educed from the animal body a spiritual body devoid of all material attributes, and even of members with sensuous functions, a body resplendent as the stars of heaven. This is possible, because in the substance of the body there is an indestructible germ which raises it up and restores it, as the germinative principle in the grain of wheat which dies in the ground restores the grain into a body having stalk and ear. The will of God who made it what it is can raise this present body of ours to the purity and splendour of a spiritual body "according as the condition of things requires, and the deserts of our rational nature shall demand."[1] The differences in the degree of glory among those who rise again are explained by the fact that the soul's new tenement is conditioned by its worth. In every case the general features will be preserved, and the body suited to its new environment.

[1] *De Princ.* ii. 10. 3 ; iii. 6. 4.

Origen holds strongly that "the end must be like the beginning," a perfect unity in God. As the result of the soul's progress through discipline, there will be effected a restoration exhibiting the perfect equilibrium of a perfect life. Law shall not clash with freedom, nor justice collide with love. But this great consummation, the complete return of the all to the original unity with God, lies still beyond the resurrection, which only brings it nearer. One by one the wholly sanctified reach their goal, no more to wander; but many must be still further instructed and purified before they can stand around God's throne. Towards this result, however, all things tend, and at length the end comes. Then all know the Father even as He is known by the Son. Evil is abolished by the conversion of the wicked, and that goal of happiness is reached in which God is said to be "all in all." Not that even then all are on a level. There are "many mansions," many degrees of blessedness. Through sin the soul may for ever be unfitted for gaining the loftiest heights, and from this standpoint, at any rate, Origen declares the eternity of punishment.

Origen looked with disfavour upon the primitive Christian eschatology, which connected blessedness with the second advent of Christ and the last judgment. For him the state of perfect felicity is reached immediately upon the severance of the believing soul from the mortal body. The brilliant attempt which he makes to convey an adequate idea of bliss, while yet eliminating all sensual delights, deserves to rank as one of the grandest efforts of genius. The notion of a purgatory or cleansing fire, based upon 1 Cor. iii. 13-15, is a legacy to the Church from the Alexandrians.

After Clement and Origen, however, the only one of the Greek Fathers who seems to have retained the idea was Gregory of Nyssa. It ultimately passed through Ambrose into the Western Church, where it soon became naturalised; and in the great poem of Dante it has received such graphic and striking expression as to secure for it a permanent place among the conceptions that have moulded and dominated theological thought. One of the least satisfactory features of the eschatology of Origen, and of the Greek theologians who followed him, is the extent to which it ignores the thought of the judgment and the responsibility before God of every individual soul. In primitive Christianity these were matters that were not allowed to slip into the background, and to cease to lay stress upon them is to reduce forgiveness to an empty name. Yet, whatever may have been the view taken by the general body of the people belonging to the Eastern Church, this was certainly the case as regards "scientific" theology. Not that the term judgment was no longer employed, but it was robbed of its real significance. In his conception of the consummation of being, it is unfortunate that Origen so frequently fails to distinguish between the close of the present world and the close of all things. Again and again the reader is confused by this mixing up of ideas belonging to two separate categories. A distinct delineation of perfect life in absolute repose is perhaps beyond the resources of human thought and language. Another criticism to which, ever since Jerome's day, this part of Origen's system has been exposed, is that the hope of final harmony is irreconcilable with the doctrine of free will. If in the future life the will is still entirely free, what security is there

REDEMPTION AND RESTORATION

that this "final restoration" will be final? The created spirit may fall again as it fell before, and under such conditions there may be a perpetual process of alternate falling and rising, which after the lapse of countless ages leaves the end as far off as ever. This objection may be logically sound, yet it is unfair to Origen, and misrepresents his meaning. Without in the slightest degree infringing upon the inalienable liberty of rational creatures, and granting that the soul is free to rebel as long as it chooses, we may yet surely with reason decline to infer from our observation of this short life that it will be eternally obdurate.

Such, then, in brief outline, is the system of Origen. It has been described by one modern writer as "sublime,"[1] and by another as "a precious repertory of profound thought."[2] Characterised by great boldness and originality, it certainly forms the high-water mark of Christian thought in that fresh and formative period. It was also calculated to exert a healing influence in view of the antagonisms then abroad. Origen was opposed alike to the unreasonable rejection of human knowledge so common in the Church of that age, and to the arbitrary use made of it by the Gnostics; and although he erred no doubt in not sufficiently sifting what he appropriated from Greek speculative philosophy, it is not to be forgotten that he writes in no hidebound spirit of dogmatism. Where divergent views are irreconcilable, the reader is invited to choose between them. If, moreover, his religious philosophy seeks to focus and present in complete form the scientific knowledge of his time, it makes no pretension

[1] Pressensé.   [2] Redepenning.

212 ORIGEN AND GREEK THEOLOGY

to be anything beyond an honest and reverent attempt to arrive at a truly spiritual conception of Christianity. He was a pioneer, and ought to be judged as such. Yet he was far more than a pioneer. "Orthodox theology of all creeds has never yet advanced beyond the circle first mapped out by his mind."[1] Within the sphere of Christian dogma he was the first, and he has been the only independent, builder. Even Augustine and the Reformers (Luther, Calvin, etc.), the only other typical builders in the history of dogma, never aimed at being anything more than rebuilders. Much of Origen's speculative thinking, which the Church was constrained to accept, has been indissolubly bound up with the simple faith itself, and the rule of faith has thus gradually assumed a more philosophic aspect. If the Church has outgrown many of his modes of doctrinal statement, his beautiful and ardent spirit will be a source of inspiration to her so long as the world endures.

[1] Harnack, *History of Dogma*, ii. p. 334.

CHAPTER IX

SUCCESSORS OF ORIGEN

IN one sense Origen had no successor. Nature is not so prolific in men of his moral and intellectual stature as to keep up an unbroken apostolical succession of this sort. Those choice spirits that tower like Alpine peaks above the general level of humanity appear only at intervals upon the stage of history. They are indeed "the world's epoch-makers," the uncrowned kings of learning, thought, and science. Origen is undoubtedly entitled to a place amongst these giant souls. What Carlyle says of Frederick the Great may with still more fitness be said of him, "his movements were polar." No one can study his life and writings without being impressed with the greatness of his personality and the versatility of his genius. His work in any single department of theological study would have brought him fame, but he excelled in all departments. He was the founder of scientific theology, the pioneer of a reverent criticism, the champion of free and unrestricted investigation, and a bold speculative thinker; but he was also at the same time a great Christian preacher, a believing expositor, a devotional writer, and an orthodox traditionalist. All parties drew material from his writings, and the champions of conflicting schools of thought claimed him with equal confidence for their side. This was perhaps partly due to the fact that "on many subjects the opinions of Origen resemble the moving statues of Dædalus, now here, now there; they are not to be fixed on a pedestal and identified by a name";[1] but, apart from the extent to which his inconsistencies may be explained by the distinction he made between exoteric and esoteric teaching, it is absurd to judge him by the rigid dogmatic standard of modern theology. Due allowance must be made for the fact that he lived in an age of freedom when as yet Christian belief was in a more or less fluid condition, and tradition was in the course of formation. Only when we regard him not in the light of later dogmatic opinion, but in that of one who furnished many stones for the future edifice of Christian thought, can we possibly do justice to Origen. Here suffice it to recognise that for long he was the dominating force in the theological world; that all subsequent theology has been largely shaped by him; and that even when every deduction has been made for his errors, he must still, as regards spirit and method, take rank as the ideal Christian theologian.

But if in respect of genius and influence Origen had no immediate successors, either at Alexandria or elsewhere, there were not wanting those upon whom to a certain extent his mantle had fallen, and who, as they were able, continued to propagate his principles. No fewer than seven teachers followed him in direct succession as presidents of the Catechetical School, namely, Heraclas, Dionysius, Pierius, Theognostus, Peter the Martyr, Didymus, and Rhodon. Although

[1] R. A. Vaughan, *Essays and Remains*, vol. i. p. 31.

SUCCESSORS OF ORIGEN 215

all of them were in sympathy with Origen's philosophy —this was true even of Peter the Martyr, who made certain corrections upon Origen's system where he considered its conclusions inconsistent with the rule of faith—the school seems to have made little headway after the disappearance of the great master himself. Indeed the tide, instead of flowing, began to ebb, and after the time of Theognostus its adherents were obliged to assume the defensive. Partly this was due to the rival attractions of Neoplatonism, which at the commencement of the fourth century became the prevailing philosophy in Christian as well as in pagan circles, and partly to the circumstance that the Church was wholly engrossed with debates upon one particular subject—that of the Trinity, and could not give a thought to the elaborate philosophy of Origenism.

It is evident that Origen's influence in Alexandria was not extinguished, or even diminished, by his condemnation at the hand of Demetrius. On the death of the latter, Heraclas, the friend and pupil of the exiled teacher, was chosen bishop. This was the reply of the Eastern Church to the unworthy treatment meted out to Origen, and a significant comment upon the exclusion of presbyters from the synod convened to pronounce sentence against him. Prior to his elevation to the leading Egyptian See, Heraclas had acted, first as colleague, then as successor, to Origen in the Catechetical School; and when the latter went into exile, it must have been some mitigation of his sorrow to reflect that the work he loved was in safe hands. Of the actual teaching of Heraclas, however, we possess no details. He died in A.D. 249.

When Heraclas became bishop, he was succeeded as

216 ORIGEN AND GREEK THEOLOGY

head of the training school by Dionysius (Alexandrinus), perhaps the most learned, and certainly not the least enthusiastic, of Origen's disciples. Distinctly inferior to him in speculative power, there is no evidence to show that he developed in any important respect the teaching of his master. He was raised to the bishopric. of Alexandria in the year 248, and died in 265. Without exceptional gifts as a professor of theology, he was undeniably a rare success in the episcopate. His ecclesiastical leadership was characterised by much wisdom, and even in his own time won for him the title of *the Great*. Calm and courageous, gentle and generous, firm and faithful, he possessed that peculiar combination of qualities which go to the making of an ideal Church ruler. No prominent ecclesiastic ever had less of the implacable, dictatorial, or official spirit. Amid the many controversies, doctrinal and ecclesiastical, in which he was called upon to take part, he bore himself with splendid moderation and unfailing brotherliness. While frankly contending for what he believed to be the right, he always favoured free discussion, and never was guilty of anything approaching to hierarchical assumption. It was by the path of free investigation that he himself had been convinced of the truth of the gospel; and to this principle he adhered alike through good report and bad, refusing to condemn what he had not read, even when less scrupulous persons represented to him that the perusal of so many heretical writings might seriously injure his own soul. He would have scorned to use against an opponent the convenient weapon of excommunication. So far from anathematising those who held millenarian views, he held a protracted conference with them, and expressed his love for Nepos their leader; and when writing to Novatus the Schismatic he was careful to call him "brother." His life, in short, is a notable illustration of the far-reaching influence of a conciliatory and self-denying spirit.

From fragments of a work written by Dionysius after the death of Nepos on the millenarian question, a work in which he argues against the genuineness of the Book of Revelation, it is clear that his ability as a critic was of no mean order, although in combating error he seems to have allowed his zeal sometimes to outrun his discretion, and so to have fallen into error himself. The same thing is true with regard to his contending against Sabellianism, which found favour with the bishops of Egypt: in his eagerness he uses language which amounts to a subordinationist denial of the unity of the three Persons in the Godhead. "The Son of God," he says, "is a creature born of God, and not identical with Him in nature. In substance He differs from the Father as does the husbandman from the vine, and the shipwright from his boat. Furthermore, as a creature the Son did not exist before His creation."[1] But when, in answer to a complaint addressed to him by the bishops of Libya, Dionysius of Rome issued a treatise in which he trenchantly exposed the erroneous expressions employed by the Alexandrian bishop, the latter, while endeavouring to explain the assertions to which exception had been taken, practically withdrew what he had so unadvisedly spoken. It is not quite clear what was his precise position with reference to the great dogmatic question of his age, but he appears to have occupied a

[1] Athanasius, *De Sententia Dionysii*, c. 4.

standpoint midway between the Unitarianism of Arius and the Trinitarianism of Athanasius.

The behaviour of Dionysius during the Decian persecution was singularly dignified, prudent, and brave. A troop of soldiers sent to seize him scoured the neighbourhood, leaving unsearched only his own house, where for four days he placidly awaited them. Having then shown himself out of doors he was arrested, only to be speedily liberated by a band of Christians whom he vainly besought to allow him to secure the martyr's crown. He knew nothing of the craven spirit displayed many centuries later by Cranmer. From the hidden fastnesses of the Libyan desert he controlled the affairs of his Church until the death of Decius. Driven again into exile under Valerian, because of his unflinching testimony to Christian truth, he became the herald of the gospel in various quarters. The accession of Gallienus in 260 reopened the way for the return of Dionysius to Alexandria, where his exertions during a time of pestilence exhausted the energies of an outworn frame and hastened his death. He remained true throughout to the spiritualism of Origen, his indebtedness to whom he was always proud to acknowledge; and when his beloved master was imprisoned, under the Decian persecution, he wrote to him a letter of consolation.

In the direction of the school of catechists Dionysius was followed by Pierius, an eloquent teacher, who was called "a second Origen." He led an ascetic life, and wrote a commentary on Hosea; but with the exception of a few fragments preserved by Photius we know nothing of his teaching. It was as a pupil of Pierius that Pamphilus imbibed his strong admiration for

SUCCESSORS OF ORIGEN

Origen's theology. Regarding the doctrine of Theognostus, his immediate successor, we are also comparatively ignorant. Photius criticises his views, but lauds his eloquence; while Athanasius speaks highly of him as a man of culture who was not satisfied with giving an exposition of dogma, but followed Origen's plan of suggesting questions for debate. His great dogmatic work (*Hypotyposes*), unhappily no longer extant, was not, however, like Origen's, written in sections, each dealing with the whole under reference to one ruling thought, but so as to form one connected and consecutive exposition. In adopting this method he anticipated all future workers in the same field. From some remaining fragments of his work it is clear that he adhered closely to Origen in his theological position. This appears particularly from his exposition of the sin against the Holy Ghost, which is founded on the view that as the sphere of the Spirit extended only to the perfect, the sin against the Holy Ghost, as the sin of the perfect, was unpardonable. Peter, the next president, was raised to the bishopric of Alexandria in recognition of his renown as an ascetic, but was cut off in the Decian persecution after three years' tenure of that office. He asserted the complete humanity of Christ, denied the pre-existence of the soul, and denounced the tenet of a premundane fall as a "precept of Greek philosophy which is foreign and alien to those who desire to live piously in Christ." But although distinctly opposed to Origen upon these points, it was his aim rather to correct than to repudiate the doctrines of the master. So far as they were in keeping with the rule of faith, he taught and upheld them.

Didymus, who also acted as catechist in Alexandria, was a prolific author in spite of his almost lifelong blindness, but few of his works are extant. Like his predecessors, he was strong in his admiration for Origen, but under the pressure of the influences of his time he was induced to tone down the doctrines of the *De Principiis*, especially those regarding the Trinity, until his theology was virtually brought into line with the prevailing orthodoxy, which was soon, by means of œcumenical councils, to gag the freedom of belief. Of Rhodon, the last of the superintendents mentioned in connection with the Catechetical School, nothing is known to us but the name.

In this connection there remains to be mentioned the great name of Athanasius. Born at Alexandria in 296, and educated doubtless at the Catechetical School, he became the most prominent Church leader of his time. In consideration of his services against Arianism, he was venerated as "the father of orthodoxy." His great talents and learning, his clear insight and his earnest spirit, his indomitable energy and strength of will, his humble faith and dauntless courage, formed a rare combination of qualities, and one by means of which he was fitted to play a most distinguished part in the history of the Christian Church. Although his gifts lay in the direction of ecclesiastical statesmanship rather than in that of speculative thought, his is essentially a Greek mind—subtle, flexible, and philosophical. In the line of Greek theologians he ranks next to Origen in importance, if not in direct chronological succession. None of those who lived in the intervening century have so indelibly left their mark upon the doctrinal standards of the Church as he has.

SUCCESSORS OF ORIGEN

Prior to the commencement of the Arian controversy in 319, Athanasius wrote two short apologetical treatises under the titles *Against the Gentiles* and *On the Incarnation of the Word*. In the former he denies the assertion of Greek polytheists, that intermediary deities are necessary to the government of the world, and maintains the divine immanence in creation; in the latter he argues that this principle lends confirmation to the fact of the incarnation, seeing that it is just as reasonable that God should dwell in a single man as that He should dwell in the world. Through the incarnation Christ as the God-Man becomes the medium by which God acts upon the universal life, and in His person the whole human race has been redeemed and raised even to the height of deification. "As when a mighty king entering some great city, although he occupies but one of its houses, positively confers great honour upon the whole city, and no enemy or robber any longer throws it into confusion by his assaults, but on account of the presence of the king in one of its houses, the city is rather thought worthy of being guarded with the greatest care; so also is it in the case of Him who is Lord over all. For when He came into our country and dwelt in the body of one like ourselves, thenceforth every plot of the enemy against mankind was defeated, and the corruption of death that formerly operated to destroy men lost its power."[1]

It was as archdeacon of Alexandria that Athanasius accompanied his bishop (Alexander) to the Council of Nicæa in 325. Although not a regular member, he seems to have been permitted to share in its discussions. He was strongly opposed to the teaching of Arius, who,

[1] *De Incar.* c. 9.

as a son of Antioch, and even more under the influence of Orientalism than of Hellenism, conceived of God as the absolutely transcendent, for whom no contact with the world or with man was possible. On such a view of Deity Arius had to deny the incarnation. Rejecting the idea of the eternal generation of the Son, he taught that He had been created by the Father in order to the creation of the world through Him. Christ therefore he regarded as higher than man but inferior to God, and the revelation made by Him not as the disclosure of the divine character, but as an ethical code for the guidance of conduct. Athanasius, on the other hand, contended that the Father and the Son participate alike in the divine essence, and that the Son is coequal with the Father. The decision of the Nicæan Council was against Arius, who was excommunicated. Alexander died shortly after his return from Nicæa to the labours of his own diocese, and at the early age of thirty Athanasius found himself installed as his successor. The morning of his episcopate seems to have dawned peacefully enough, but long ere noon dark stormclouds filled the sky, and continued to loom overhead until the sunset was at hand.

His life and writings were really devoted to one great cause—the fight against Arianism. It is a very significant commentary upon the strenuousness with which he maintained the conflict, that nearly one half of the forty-five years of his episcopate should have been spent in exile. Deposed and banished by Constantine I. to Gaul, he was restored to his flock by Constantine II., only to be expelled once more by Constantius, another son of the elder Constantine, who reigned in the East. In the latter case a Cappadocian,

SUCCESSORS OF ORIGEN

Gregory by name, was by force of arms installed in the office of the uncompromising defender of the faith. But Athanasius appealed to Rome, which so warmly espoused his cause that a regular rupture took place between the Eastern and the Western Church. At the Council of Sardica in 343 the Eastern bishops declined to confer with their compeers of the West, because the latter were resolved upon ignoring the sentence of deposition that had been pronounced against Athanasius. Meanwhile, the intruded bishop, Gregory, a man of harsh and tyrannical spirit, having been murdered by an infuriated Alexandrian mob, the emperor consented to the return of the much-loved bishop. This took place amid great public rejoicing in the year 346. According to Gregory of Nazianzen, the inhabitants went streaming forth "like another Nile" to welcome him. For a whole decade Athanasius continued at his post, but in the year 356, owing to the machinations of the Arian party, he was condemned at the Council of Milan, while those bishops who were friendly to him were driven into exile. That his own life was once more in jeopardy was proved by the intrusion of an armed band into a church where he was conducting service. He succeeded, however, in escaping to the wilds of the Egyptian desert, where he composed his *Discourses against the Arians*. Six years later, the death of Constantius and the accession of Julian enabled Athanasius to return to his See. But the success of the Christian bishop soon proved distasteful to an emperor who desired the supremacy of paganism, and on the pretext that he acted as a disturbing influence, Athanasius was banished yet again. Within the year, however, Julian died, and the next emperor,

Jovian, was prepared to tolerate the Arians and the Nicene party alike. Accordingly, Athanasius again took up his episcopal duties, but under Valens was once more obliged to flee. This was his last period of exile. After four months' absence he was recalled, and from this date (366) he carried on the manifold work of his diocese without further molestation. He laboured incessantly until his death in 373, manifesting to the last that intrepid spirit which has received fit commemoration in the saying, *Athanasius contra mundum*.

The significance of Athanasius for theology lies in the leading part which he took in the great controversy regarding the Trinity. On this subject three views were propounded and discussed with the keenest dialectic subtlety. Christ was declared by some to be of a different essence from the Father, by others to be of a similar essence, and by others still to be of the same essence. The last was the view espoused by Athanasius, and that it ultimately triumphed was largely due to his strenuous advocacy. Origen's idea of an economic and relative trinity he discarded in favour of the immanent and absolute trinity.

Origen's influence, however, was by no means limited to Alexandria; it was equally strong in Arabia, Palestine, and Asia Minor. He was on terms of intimate friendship with such men as Theoktistus bishop of Cæsarea, and Alexander, bishop of Jerusalem, who not only opened to him their pulpits, but venerated him as their master; Firmilian, bishop of Cæsarea in Cappadocia, who sheltered him during the persecution under Maximin the Thracian; and Julius Africanus, bishop of Nicopolis, whose correspondence with him regarding the authenticity of the *History of*

SUCCESSORS OF ORIGEN

Susannah has been preserved.[1] But the most distinguished of Origen's disciples in Asia was Gregory Thaumaturgus, to whose touching panegyric upon his master we have already referred. Originally he bore the name of Theodorus, and belonged to a noble and wealthy heathen family of Neocæsarea in Pontus. His parents had chosen for him the profession of an advocate, and he became a diligent student of Roman law. But his accidental meeting with Origen under the circumstances mentioned[2] changed the whole current of his life, and led him to consecrate his energies to higher ends. That great master, perceiving him to be a youth of talent, set himself to draw out his thinking powers, imbued him with the spirit of free investigation, and initiated him into the sweets of intellect. A course of geometry and astronomy, so far as calculated to explain the Sacred Scriptures, and one of Greek philosophy, in which its various systems were made to cast their mites into the treasury of truth, was followed by instruction in the revealed oracles of God. The earnest study of Holy Scripture, with Origen as interpreter, opened up to Gregory's vision a new and higher world, and in his parting address to his beloved teacher he thanks "that God who conducted us to thee." It was with most poignant regret that he separated himself from one to whom his soul was knit, as was the soul of Jonathan to that of David. But he did so in the consciousness that he went forth bearing as a lasting possession those seeds of truth which he had received from him, and in the hope that God would permit him to return to him, bringing with him the fruits and sheaves yielded by those seeds. In a letter

[1] See above, p. 58 f.   [2] See above, p. 56.

still extant Origen expresses his conviction that Gregory's natural abilities were such as to ensure him success either as a Roman lawyer or as a professor of Greek philosophy, but at the same time intimates his desire that he should devote his talents to Christianity, and employ his scientific knowledge in the service of theology, so as to make everything else subserve the divine calling. He exhorts him to bend all his energies in the direction of biblical study, and prayerfully to investigate the sense of the sacred word, which so many have missed.

Sometime after his return to his own country Gregory was, by the joint influence of Origen and Phædimus, bishop of Amasia, literally dragged from his life of quiet asceticism, and installed as bishop of his own town of Neocæsarea, an office which he held and adorned for about thirty years. The legendary element has unfortunately entered largely into the story of his episcopate, and in the account of his life and labours composed by Gregory of Nyssa, the distance of a century lent so much enchantment to the view that the result is not a sober narrative of facts, but a highly coloured portrait of a Christian wizard at whose word the rocks are moved and the plague ravages the city. But, apart from such spurious fables, there is no reason to doubt that Gregory was a conspicuously pious and influential servant of the Church. This is the real meaning of the tradition that at his death the number of pagans in Neocæsarea was only seventeen, or precisely the number of Christians resident there when he assumed the bishopric. It is a singular testimony to his worth, that, notwithstanding the interruption of his work caused by the Decian persecution, and the debasing influences connected with an invasion of the Goths, he should have so impressed himself as a moral force upon the men of his time. In his general views upon the Trinity and the Person of Christ Gregory's position may be described as Origenistic. But, in face of a decided tendency towards a polytheistic conception of the Trinity, he felt constrained to lay special stress on the unity of God. According to Basil, he spoke of the Father and the Son as "two in thought, but one in substance"; at any rate he was accused of Sabellianism. Although his gifts were administrative rather than speculative, he took his fair share in the doctrinal controversies of the period, and won for himself an assured place among the leading Fathers of the Church. Besides his *Panegyric upon Origen,* he wrote what Jerome styles a "short but useful" *Paraphrase of Ecclesiastes,* and a *Canonical Letter* dealing with the exercise of discipline in the case of Christians who had abandoned the faith under stress of persecution, but were desirous of being restored to Church fellowship. Gregory died in 270, so that he survived Origen by about seventeen years.

CHAPTER X

HISTORICAL SERVICES, GENERAL CHARACTERISTICS, AND DISTINCTIVE DOCTRINAL COMPLEXION OF THE GREEK THEOLOGY

FROM Justin to Gregory the Greek Fathers had opposed the Gnostics, and so rescued the Church from being paganised. It was through their conflict with Gnosticism that they first became theologians. Ever since the days of St. Paul the Church had produced saints and martyrs, but not thinkers; the task of the Christian had been to love God and his neighbour, but not to unravel hard questions or engage in bold speculations. When, however, the Gnostics began to discuss the deepest problems of existence—the nature of God, the origin of evil, the redemption of the world—the Greek Fathers were compelled to formulate their own theology in reply to the erroneous views that were being disseminated.

They were further led to combat the frenzied extravagances of the Montanists, a sect claiming to have the spirit of prophecy in active operation amongst its adherents, and somewhat resembling the Irvingites of a later time. Montanism had its rise in Phrygia, but its influence extended to North Africa, Italy, and even Gaul. Ecclesiastical rather than doctrinal questions

HISTORICAL SERVICES 229

underlay the movement. The disorders which St. Paul rebukes in his letters to the Thessalonians were reproduced under Montanistic teaching, which placed in the forefront the nearness of Christ's second advent in the flesh. The movement was chiefly a protest against the growing hierarchical assumption of the clergy. It condemned as a pure figment the doctrine of apostolical succession, which was first formulated by Cyprian, bishop of Carthage. The Montanists maintained that Christ had no successor save the Holy Spirit, and by way of emphasising their belief that in His communications to men the Spirit was not necessarily limited to the clergy, they appear to have found their chosen oracles in women rather than in men. They had certainly some reason for protesting against the encroaching secularism and sacerdotalism of the Church. But they soon developed a proud spirit of Pharisaic legalism. While standing for much that was true, Montanism contained also many false elements which operated as seeds of dissolution. More especially it was characterised by an element of fanaticism; it lacked the virtue of self-restraint. After they broke with the Church the Montanists "became narrower and pettier in their conception of Christianity,"[1] until in the fourth century their conventicles were deserted even in the land of their origin. Although in many respects strictly orthodox, in popular estimation they were usually regarded as equally heretical with the Gnostics. It was by defeating these two "isms"—Gnosticism and Montanism—that the Greek Fathers made the "Catholic" Church.

They also overthrew Chiliasm. This is the rather

[1] Harnack.

inappropriate name given to the ancient Christian eschatology, from the circumstance that one of its tenets was the doctrine of the millennium. It embraced, however, many other features, of which some were fixed, and some were being continually modified. Of the latter sort were the ideas about the Antichrist, and about the place, extent, and duration of Christ's glorious kingdom. After the decay of Montanism, Chiliastic views lost caste, so to speak, and were denounced as Jewish; and the early Christian hope with respect to the future was gradually undermined by the speculative mysticism of the Alexandrians.

Such were the main currents of controversy in which the Greek theology took shape, and such the conditions amid which it rendered effective and lasting service to Christianity. A few words will suffice to indicate its more general characteristics. As we have already seen, it overdid the use of allegory in the interpretation of Scripture, and made it easy to discount the conclusions arrived at by any other sort of exposition. There lay also in its doctrine of reserve a source of potential mischief which has oftener than once in the history of the Church ceased to be potential and become actual. Moreover, all the Greek Fathers, not excepting Methodius himself, were intellectualists; neither Justin nor any of his successors ever renounced philosophy as did the teachers of the Latin Church. But while it may with truth be said that they were too intellectual, too subtle, and that they developed mind at the expense of heart, they were thereby saved at all events from mawkish sentimentality. They breathed the air of intellectual freedom, and their writings are healthy, breezy, and manly. Another noteworthy feature of the

Greek theology is its true catholicity. "As the soul is the principle which holds the body together, so Christians hold together the world itself." What finer expression could we have of the idea of the Church's worth and universal mission than in this saying from the Epistle to Diognetus, penned even before the days of Clement and Origen, but bearing distinct marks of the same Hellenic culture that influenced them? The writings of the Greek Fathers are further marked by a high moral tone and a deep spirituality; in this respect they are fit to be our teachers still. We may note also their pronounced humanitarianism, and their unquenchable optimism, which was really part of their creed. Believing as they did in the ultimate restitution of all rational beings, and unoppressed with thoughts of total depravity or eternal punishment, they knew no morbid feeling of dread or despair, and were as joyous in spirit as they were daring in thought. Bright and in some respects truly Christian as is this optimistic vein in the Greek patristic writers, there is another side—the eschatological—from which it appears in a less satisfactory light. Their conceptions of the intermediate state are anything but clear and precise. It was only the final goal of the deification of humanity that they were really concerned with; all else was of minor importance. Thus the great Christian truth, that a time will arrive when at the judgment-seat of Christ every one shall receive according to his deeds, was relegated to the background as a mere mode of redemption, one of the "channels through which it works." Augustine, on the other hand, sought to emphasise this truth, with the result that the Western Church continued to be inspired by one great motive to which the Eastern Church became in large measure indifferent—the fear of the Judge. Closely connected with the certainty of the judgment is the sense of sin, which was also much stronger in the Latin Church than in the Greek. The latter had no doctrine of original sin, saw no such schism in the divine nature as to require the appeasing by sacrifice of outraged justice before love could pardon, and gave no place to the idea that Christ endured sufferings equal in significance to the eternal sufferings of the whole human race. But when complaints are made of the deficient sense of sin manifested by the Greek theologians, it would perhaps be fairer to speak of their overmastering appreciation of Christ's redemption. That this charge, although not altogether groundless, is nevertheless more ancient than forcible, is shown by the fact that it was levelled by Judaisers against the Apostle Paul for proclaiming the doctrine of justification by faith. The truth is that the doctrine of grace as taught in the Western Church is simply the Latin substitute for the Greek principle of the indwelling of God in humanity.

It is the Latin conception of the gospel that has been embodied in the traditional creed of the Western Church. It was first formulated by the acute and profound mind of Augustine, whose writings constitute an epoch in theological literature and thought. Strongly favoured by Rome, it soon impressed itself upon the entire West, and for many centuries has presented the appearance of an impregnable fortress. Yet it is certainly not the oldest type of Christianity. In the history of Christian thought the Hellenistic theology occupies a prior place, and in recent times many have declared it to be based upon a truer philosophy of God and man. The very fact that a reversion to the earlier conception of gospel truth should have been seriously advocated, and that the Augustinian theology should have been condemned as by comparison narrow and pessimistic, "harsh and loveless," makes it doubly interesting and important to inquire as to what is doctrinally distinctive in the school of Origen. It will be obvious that those whose motto is "Back to the Greek theology" are for the most part universalists. Their whole standpoint necessarily conflicts with the Augustinian doctrines of total depravity, predestination, the loss of freedom, and eternal punishment, and is virtually that reflected in the closing lines of Tennyson's *In Memoriam*, where he speaks of

> "One God, one law, one element,
> And one far-off divine event,
> To which the whole creation moves."

The following brief outline of the Hellenistic position is from the pen of one of its champions: "In the thought of Hellenism a profound unity underlies all phenomena, and works steadily and surely towards the elimination of all discord and evil. This purpose, namely, 'The Restoration of all things,' is clearly revealed in Holy Scripture; this larger hope or certainty is indeed 'the glad tidings of great joy' which the gospel promises. The agent in this process is the immanent Logos manifested in the flesh, made man for us and for our salvation. But as the universe is really *One*, the work of the Logos cannot be confined to this earth; it extends to the entire spiritual world, and is effective wherever the *logical, i.e.* rational, creature sins and suffers. The Incarnation is thus the expression of a universal purpose of unification, education, restoration. This plan may be traced in all God's dealings with us. His wrath and vengeance are really the expressions of love eternal. Fire, penalty, judgment, are but moments in the great *redemptive* process. The resurrection is its climax.

"In the Hellenistic vocabulary, such Western phrases as imputation, satisfaction, substitution, probation, are wanting; sin, however grievous, is always curable, because residing in the will, and not penetrating to the nature of man. While the ties of heredity are recognised, yet infant innocence is firmly held. The Church, if not technically, is yet potentially and vitally a synonym for the whole human family. The crude absolutism which has always characterised the Latin ideal of God, and which is reflected in the claims of the Pope as God's vicegerent, is also wanting in Hellenistic theology. This indeed recognised the divine sovereignty, but it is the supremacy of a reasonable and loving Creator and Parent. To man a special interest and dignity is assigned, stamped as he is indelibly with the divine image, a child of the All Father, a pupil whom the Heavenly Tutor is educating. But man is more than this. He is the microcosm or mirror of the universe, God's representative and vicegerent, a common bond and centre uniting the spiritual and sensible universe."[1]

We quote this statement not only on account of its intrinsic interest, but also because it is fair to let the advocate of a new (if likewise old) theology speak for himself. While we cannot here discuss the merits of the question raised, we may briefly advert to the three

[1] Allin, *Race and Religion*, Preface, p. 7 ff.

HISTORICAL SERVICES

great pillars on which the Greek theology seems to rest.

The first is the immanence of God in the universe. This is a root principle with far-reaching consequences, for in theology everything must ultimately depend upon our conception of God. History and experience go to show that there are two fundamentally different ways of regarding Him. He may be viewed as dwelling within His creation, or as transcendently exalted above it. In the Mosaic period the people thought of Him as dwelling among them by the shechinah, but in the later days of post-exilic Judaism God was absolutely conceived as reigning in the remote heaven. It was the latter view that commended itself to Latin Christianity. Augustine found it dominant in the Church at the time of his conversion, accepted it as part and parcel of the divine revelation, and defended it with all the resources of a powerful intellect. The history of the Christian Church resembles that of the Jewish in so far as it, too, shows a transition from the one standpoint to the other. The earlier interpretation of Christianity adopted by the Greek Fathers and rejected by the Western Church in favour of a theological system of which the transcendence of Deity is the ruling principle, was based upon the thought of the divine immanence in creation and in the life of man. In the two ways of looking at the subject is reflected the spirit of the two races as exhibited in their respective mythologies. While for the Roman the gods were distant and unfamiliar beings, for the Greek they were gracious presences ever by his side. There can be no doubt as to which of the two conceptions of Deity is the higher and more worthy. It was surely a retrograde step for the Church of the West to abandon that of the Greek theology in order to set on a far distant throne Him who is "not far from every one of us," and through whose indwelling spirit men become "the temple of God." Yet there was one great danger to which the Greek conception of Deity exposed its adherents—that of pantheism. They did not always find it easy so to hold the divine immanence as to avoid identifying God with the world.

The second keystone of the Greek theology is the Incarnation. Stress is laid upon this, however, not as a device for repairing the injury wrought by the Fall, but as the completion of God's eternal purpose "before the foundation of the world." The divine revelation in Jesus is the complement of the divine revelation in nature. This view is already propounded by Clement. "Since Christ is the indwelling God, His incarnation is not a thing new or strange, an abrupt break in the continuity of man's moral history; it had not been decreed in the divine counsels in order to avoid some impending catastrophe which suddenly confronted or threatened to disappoint the divine purpose; it was not merely an historical incident by which he came into the world from a distance, and, having done His work, retired again from it. He was in the world before He came in the flesh, and was preparing the world for his visible advent. As indwelling Deity, He was to a certain extent already universally incarnated, as the light that lighteth every man, the light shining in the darkness, the light and life of men in every age."[1] To the Greek theologian, then, the incarnation is not only a natural, but almost a necessary redemptive

[1] Allen, *The Continuity of Christian Thought*, p. 47.

manifestation in order to succour sinful and suffering humanity, and carries with it the salvation of the race. He is not careful, like the writers of the West, to construct theories of the atonement, which is viewed virtually as an extension of the incarnation. For him the point of consequence is not that Christ was crucified, but that Christ became flesh. "Hellenism sat by the cradle, while Latinism stood by the cross of the Lord."

The third cardinal principle in the Greek theology is that of the All-Fatherhood of God. Christ's life and death are viewed as the proof of God's identification with, and love for, mankind. The thought of God's justice is not allowed to dwarf that of His goodness; man does not quail before an angry judge, for the Just One is good, and the Parent-source of every blessing, including that of redemption. In taking this ground the Greek Fathers were at all events true to the fundamental idea of the gospel as a revelation of divine love. Whatever may be its merits otherwise, the Latin theology, which built upon sin and fear and propitiation, undoubtedly erred in permitting the great truth that God is love to slip too much into the background. And in these days when this fact is growingly recognised it will be reckoned to the credit of the Greek theology that it did justice to the "magnetic force and universal range and efficacy" of that Love which said: "I, if I be lifted up, will draw all men unto Me."

CHAPTER XI

REACTION AGAINST ORIGENISM

LOVE and hatred encircle the name of Origen. This was the case already in his lifetime. Some distrusted him as a heretic, others invoked his aid to silence heretics; by some he was almost worshipped, by others he was bitterly disliked. And sometimes he suffered as much at the hands of injudicious partisans as from the opposition of his deadliest enemies; for if the latter unscrupulously misrepresented his views, the former frequently refined upon them. Generally speaking, however, for at least a century and a half after his death, he was regarded with respect and even with veneration. It was towards the end of the fourth century that Origen's doctrinal position began to be viewed in many quarters with disapprobation. Substantially, it was still adopted by Gregory of Nyssa, although Jerome bitterly accuses him of having abandoned the orthodox faith. On the subject of the Trinity in particular, Origen had held that the Son was eternally begotten of, and yet subordinate to, the Father. It came to be felt that these were two incompatible propositions. Those who adhered to the first asserted that the Son was of the same substance with the Father (*Homoousia*); those who adopted the

REACTION AGAINST ORIGENISM

second taught that there were two natures. Many Origenists were prepared to accept a compromise, and propounded the view that while there was not identity, there was similarity, of substance (*Homoiousia*). Subsequently, when to the Nicene Creed there had been added a declaration of the equality of the Holy Spirit with the Father and the Son, there took place in the theological thought of the period a vigorous reaction against the speculative spiritualism of the school of Origen, and a strong drift in favour of primitive and traditional belief. Thus it came about that, in the fifth century, Origen was reckoned a heretic in respect of his teaching upon many points. Particular exception was taken, however, to his views with reference to (1) the pre-existence of the soul, and its incarceration in the body after rebellion against God; (2) the human soul of Jesus; (3) the resurrection of the body; (4) the ultimate restoration of all, and the possibility of redemption for the devil; and (5) the continued creation of new worlds. "The Church," says Harnack, "has produced two fundamental systems, Origen's and Augustine's. But the history of theology in the East is the history of the setting aside of Origen's system, and the same is to be said of the Augustinian in the Catholic West. Only the procedure in the East was more thoroughgoing and open than in the West. In the former Origen was condemned, in the latter Augustine was constantly celebrated as the greatest *doctor ecclesiæ*. In both cases, however, the rejection of the theological system caused the loss of a coherent and uniform Christian conception of the world."[1]

The first regular attack upon the writings of Origen

[1] *History of Dogma*, iii. p. 139.

was made in the last decade of the third century by Methodius, bishop of Olympus and Patara in Lycia, and subsequently of Tyre in Phœnicia. In a treatise on *Things Created*, fragments of which have been preserved by Photius, he assails the cosmology of Origen, and charges him with having "fabled many things concerning the eternity of the universe." But his criticism is so ineffective as almost to justify the remark that it is sometimes difficult to know whether he is imitating or opposing Origen.[1] This is probably due to the fact that, while strongly advocating the popular conception of the Church's creed, and maintaining the literal truth of sacred history, Methodius is as much a Platonist as Origen himself. His antagonism finds, however, more pronounced expression in a work upon the *Resurrection*. Although an allegorist himself, he condemns Origen's method as well as his doctrine. On the question at issue he denies that the soul alone is man, and that the body was given to the soul as a fetter after the Fall, and maintains that if there were no resurrection of the flesh Christ would have agreed with the Sadducees who invented the parable about the woman and the seven brethren. "If," he argues, "the soul be immortal, and the body be the corpse, those who say that there is a resurrection, but not of the flesh, deny any resurrection." Methodius also rejects the teaching of Origen with respect to the eternity of the Logos, the pre-existence of the soul, and the merely temporary character of the bodily nature as a moment in the process of development. All God's creatures are capable of permanence. So far from salvation necessitating separation of soul and

[1] Schnitzer, *Origenes*, p. 43.

body, it implies the reverse; it is a union of elements in the constitution of man which had been unnaturally divorced. Unfortunately the strictures of Methodius are conceived more in the spirit of a champion of orthodoxy than in that of a disinterested seeker after truth. He misrepresents, as well as assails, the views of Origen. His aim was to "unite the theology of Irenæus and Origen, ecclesiastical realism and philosophic spiritualism, under the badge of monastic mysticism."[1] In the praise of virginity, and in the reverence for "mother Church" enjoined upon the individual soul that would become the bride of Christ, we have undoubtedly the distinctive notes of the mysticism associated with the cloister. Methodius was not alone in his attacks, his aversion to the spiritualism of Origen being shared by, among others, Diodorus of Tarsus, Eustathius of Antioch, Theophilus of Alexandria, and Nepos the cultured bishop of Arsinoe, who wrote a work against "the allegorists."

The defence of Origen was taken up with great zest by his pupils Pamphilus the Martyr, and Eusebius the historian, bishop of Cæsarea. Out of loving devotion to his memory they made a collection of his works for the Church library of the city to which he had brought so much renown, and wrote in six books, of which only the first is extant in a translation by Rufinus, an elaborate *Apology* for Origen. Their enthusiasm for their master was genuine and lifelong, and led them occasionally to run riot in directions unsanctioned by him. In his views of Christ, for instance, Eusebius is loose and unsatisfactory; he virtually represents the Mediator as a created and secondary God. Pamphilus

[1] Harnack, *History of Dogma*, ii. p. 13.

relieved the tedium of imprisonment during the Maximinian persecution by working at the *Apology*. It was his last task before his martyrdom. In meeting the charge of subordinationism in the Son's relation to the Father, Pamphilus adduces evidence from Origen's writings to show that he accepts the divinity of Christ, and that his views are neither of an emanationist nor of a docetic character. It is further asserted by this loyal disciple that many loud accusers of his master had no better foundation for their charges than that of idle rumour. Considering it heretical to read Origen's works at all, they were not only for the most part quite ignorant of the writings they denounced, but they even charged him with errors which he had been at pains to refute. It was impossible that these silly slanders could produce much effect so long as Origen's own pupils lived to contradict them, and for a time his authority was not sensibly diminished; in the West it even seemed to grow. Nearly all the leading Fathers of the fourth century regarded him with honour, and even down to the middle of the fifth century there was no one whose prestige was comparable to his own. At the Council of Nice Athanasius appealed to him in support of his doctrine of the Trinity, and his testimony is quoted by the Church historian Socrates against Origen's critics and enemies, whom he stigmatises as "vain and ambitious obscurantists, hero-levelling fellows."[1] Hilary of Poitiers rendered into Latin his commentaries on Job and St. Matthew; Ambrose of Milan and Eusebius of Vercelli did the same for certain of the Commentaries or Homilies. Jerome, too, whose early enthusiasm led

[1] See Harnack, *History of Dogma*, iii. p. 146.

REACTION AGAINST ORIGENISM

him to regard Origen as "a Church teacher second only to the apostles," translated into Latin his discourses on St. Luke and Canticles, and in his biblical works avowedly "pilfered" from the exegetical treasure-stores of the great Alexandrian. Origen's theological views were also espoused by the three Cappadocian Fathers, the philosophical Gregory of Nyssa, his elder brother Basil, and Gregory Nazianzus. By writing in the spirit of the *De Principiis* a guide towards the apologetic presentation of Christian doctrine, the first-mentioned of these Fathers seriously imperilled his reputation for orthodoxy. To the two latter we owe the *Philocalia*, which has preserved for us a considerable portion of the *De Principiis* in the original Greek.

In the East neither the onslaughts of Peter, bishop of Alexandria, nor the hostile attitude of Eustathius of Antioch had seriously injured Origen's reputation. Towards the close of the fourth century, however, the tide began to turn. A strong feeling of antipathy to his views was developed among a section of the Egyptian monks. While those of the Nitrian desert, who were distinguished for their mystical spiritualism, were enamoured of his doctrines, those of the Scetian desert regarded them with aversion, and in their recoil from his idealistic speculations embraced the grossest anthropomorphism. As the Arians had claimed the support of Origen for their side, the fanatical opponents of Arianism had gradually come to regard him as the source of all heresy. His name was dragged into all the subsequent controversies of the period,—the Pelagian, the Nestorian, the Eutychian, —and this very circumstance tended to increase the suspicion fostered by his views about pre-existence and the resurrection. His teaching on the subject of the eternal gospel had also excited the imagination of many of the Palestinian and Egyptian monks to an extent that led the ecclesiastical authorities to look with disfavour upon writings that produced such effects. So palpably did those monks who favoured Origenistic views exaggerate everything, that they must be carefully distinguished from what may be termed the orthodox Origenists, who held by the genuine doctrines of the master. It was, however, an unhappy thought on the part of the latter to attempt to adduce evidence from Origen's writings to show that he was orthodox according to the standard of the Nicene Creed. With this design, towards the end of the fourth century, Didymus of Alexandria wrote commentaries on the *De Principiis*, and more than a century later Evagrius and others were still writing in a similar vein. Apart from the fact that fetters were thus placed upon individual freedom of thought, this whole policy lent itself too readily to the manipulation of the text of Origen's writings, and in consequence to the lasting injury of theological learning. As time passed, the controversial din over the grave of Origen waxed louder and louder. The bitterest invectives were used; Church fellowships were broken up; private friendships were dissolved. Ultimately the orthodox party triumphed; but their victory did them little honour. If they were actuated by zeal for truth, it was a zeal untempered by Christian charity.

Owing to their increasingly complex character, it is somewhat difficult to trace the course of these Origenistic wrangles. In not a few instances the

REACTION AGAINST ORIGENISM

main issues disappeared in the vortex of personal disputes. One of these quarrels arose in Palestine. John, bishop of Jerusalem, lived on terms of intimate friendship with the two Latin theologians Rufinus and Jerome, both of whom shared his admiration for Origen. The latter, in particular, was an eager collector and translator of the master's works. To appreciate Origen as a writer he considered a sign of intelligence; his detractors he designated "barking dogs." To be his peer in scholarship was his great ambition. But suddenly, in the year 394, the spirit of his dream was changed. A Western theologian Vigilantius, and an Egyptian monk Aterbius, having arrived in Jerusalem and commented adversely upon Rufinus's and Jerome's attitude towards Origenistic heresy, the latter, dreading any imputation upon his orthodoxy, began to kick his former idol. Writing to Theophilus he says, "If you believe me, I never was an Origenist; if you do not believe me, I have now ceased to be one." He was further incited to resile from his partiality for Origen by the heated diatribes of Epiphanius, bishop of Salamis, who, at the instigation of the Scetian monks, had sailed for Palestine. Invited or permitted to preach, this prelate uttered a violent tirade against Origenism, to which John made a spirited reply, vindicating the credit of Origen, and denouncing anthropomorphism. After vainly endeavouring to get him to abandon his Origenistic views, Epiphanius induced Jerome and the monks at Bethlehem to renounce Church fellowship with John and his sympathiser Rufinus. The controversy was further embittered through the action of Epiphanius in invading John's episcopal rights by ordaining Paulinianus, a brother of Jerome, as presbyter for the recalcitrant monks at Bethlehem. Ultimately, in 396, Theophilus of Alexandria was called in as arbiter, and Jerome and Rufinus were reconciled before the altar.

A new storm-centre now arose in the West. Rufinus returned to Rome, and in 397 published a translation of the *De Principiis*. While avowedly omitting several of the most compromising passages, and affirming that Origen's works in general, and this book in particular, had been maliciously corrupted by heretics, he rather maladroitly recalled in his preface Jerome's early enthusiasm for Origen. The wrath of the latter, on hearing of this, knew no bounds. He issued a literal translation of the work in question, and continued to fulminate furiously not only against Origenism, but also against his old friend and associate. As a Pelagian, Rufinus adhered to Origen's teaching with respect to pre-existence and free will, but being no Arian, he rejected his doctrine of the Trinity. On the latter point, as well as with regard to the resurrection, he asserted the orthodoxy alike of himself and of the Bishop of Jerusalem. At the same time he severely condemned the detractors of Origen, and the controversy grew hotter than ever. Rufinus devoted three years to a treatise in which he defended himself and attacked Jerome; the latter replied in a similar vein and at equal length. Partisans on both sides rushed into the fray. The Roman bishop Siricius, who had no great liking for Jerome, threw his ægis over Rufinus; but in the year 400, under his successor Anastasius, he was formally censured for translating the *De Principiis*. His friend John of Jerusalem fared worse, a Bull of excommunication having been issued against him. The odd thing about these proceedings was that, according to his own naïve confession, Anastasius had never even heard of Origen before the translations of Rufinus appeared. Perhaps this absolute ignorance of his works made it easier for him to gratify Jerome's disciple Marcella, who called for their condemnation.

In Egypt, too, Origenism had come under a cloud. Compelled at first by the violence of the Scetian monks to anathematise Origen's writings, Theophilus of Alexandria afterwards became of one spirit with them, and, breaking away from his former predilection for their rivals of the Nitrian desert, condemned Origen at a synod held in Alexandria in 399. Epiphanius, who had a keen scent in such matters, made it convenient to attend and assist, and greatly rejoiced over the defeat of Amalek. According to Jerome, the sentence was adopted by many other bishops both in the East and in the West. Two years later, Theophilus, who was a scheming, vindictive prelate rather than a theologian, denounced Origenistic views in a violent manifesto, which Epiphanius blessed and Jerome rendered into Latin. Troops were employed forcibly to dislodge from the Nitrian mountains the monks who refused to renounce the writings of Origen. Although, however, Theophilus ordered Origen's works to be destroyed, he continued to read them himself, on the plea that he "culled the flower and passed by the thorn."[1] Many of the monks took refuge in Constantinople, where they hoped to plead their cause before the emperor. There, too, they enjoyed the kindly protection of the noble-minded Chrysostom, who, without being exactly an Origenist, put a high value on the service

[1] Socrates, *H. E.* vi. 7.

rendered by Origen, and apparently had little idea of the fierce emnity directed against his admirers.

The Byzantine capital now became the headquarters of the Origenistic controversy. Theophilus forgot everything else in the desire to humiliate Chrysostom. At first it did not look as if he would succeed, for at the instance of the monks the empress Eudoxia induced Arcadius the emperor to cite Theophilus to appear before a synod to be presided over by his hated rival. The Alexandrian prelate invoked the aid of the ever zealous Epiphanius, who, however, being an honest bigot, withdrew from Constantinople on ascertaining that he had been misled by false pretences. But Theophilus, finding another ally in the faithful preaching of Chrysostom, who had not shrunk from rebuking the vices of a licentious court, contrived to turn the tables upon his opponent, and to become the accuser instead of the accused. In the year 403 Chrysostom, after refusing to attend a council organised and packed by Theophilus, was excommunicated and sent into exile. The Alexandrian bishop wrote to Theotimus of Scythia requesting his concurrence, but only to get the retort that "he would neither besmirch the fair fame of a sainted man long since gone to his rest, nor have the presumption to condemn what none of his predecessors had rejected."[1] Within a few days of his banishment an earthquake, together with the indignation of the populace, led to the recall of Chrysostom and to the flight of Theophilus. Ere long, however, on St. John's day, Chrysostom was rash enough to compare the empress to Herodias, and the friends of Theophilus at court took care to foster her indignation, with the

[1] Socrates, *H. E.* vi. 12.

REACTION AGAINST ORIGENISM

result that at Easter, in the year 404, Chrysostom was seized and deported to Armenia. Thereupon the brutal Theophilus had the effrontery to write, "Babylon is fallen, is fallen."[1] This second exile Chrysostom endured with Christian heroism, and to his attached flock he continued to write words of comfort until his death, which occurred in 407 while he was on the march to a still drearier place of exile by the Black Sea. A generation later, under Theodosius II., the protests of his flock were still loud enough to secure that his bones should be brought to Constantinople and laid in an honoured grave.

During the fifth century there was a comparative lull in the storm that raged around Origen and his writings. It was, however, marked by two incidents worth noting, the one at its commencement, the other at its close. In Spain, where Pelagianism had already obtained a footing, a certain Avitus sought to introduce the doctrines of Origen; but about the year 410 this attempt was thwarted by Orosius, a presbyter of that country. Eighty-six years later, in A.D. 496, by a decree of the Roman bishop Gelasius, he was pronounced a schismatic (!), and all his works were abjured except those which had been translated by Jerome.

In the sixth century the controversy was renewed in all its bitterness. About the year 530 the convent of St. Sabas, in Palestine, became a hotbed of Origenism. Among the abbots there, Domitian and Theodore (Askidas) were especially distinguished for their de-

[1] By some the letter in which this occurs is ascribed to Jerome. But one is loth to think that, fiery fanatic as he could sometimes be, that learned Father could thus glory over the ruin of a great man of God, whose only offence consisted in the practice of Christian charity towards the persecuted.

votion to Origen. Some of the more fanatical of the party even had it in view to demolish the monasteries of their antagonists. Before his death, however, Sabas himself requested the emperor Justinian formally to condemn the arch-heretic. In a famous letter to Mennas, patriarch of Constantinople (*c.* 538), Justinian tabulated the errors of Origen and gave instructions to have him condemned, and his works suppressed, by synodal decree. The stress laid in this document upon the heresy of pre-existence is in itself eloquently suggestive of the period of the Monophysite controversy, and of the opposing camps of the *Protoktists* and the *Isochrists*, into which the Origenists were divided. The former were so called with respect to the doctrine of the pre-existence of the soul of Jesus; the name applied to the latter marked them out as defenders of the view that all souls will ultimately be restored and be on a level with Christ. The diocesan synod called for by Justinian was held at Constantinople in 541, and expanded the emperor's nine anathemas against Origen and his works into fifteen.[1] There were still, however, at court secret disciples of the Alexandrian teacher. Through the empress Theodora and bishop Theodore of Cæsarea, whose sympathies were with the Monophysites, these were able to devise retaliatory measures. Anxious to put an end to the unrest caused by the Monophysite controversy in Egypt, Justinian was led to expect that his object could be achieved provided "the three chapters"—the Nestorian writings of Theodore of Mopsuestia, the polemical tractates of Theodoret of Cyrus against Cyril, and the letter of

---

[1] The student will find these enumerated in Harnack's *History of Dogma*, iv. p. 348 f.

REACTION AGAINST ORIGENISM

Ibas of Edessa to Maris—were condemned. Action was accordingly taken on these lines in 544; but the bishops of the West refused to subscribe the edict, as being derogatory to the authority of the Council of Chalcedon. In 547 Vigilius of Rome, a weak and vacillating man, who had climbed to place and power as the tool of the empress, was summoned to Constantinople and compelled to acquiesce; but shortly after, finding that the African bishops and others had renounced Church communion with him, he withdrew this approval. Thereupon Justinian condemned the three chapters afresh (551). After much dissension matters were at length settled at the Fifth General Council, which Justinian summoned to meet at Constantinople in the year 553. The three chapters were condemned. Origen also, it would appear, was anathematised. He was not, however, singled out for special treatment, his name being mentioned only in a list of more ancient heretics. With this deliverance the long and bitter series of Origenistic disputes came to a close.

CHAPTER XII

Subsequent History of Origenism

THE subsequent history of Origenism is disappointing. It no longer, indeed, had a history in the same sense as formerly; but it had, or rather remained, an influence that could never die out. Like Hellenism, it was an atmosphere, a spirit, a subtle force pervading thought and life. But although all down the centuries it has lacked neither advocates nor assailants, it has never again become the battle-cry of opposing parties in the Church. For a time, in the domain of theology, it remained

> " The imperial ensign; which, full high advanced,
> Shone like a meteor, streaming to the wind."

But only afterwards to disappear in a bog; irrecoverably, as a complete scientific system, yet, happily, not so as a storehouse of great thoughts fraught with blessing for the world still.

In the Eastern Church, after Gregory of Nyssa, the most prominent names associated with Origen down to the seventh century were those of Æneas of Gaza, Zacharias of Mitylene, and "the divine philosopher" Maximus Confessor. Æneas and Zacharias, who lived in the fifth and sixth centuries respectively, exhibit,

SUBSEQUENT HISTORY OF ORIGENISM 253

according to Denis, "incontestable traces of Origenism, but they are only disjointed reminiscences, and consequently of no great significance."[1] They were rhetoricians rather than theologians. In the seventh century Origenism was represented by Maximus, an Eastern monk, an able thinker, a learned scholar, and a fearless controversialist. By denying the right of the emperor to intermeddle in disputed questions of dogmatic, he anticipated the contendings of later reformers with respect to the Church's independence of the State. In common with others who upheld the affirmations of the Chalcedonian creed regarding two natures and two wills, he denounced the imperial "Typus"—a document forbidding all controversy as to whether Christ had only one will or two—on the ground that it robbed Him not only of His wills, but also of His action, and therefore of His natures generally. His theology was of the scholastic type, and a combination of Aristotelian philosophy and Alexandrian mysticism. His great theme is the soul's receptivity; he has little to say about active effort. In his doctrine of grace he resembles Origen rather than Augustine, holding that whatever of being there is in us is good, because being comes from God. Even though the taint of sin has tarnished our race, there always remains in us "the germ and the faculty of good." Maximus adhered likewise to the teaching of Origen and Gregory of Nyssa with regard to universal salvation. The labours of the Cappadocians and of Maximus, together with the philosophy of Aristotle, prepared the way for Greek scholasticism as represented by John of Damascus. It would appear that by the

[1] *De la Philosophie d'Origène*, p. 549.

254 ORIGEN AND GREEK THEOLOGY

end of the fourth century the Hellenistic spirit had virtually exhausted itself. It no longer welled up in living and creative power. Even the writings of Maximus are largely a *mélange* of the ideas of Gregory of Nyssa and those of the pseudo-Dionysius, who lived early in the fifth century. But naturally, as independent thinking waned, increased attention was bestowed upon form and method. The intellectual treasures, of which they were the custodians, no longer stimulated the Greek theologians to add to their bulk and their beauty; rather did they constitute a burdensome, if sacred, heritage, which it cost much labour to preserve and transmit. John is not an independent author; he is a diligent editor, a scholastic through whose dialectic skill orthodox Christianity attained a fixed form in the Greek Church. But with this it lost much of its living interest, and men's minds began to be occupied with questions of worship rather than with problems of theology. As Harnack says, "The history of dogma came to a close in the Greek Church a thousand years ago, and its reanimation cannot easily be conceived."[1] Such a situation must ever appear regrettable in view of the sparkle and brightness which the Greek mind might have imparted to Christianity.

Until the time of the Pelagian controversies Origen was scarcely known in the West; and even then, if we except the accusations of Jerome, his name was not much canvassed either in orthodox or in heterodox circles. The welcome extended to the writings of Augustine was tantamount to the rejection of those of Origen. What more particularly sapped the foundations of Origenism was Augustine's doctrine of sin and

[1] *History of Dogma*, iv. p. 352.

SUBSEQUENT HISTORY OF ORIGENISM 255

grace, with its literal acceptance both of the tradition of original sin and of St. Paul's Epistle to the Romans. For fully three hundred years the Augustinian position was scarcely challenged; yet this apparently complete victory of the great Latin Father's teaching over that of the Greek was due not so much to its own superiority in depth and logic, as to the gross darkness induced by the disintegration of the empire of the West. Amid the chaotic confusion of the revolutionary period that witnessed the general overthrow of institutions and customs, there was no disposition to investigate the foundations of belief or to stir new questions for debate. What mental energy was left to those who represented theological study had to be expended in the summarising of results already reached. The only real trace of Origen's influence in the Middle Ages is found in the writings of John Scotus Erigena (†1308). It is uncertain whether his knowledge of Origen was gained at first-hand or not. There is nothing improbable in the supposition that through Theodore of Tarsus, who became archbishop of Canterbury, he may have had access to the writings of the Alexandrian Father. But although Scotus frequently mentions Origen by name, and uses language closely akin to his, he does not appear ever to quote him directly. While referring freely to other Greek Fathers also, he studiously ignores the Latin Fathers, with the exception of Augustine ("who is really mentioned only *honoris causa*") and Ambrose. The latter attracted him chiefly through his *Hexameron*, an allegorical treatise of more pronouncedly Alexandrian type than any other of his writings, and possibly John's knowledge of Origen may have been wholly derived from

Ambrose and Gregory of Nyssa. In affirming that "true philosophy is true religion, and true religion is true philosophy," Scotus at once reveals his affinity to Origen, whom he specially resembles in speculative boldness. Nor is the similarity between the two men confined to a mere general bent of mind; it is doctrinal as well. For instance, he summarily rejects the Augustinian doctrine of predestination. Like Origen, too, Scotus asserted the eternity of the world, and held that had God existed before and without the world, creation would have been an accident in the divine life. Only in the sense in which cause must exist anterior to effect, *i.e.* by a logical interval, but not an interval of measurable time, did God exist before the world. His position is exactly that of Origen, except that for him creation is an emanation, and not a real creation by an act of will. In his spiritualising tendency he even goes beyond Origen. For him the popular notions about a material hell are simply a relic of paganism. Conscience constitutes both heaven and hell: "there is no other joy than to see Christ, no other punishment than not to see Him." In the soul's return to God he distinguishes five stages— death, resurrection, the transformation of the fleshly body into a spiritual body, the return of the spirit to first causes, and finally deification. On the other hand, in his doctrine of man, whom he views as a microcosm, Scotus deviates from Origen; and on various topics he takes for his master the pseudo-Dionysius, who was a theosophic mystic. To a certain extent the spirit of Origen reappears also in the Neapolitan monk Joachim, more especially in his free interpretation of the sacred text, but it is doubtful

SUBSEQUENT HISTORY OF ORIGENISM 257

whether he had any acquaintance with the writings of the great Alexandrian.

Enough has been said to show that Origen's influence upon succeeding ages was by no means commensurate with the boldness and grandeur of his system. This may be accounted for in several ways. For one thing it was not "compactly built together"; through its looseness and discursiveness it was at a disadvantage as compared with the more firmly welded Neoplatonism of Plotinus. The furious strife that raged round his name from the time of his death until the middle of the sixth century was due more to personal antipathies than to any great living force in his philosophy. No great book was produced on either side. The doctrines of pre-existence and of the eternity of the world were no doubt taught in many of the philosophical schools,—the former, in particular, has shown a persistent tendency to assert itself at intervals in the subsequent history of the Church,—and that of the final restoration of all spirits received the support of Gregory of Nyssa and of Maximus the Confessor. It is clear from the Church history of Socrates that in the fifth century Origen's influence was in certain circles still undiminished; but if the Greek Church as a whole had held him in much esteem, it would surely have been at more pains to preserve his works. The truth is, his name was no longer one to conjure with in the East; and it was still less so in the West. The thunders of Jerome rendered him an object of general suspicion. The prestige of the Augustinian theology, which had occupied the field, as well as the barbarism and ignorance fostered by repeated invasions on almost every side, likewise

258 ORIGEN AND GREEK THEOLOGY

tended to bring about the general neglect of Origen's writings even after they were accessible to readers in the Latin tongue. Not until the ninth century did any gleam of his influence appear; and if three centuries later it manifested itself with greater strength in the pages of Duns Scotus, it was overlaid and virtually stifled with Neoplatonic mysticism drawn from the pseudo-Dionysius the Areopagite. "During the Middle Ages Origen was only a name. In modern times his writings have been restored to the light of day, but life has not been restored to his doctrines. Some of his ideas have crept into Jacob Behmen, into Poiret, into St. Martin; his system has remained alien to them." So writes Denis,[1] who is probably correct in thinking that, owing to the cosmology of its founder, the reconciliation of the modern spirit with Origenism is almost inconceivable.

Apart altogether from the question of the influence exerted by him, it may be noted that the West has been much more generous in its treatment of Origen than the East. This is curious enough, and yet it is only another illustration of the well-attested principle that "no prophet is accepted in his own country." During the Middle Ages, throughout the Greek Church, his name was held in execration, and the margins of his MSS. were covered with the bitter denunciations of anonymous scribblers, who were greatly shocked at what they considered his deadly heresies and intolerable blasphemies. Even yet the Church whose creed he did so much to mould regards him with decided aversion. In the Latin Church opinion has always been more divided as to his merits, some having

[1] *De la Philosophie d'Origène*, p. 611.

written in condemnation, others in defence, of his views. Augustine, though opposed to his theology, had that respect for his memory which it was fit that one great man should entertain in relation to another. Vincentius of Lerinum pointed to Origen as a warning example of how the most scholarly and illustrious teacher might deviate from the highway of truth. Others, doubtless, have considered him literally beyond redemption, and the question of his salvation has been discussed in more than one printed treatise. But those who doubted of his salvation did not scruple to help themselves to the fruit of his labours; they were adherents of that type of ecclesiastical "science" which cares little for historical truth, and "lives on fragments of the men whom it declares to be heretics." But at the beginning of the ninth century Pope Leo III. included among the patristic readings in the Roman breviary several selections from his writings, and all along many were disposed to regard as wanton interpolations by heretics what of heterodoxy they contained. In the fourteenth century the pious Mechtildis claimed to have had it revealed to her in a vision that in spite of his errors God had shown him mercy.

Among the admirers of Origen in more recent times special mention is due to the learned Erasmus. Besides writing his life, this greatest of all the Humanists translated some of his Commentaries into Latin, thereby confirming his declaration that he "learned more Christian philosophy from a single page of Origen than from ten of Augustine." Luther took a diametrically opposite view: *Origenem jamdudum diris devovi*; but Luther was not without strong dogmatic bias—witness the fact that he called the

Epistle of St. James "an Epistle of straw." The great Reformer's unfavourable estimate of Origen was possibly due, however, more to the impatience with which a practical mind is apt to view the idealist and his long-spun theories than to anything else. It is worth recalling that in his *Table Talk* he quotes with approval what Origen says about the power of devils being broken by the saints.[1] Beza, the friend of Calvin, had also a poor opinion of Origen. Melanchthon regarded him with mixed feelings, approving of his doctrine of the Trinity, but rejecting his view of Justification. While not homologating his opinions, the venerable Bede and the saintly Bernard revered his memory. In Genebrard he found a zealous defender and industrious editor of his works.[2] Since the seventeenth century, when Augustinian divines still referred to Origen in terms of heavy censure, there has been a disposition to extend to him a kindlier judgment. In some quarters he is even

[1] *Of the Devil and his Works*, DCVII.

[2] These were first printed by Merlin in 1512. His emendations are quite uncritical. Although finely printed, the edition of Erasmus (Basel, 1545) is lacking in care and exactness. Rather better than these is the edition of Genebrard (Paris, 1574). A great advance in every respect is shown in that of the *Benedictine De la Rue*, 4 vols. fol., Paris, 1656–1659,—reprinted by Lommatzsch, 25 vols. 8vo, Berlin, 1831–1848, and by Migne, *Patrologiæ Cursus Completus*, ser. Græce, vols. xi.–xvii. The splendid edition of the Greek Fathers now being issued by the Berlin Academy provides the world at last with a complete critical edition of Origen's extant writings. In the *Journal of Theological Studies* (October, 1900) there is an article by E. C. Butler upon "The New Tractatus Origenis,"—"a series of twenty homilies in Latin discovered in two manuscripts (10th and 12th centuries respectively), by Mgr. Batiffol, Rector of the Institut Catholique of Toulouse," and published by him in the early part of last year. The probability appears to be that they are of purely Latin origin.

hailed as the real author of much that is accounted modern in the religious thought of the present day. For our own part, we are inclined to accept as just and Christian the calmly conceived and finely expressed estimate of the author of *Hours with the Mystics*: "Of the merits of Origen we must judge in the spirit of charity. His labours entitle him to no less at our hands. Of this victim of unmeasured censure—this idol of indiscriminate praise, we can now form a dispassionate estimate. The uproar of the contests which ensued upon his death has died away. Those funeral games are ended. We are not, like his contemporaries, applauding now Jerome and now Rufinus, as they strain and turn in their grapple of hatred. Let not the evil which was no part of his design be laid to his charge. Let his love to the Most Holy, whom he wished to serve, be present with us when we think upon the multitude of his errors. His whole life he offered up as a sacrifice to his Maker—calumny alone would snatch the offering from the altar. 'I shall know after death,' said he, 'whether those stars are indeed animated.' We believe that he now does know —in heaven."[1]

[1] R. A. Vaughan, *Essays and Remains*, vol. i. p. 44.

INDEX

ABELARD, 146 n.
Achaia, Church of, 50.
Adamantius, 98.
Adamantius = Origen, 104.
Æneas of Gaza, 252.
Alexander, bishop of Alexandria, 221 f.
Alexander, bishop of Jerusalem, 13, 37, 50, 56, 63, 224.
Alexandria, 2, 14, 24, 35, 44, 46, 49 ff., 54 f., 58, 220 f., 224, 247.
Alexandrian Church, 8, 37, 52, 62.
Alexandrian Fathers, 8, 81, 93, 209.
Allen, quoted, *Pref.*, 236.
Allin, quoted, 223 f.
Ambrose, 210, 242, 255 f.
Ambrosius, 9, 47, 58, 62 f., 100, 110, 133, 138.
Ammonius Saccas, 6, 44.
Anastasius, bishop of Rome, 246 f.
Anselm, 188.
Antichrist, 206, 230.
Antioch, 3, 13, 49, 51, 62, 222.
Apologists, the, 148.
Aquila, proconsul of Egypt, 40.
Aquila, translator of LXX, 99, 101 ff.
Aquileia, 58.
Arabia, 49, 53, 56, 61, 224.
Arabian Church, 60.
Arcadius, 248.
Arianism, 220, 222, 243.
Aristides, 10.
Aristotle, 253.
Arius, 218, 221 f.
Asia Minor, 224 f.

Aterbius, 245.
Athanasius, 2, 217 n., 218 ff.
Athenagoras, 148.
Athenodorus, 56.
Athens, 3, 10, 12, 36, 51, 58 f.
Atonement, Origen's theory of the, 186 ff.
Augustine, 63, 212, 231 f., 235, 239, 254 f., 259.
Augustinian theology, 257.
Aurelius, Marcus, 105.
Avitus, 249.

BARNABAS, 27.
Basil the Great, 126, 243.
Basilides, 4, 28.
Baur, referred to, 43 n., 45 n.
Baxter, Richard, 98.
Bede, 260.
Behmen, 192 n., 258.
Bernard, 192 n., 260.
Beryllus, 59 f.
Berytus, 56.
Beza, 260.
Bigg, quoted or referred to, 110, 121, 125, 198.
Bithynia, 58.
Bostra, 59 f.
Bruce, quoted, 119.
Burns, quoted, 207.
Butler, 74.

CÆSAREA, 50, 54 ff., 103, 175.
Cæsarea in Cappadocia, 57, 224.
Calvin, 98, 212, 260.

INDEX

Candidus, the Valentinian, 55.
Cappadocia, 53, 56.
Cappadocian Fathers, 243, 253.
Caracalla, 46, 49.
Carlyle, 213.
Carthage, Church of, 17.
Catechetical School, 2, 8, 12, 19 f., 40 f., 43, 46, 214 f., 220.
Celsus, 9, 61, 105 ff., 150, 159.
Celsus the Epicurean, 105.
Chalcedon, Council of, 2, 251.
Chaldæans, the, 84.
Chiliasm, 229 f.
Christianity, 1, 4, 7, 13, 15 ff., 19, 23 ff., 36 ff., 49, 61, 84, 89 f., 93 f., 99, 105 f., 109, 111 ff., 127, 159, 229, 232, 254.
Chrysostom, 247 ff.
Church, Origen's idea of the, 196 f.
Clement of Alexandria, 2, 13 ff.; attitude of towards Greek philosophy, 14 ff.; place assigned by to reason, 16 ; his views of Holy Scripture, 17 ff.; his distinction of the true Gnostic from the ordinary disciple, 19 f.; his influence on Origen, 20 ; his writings, 20 ff.; apologetic trend of his teaching, 23 f.; founder of a scientific Christian dogmatic, 24 ; his theology, 26 ff., 37, 40, 44, 73, 79, 81, 84 ff., 90, 120, 131, 148, 158, 189 f., 196 ff., 210, 236.
Constantine I., 105, 222.
Constantine II., 222.
Constantinople, 247 f., 250 f.
Constantius, 222.
Cranmer, 218.
Cunningham, referred to, 26.
Cyprian, 196, 229.
Cyril, 250.

DANTE, quoted or referred to, 39, 170 n., 203 ff., 210.
Decian persecution, 61 f., 218 f.
Demetrius, bishop of Alexandria, 41, 43, 46, 49 ff., 60, 63, 215.
Denis, quoted or referred to, 3 f., 77, 80, 87 f., 92, 97, 121, 253, 258.

Didymus, 214, 220, 244.
Diodorus of Tarsus, 241.
Diognetus, Epistle to, 231.
Dionysius of Alexandria, 62, 214, 216 ff.
Dionysius of Rome, 217.
Discourse, The True, 105, 107, 109 ff.
Dods, referred to, 23.
Domitian, abbot of St. Sabas, 249.

EASTERN Church, 210, 215, 223, 231, 252.
Egypt, 13, 35, 49, 55, 247, 250.
Egyptian Church, 37, 41, 50, 63.
Egyptian monks, 243.
Egyptians, 84, 163.
Eleazar, 139.
Elkesaites, the, 59, 61.
Emmaus (Nicopolis), 58.
Ephesus, 51, 101.
Epicureanism, 42, 84.
Epicureans, 108.
Epiphanius, 245, 247 f.
Erasmus, 259.
Ernesti, 123.
Eudoxia, 248.
Eusebius of Cæsarea, 42, 45, 49, 53, 60, 62, 66, 92, 103, 105, 111, 152 n., 198 n., 241.
Eusebius of Vercelli, 242.
Eustathius of Antioch, 241, 243.
Eutychian controversy, 243 f.
Evagrius, 244.

FABIAN, bishop of Rome, 53, 198 n.
Fénélon, 192 n.
Fifth General Council, 251.
Firmilian, 57, 224.
Free will, the doctrine of, 132, 161 ff.

GALLIENUS, 218.
Gaul, 228.
Gelasius of Rome, 249.
Genebrard, 260.
Gennadius, 54.
Geta, 49.
Gnostics, 2, 4, 6, 14, 18, 48, 78 f., 88, 139, 144, 162 f., 169, 189, 211, 228.

INDEX

Gordian, 110.
Gospel, The Eternal, 179, 190, 244.
Gospels, the, 67, 104.
Goths, the, 227.
Greece, 50, 53, 58, 101.
Greek Church, 232, 257 f.
Greek Fathers, 210, 220, 228 f., 230 f., 237, 255.
Greek philosophy, 82, 84 ff., 94, 115, 211, 219, 225 f.
Greek theology, 228 f.
Gregory the Cappadocian, 223.
Gregory of Nazianzen, 126, 223, 243.
Gregory of Nyssa, 210, 226, 238, 243, 252 ff., 257.
Gregory Thaumaturgus, 11, 56 f., 59, 64, 133, 225 ff.
Guyon, Madame de, 192 n.

Hades, 204 f.
Hadrian, 100.
Harnack, quoted or referred to, 25, 53, 85, 91, 97, 126, 153, 172 f., 190, 212, 239, 241 f., 250, 254.
Hellenism, 233, 252.
Hellenistic theology, 232 ff.
Heraclas, 2, 9, 39, 44 ff., 53 f., 62, 214 f.
Heraclitus, 107 f.
Hermas, The Shepherd of, 74.
Herod the Great, 54.
Hexapla, The, 47, 50, 55, 58, 101 ff.
Hilary of Poitiers, 242.
Hippolytus, 49.

Ibas of Edessa, 250.
Incarnation, doctrine of the, 117 ff., 131, 180 ff., 236.
India, 37.
Irenæus, 17, 145, 241.
Irvingites, the, 228.
Italy, 228.

Jericho, 50, 101.
Jerome, 12, 35, 52, 56, 98, 103 f., 120, 125, 171, 210, 227, 238, 542, 245 ff., 254, 257, 261.
Jerusalem, 3, 63, 203, 224, 245 f.
Jesus Christ, 12, 18, 24, 54, 86 f., 95 f., 108 f., 116 f., 135 ff., 145 f., 149, 151 ff., 163, 172, 178 f., 181 ff., 229, 250.
Joachim, 256.
John of Damascus, 253 f.
John of Jerusalem, 245 f.
John Scotus Erigena, 255 f., 258.
Josephus, 99.
Jovian, 224.
Judaism, 3, 99, 109, 116 f., 195.
Julia Mammæa, 49.
Julian, 223.
Juliana, 57.
Julius Africanus, 58 f., 133, 224.
Justin, 8, 10, 15, 24, 99, 148, 228, 230.
Justinian, 250 f.

Kronius, 45.

Lætus, 40.
Latin Church, 230, 232.
Latin Fathers, 255.
Leibnitz, 150.
Leo III., Pope, 259.
Leonides, 35 ff.
Libya, bishops of, 217; desert of, 218.
Logos, the, 3, 14 f., 17, 24 ff., 86, 94, 131, 144, 151 f., 155, 172, 182 ff., 240.
Lucian, 105.
Luther, 212, 259 f.

Marcella, 247.
Maris, 251.
Martin, St., 258.
Maximinus Thrax, 138, 224.
Maximus Confessor, 252 ff.
Mechtildis, 259.
Melanchthon, 64, 260.
Melito, bishop of Sardis, 65, 120.
Mennas of Constantinople, 250.
Methodius, 230, 240 f.
Milan, Council of, 223.
Moderatus, 45.
Monophysite controversy, 250.
Montanists, the, 123, 228 ff.
Morinus, Petrus, 103.
Moses, 82, 86, 109.
Mystics, the, 17.

NEANDER, 20 f., 44 n.
Neocæsarea in Pontus, 225 f.
Neoplatonism, 6, 23, 44, 215, 257.
Neoplatonists, 96, 144.
Nepos of Arsinoe, 217, 241.
Nestorian controversy, 243.
Nicæa, Council of, 2, 221 f., 242.
Nicomachus, 45.
Nicomedia, 58 f.
Nicopolis, 58, 101, 224.
Nitrian monks, 243, 247.
Noetus, 160.
Novatus, 217.
Numenius, 45.

ORIGEN, 2, 11 ff., 18, 20, 34; his birth, surname, parentage, and early education, 35 ff.; meaning of the name, 35; Origen as a teacher, 39; his sympathy with Christian martyrs, 40; his unworldliness, 41; his asceticism, 42 f.; his self-mutilation, 43; his devotion to Greek philosophy, 43 ff.; his knowledge of Hebrew, 46 f.; his literary labours, 47 f.; journeys to Arabia and Antioch, 49; sojourn in Palestine, 50; his ordination by the Palestinian bishops, 50; visit to the Church of Achaia, 50 f.; his final departure from Alexandria, 52; his deposition from the rank of presbyter, 52; settlement at Cæsarea, and establishment of a theological school there, 54 f.; the counsellor of foreign Churches, 56, 60; his magnetic influence over his pupils, 56 f.; his two years' concealment in the Cappadocian Cæsarea, 57 f.; second visit to Greece, 58; letters to Julius Africanus and to Gregory, 59; his exegetical work, 59; his mediation in the case of Beryllus, 60; correspondence with Philip the Arabian, 61; imprisonment and torture under Decius, 62; his death, 62; his character, 62 ff. Origen's *view of Holy Scripture*, 65 ff.; his belief in inspiration, 67 ff.; unity of the sacred writings, 69 f.; the Spirit's twofold object in Scripture, 70 ff.; the allegorical method, 73 f.; his ruling principle of interpretation, or the threefold sense, 74 f.; the function of allegorism to discover "mysteries," 76; his reasons for adopting an allegorical exegesis, 77, 80; futility of this method, 77; relation between the law and the gospel, 77; his negative use of allegorism as an apologetic weapon, 79; the doctrine of economy or reserve, 81; Origen's failure to recognise historical development in revelation, 82.

Origen's *religious philosophy*, 84 ff.; relation of Christian doctrine to Greek philosophy, 84 f.; philosophy relatively true, but inadequate, 85 f.; the incarnation of Jesus the true goal alike of Greek philosophy and of revealed wisdom, 86; Gnostic and Neoplatonic features of Origen's theological system, 87; his doctrines, as distinguished from their philosophical dress, derived from Scripture, 87 f.; value attached by him to a scientific conception of Christianity, 89; his distinction between exoteric and esoteric Christianity, 90; drawbacks of Origen's conception of Christianity, 91; his use of the Greek cosmology, 91 f.; his moral and religious ideal partly Neoplatonic, partly scriptural, 92 f.; his theory of knowledge and its relation to faith, 94; relation of faith to obedience, 94 f.; imperfection of all human knowledge, 95 f.; the deification of humanity, 96; main outlines of Origen's philosophy, 97.

Origen, *writings of*, 98 ff.; contributions to textual criticism, 99 ff.; his apologetic work—the

INDEX

Contra Celsum, 105 ff.; exegetical writings, 120 ff.; dogmatic works — the *De Principiis*, 125 ff.; letters, and treatises on *Prayer* and *Martyrdom*, 133 ff.

Origen's *Theology*, 142-212; nature of God, 142 ff.; doctrine of the Trinity, 148 ff.; the world of created spirits and the conception of formal freedom, 161 ff.; Creation and the Fall, 168 ff.; the doctrine of man, 171 ff.; the Four Revelations, 177 ff.; the Incarnation, 180 ff.; the sacrifice of Christ, 185 ff.; the soul's return to God, 190 ff.; the last things, 202 ff.

Origen, versatility of his genius, 213; successors of Origen, 213 ff.; his influence in Alexandria, 215 ff.; in Asia Minor, 224 ff.; decay of his influence towards the end of the fourth century, 243; attack on his writings by Methodius, 239 ff.; his defence undertaken by Pamphilus and Eusebius, 241 f.; further Origenistic controversies, 243 ff.

Orosius, 249.

PALESTINE, 50, 53 f., 58, 103, 224, 245.
Pamphilus, 53, 103, 105, 126 133, 218, 241 f.
Pantænus, 2, 10, 12 f., 36 f., 44, 120.
Patrick, quoted or referred to, 109, 111.
Paul, the Apostle, 32, 77, 163, 165, 228 f., 232; his theology, 13, 33, 172; his writings, 206.
Paul, the Gnostic, 38, 62.
Paulinianus, 245.
Pelagian controversy, 243, 249, 254.
Peter the Martyr, 214 f., 219, 243.
Phædimus of Amasia, 226.
Philip the Arabian, 55, 61, 110.
Philo, 3, 26 f., 32, 78, 148.
Philocalia, The, 126, 243.
Phœnicia, 53, 240.

Photius, 12, 126, 218 f., 240.
Phrygia, 228.
Pierius, 214, 218.
Plato, 86 ff., 114 ff., 150 *n*., 156, 172, 196.
Platonism, 6 ff., 34, 42 f., 46, 84, 87, 171 f.
Platonists, 6, 26, 107.
Plotinus, 108, 257.
Plutarch, 39.
Poiret, 258.
Porphyry, 9, 44, 92, 108.
Prayer to Christ, 136 f.
Pressensé, quoted or referred to, 48 *n*., 167, 211.
Protestantism, 17.
Protoktetus, 58.
Pseudo-Dionysius, 254, 256, 258.
Pythagoras, 87, 107.

REDEPENNING, quoted or referred to, 8, 44 *n*., 53, 67, 73, 97, 126, 211.
Reuss, quoted, 65 f.
Rhodon, 214, 220.
Rome, 46, 149, 197, 246; Church of, 17, 53, 197 f., 232.
Rufinus, 98, 120, 122, 125, 158, 241, 245 ff., 261.

SABAS, St., monks of, 249.
Sabellianism, 217, 227.
Sacraments, Origen's view of the, 199 ff.
Salmond, quoted, 83.
Sarapieion, the, 14.
Sardia, Council of, 223.
Scetian monks, 243, 245, 247 f.
Schnitzer, quoted or referred to, 10, 43, 45, 126 f., 240.
Septuagint, 99 ff., 121.
Serapis, 40.
Severa, wife of Philip the Arabian, 61.
Severus, Alexander, 49, 57, 61.
Severus, Septimius, 13, 37, 46.
Sinope, 100.
Siricius, bishop of Rome, 246.
Socrates, the historian, 242, 247, 257.
Southey, 74.

Stoicism, 42, 97.
Stoics, 88 f.
Suidas, 35.
Symmachus, 57, 101.

TATIANA, 133.
Tauler, 192 n.
Tennyson, quoted or referred to, 173, 233.
Tertullian, 5, 14, 17, 145, 148.
Tetrapla, The, 103.
Theodora, the empress, 250.
Theodore (Askidas), 249.
Theodore of Cæsarea, 250.
Theodore of Mopsuestia, 250.
Theodore of Tarsus, 255.
Theodoret of Cyrus, 250.
Theodosius II., 249.
Theodotion, 101 f.
Theognostus, 214 f., 219.
Theoktetus, 138.
Theoktistus of Cæsarea, 50, 56.
Theophilus of Alexandria, 241, 245 ff.

Theophilus of Antioch, 120.
Theotimus of Scythia, 248.
"The Three Chapters," 250 f.
Timothy, 36.
Tractarian Movement, the, 82.
"Typus," 253.
Tyre, 62, 240.

VALENS, 224.
Valentinus, 4, 28, 87, 97.
Valerian, 218.
Vaughan, R. A., quoted or referred to, 51, 214, 261.
Vigilantius, 245.
Vigilius of Rome, 251.
Vincentius of Lerinum, 259.
Voltaire, 108.

WESTERN Church, 210, 223, 231 f., 235.
Wiclif, 198.

ZACHARIAS of Mitylene, 252.
Zephyrinus, 46.

www.ingramcontent.com/pod-product-compliance
Lightning Source LLC
Chambersburg PA
CBHW051631230426
43669CB00013B/2257